Sportista

In the series **Politics, History, and Social Change,**
edited by John C. Torpey

Also in this series:

Kenneth H. Tucker, Jr., *Workers of the World, Enjoy!: Aesthetic Politics from Revolutionary Syndicalism to the Global Justice Movement*

Hans-Lukas Kieser, *Nearest East: American Millennialism and Mission to the Middle East*

Ernesto Verdeja, *Unchopping a Tree: Reconciliation in the Aftermath of Political Violence*

Rebecca Jean Emigh, *The Undevelopment of Capitalism: Sectors and Markets in Fifteenth-Century Tuscany*

Aristide R. Zolberg, *How Many Exceptionalisms? Explorations in Comparative Macroanalysis*

Thomas Brudholm, *Resentment's Virtue: Jean Améry and the Refusal to Forgive*

Patricia Hill Collins, *From Black Power to Hip Hop: Racism, Nationalism, and Feminism*

Daniel Levy and Natan Sznaider, translated by Assenka Oksiloff, *The Holocaust and Memory in the Global Age*

Brian A. Weiner, *Sins of the Parents: The Politics of National Apologies in the United States*

Heribert Adam and Kogila Moodley, *Seeking Mandela: Peacemaking Between Israelis and Palestinians*

Marc Garcelon, *Revolutionary Passage: From Soviet to Post-Soviet Russia, 1985–2000*

Götz Aly and Karl Heinz Roth, translated by Assenka Oksiloff, *The Nazi Census: Identification and Control in the Third Reich*

Immanuel Wallerstein, *The Uncertainties of Knowledge*

Michael R. Marrus, *The Unwanted: European Refugees from the First World War Through the Cold War*

Andrei S. Markovits
Emily K. Albertson

Sportista

*Female Fandom
in the United States*

TEMPLE UNIVERSITY PRESS
Philadelphia

Andrei S. Markovits is Arthur F. Thurnau Professor and The Karl W. Deutsch Collegiate Professor of Comparative Politics and German Studies at the University of Michigan. He has published prolifically on German and European politics and on sports. His latest book is *Gaming the World: How Sports Are Reshaping Global Politics and Culture.*

Emily K. Albertson graduated from the University of Michigan with a Bachelor's degree in sociology and is currently a student at the University of Michigan Law School.

TEMPLE UNIVERSITY PRESS
Philadelphia, Pennsylvania 19122
www.temple.edu/tempress

Copyright © 2012 by Temple University
All rights reserved
Published 2012

Cataloging-in-Publication data available from the Library of Congress

ISBN 978-1-4399-0963-8 cloth
ISBN 978-1-4399-0964-5 paper
ISBN 978-1-4399-0965-2 e-book

Printed in the United States of America
091312P

Contents

Preface and Acknowledgments   vii

Introduction   1

1   Youth   13
The Origins of Gender Difference in Sport

2   Women in Men's Worlds   38
*Process of Exclusion and Suppression of Females
in Male-Dominated Realms Other Than Sport*

3   Women as Sports Producers   66
Progress and Problems

4   Fandom and the Typical Female Sports Fan   118

5   Sportista I: Professional Women   167
in the Contested Space of Sports Media
Issues of Entry and Acceptance

6   Sportista II: Following as a Hobby,   201
the A-Typical Female Sports Fan
*Superfans in Their Own Right, with Their Own Voice,
and Speaking Their Own Language*

Conclusion   239

Appendix: Lists of Interviewees   245

Index   247

Preface and Acknowledgments

In an odd but telling way, I date the origins of this book back to my childhood in the west Romanian city of Timișoara (also known by its Hungarian appellation of Temesvár) in the 1950s where our small family—my father, mother, and I—seemed to do everything together. We went to the local opera together, just as we did to the theater and to classical concerts. My parents took me to art history classes, which they attended on a weekly basis, taught by an old, immensely impressive and learned lady who had once studied the subject in Vienna and Budapest. And, of course, the works of Shakespeare, Goethe, Schiller, as well as Petöfi, Arany, and Madách, their Hungarian equivalents, were always read out loud by my father and mother, just as operatic and symphonic music was always listened to with all three of us in the room. I was never quite sure whether my parents did all this because they really enjoyed each other's company so much, never wanting to be apart, or whether they somehow believed that I could best be imparted all this cultural capital via their collective efforts, in stereo as it were. In fact, I can never remember my father and mother being apart other than when he was at work and she was at home with me—with one profound exception: the world of sports. Indeed, the gender segregation in our small two-room flat appeared so pronounced around this topic that I still believe that my mother somehow vanished into the deepest corner of our pantry in the kitchen or speedily fled to the neighbors across the hallway when my father and I gathered around our radio to listen to soccer games broadcast from as far away as Belgrade, Budapest, Bucharest, even Vienna on rare occasions. Whatever she did, wherever she went, my mother vanished into thin air when sports appeared on the agenda. She just disappeared, became a nonperson. Of course, my mother never accompanied my father and me to the ground of my beloved soccer team "Stinţa," whose games my father and I attended with regularity throughout my childhood. Indeed, when my mother died and my father and I left Romania for good, emigrating first to Vienna and then to New York City, as a nine-year-old boy literally everything in my life changed with one exception: my consumption of sports, for which my mother never existed even when she lived right next to me. And even though the content of the sports changed when we crossed the ocean, and soccer's cultural salience mutated into baseball's—with the New York Yankees assuming the emotional space formerly occupied by Stinţa of Timişoara—sports' overall gestalt and role in my life did not alter one bit. Indeed, sports have remained a constant, perhaps the only one throughout my life's many vicissitudes. Above all, with all the tensions and turmoil informing the standard father-son relationship that, quite probably, attained an added edge by the cultural upheaval wrought by the late 1960s, sports, even more than classical music, remained the sole uncontested space, the only place of succor and comfort between my father and me until his death.

Somehow I was always a tad confused about the virtual absence of women in this all-too-important space for me. Indeed I was incredulous. Why were women present in every aspect of my life other than sports? Why did the counterculture change so many areas of our quotidian lives without seemingly diminishing the male monopoly of sports following in any meaningful way? I began to ponder these questions when I commenced my scholarly pursuits in sports matters in the late 1980s. But it was not until a summer seminar I taught in Germany in August 1995 that I began earnest research on this topic. It was via a survey of my students designed to ascertain their knowledge of and involvement with soccer in Germany that I seriously began to pursue the topic of gender in sports consumption. The gaps between my male and female students—Germany's equivalent of our National Merit Scholars all—was immense and clearly more pronounced than in any other area of interest and concern. We refer to this early study in our book. I then did considerable work on women's soccer in the United States, and this research appeared in various publications in the late 1990s and early 2000s. But it was not until my supervision of Gillian Warmflash's thesis for the Committee on Degrees in Social Studies at Harvard University in the academic year 2003–2004 that I became seriously immersed in the study of women's relations to sports. As the reader will notice, some core parts of this book owe a great debt to Gillian's incisive work. Her thesis is without a doubt this book's intellectual precursor. In the process of writing her thesis and during the many conversations that we had in the course of that year, Gillian mutated from my student to my friend, and she remains this to this day. I cherish her friendship deeply.

It is through my continued work on the topic of women as sports consumers at the University of Michigan that I encountered many bright female students involved with sports in some fashion, and none brighter than Emily Albertson. Emily went from being a student in my large sports, society, and culture class to becoming a participant in one of my studies of female sports fans, and then transformed herself into a full-fledged coauthor of this book. I am thankful to the University of Michigan for providing me with the financial assistance to conduct these various studies. But much more significantly, I owe a great debt to this institution for being the home of some of the most intellectually challenging and academically exciting students imaginable. Emily is a case in point. Working with her on this book was sheer joy, especially because she was not only a delightful and conscientious coauthor but also its subject in that she is an inveterate fan and connoisseur of sports, in other words a real sportista. All the book's shortcomings are mine, none hers. Emily will commence her second year of study at the University of Michigan Law School by the time this book is published. Even though she decided to embark on a career away from the academy, she will always be first and foremost a consummate scholar in my view. There can be no higher praise.

I would also like to thank my esteemed colleague John Torpey for having encouraged me throughout our twenty-five-year friendship to work on topics that might not be the most rewarded by the conventional metrics of the established academic disciplines but that I found interesting and challenging. John's exceptionally fertile mind and his immense erudition in many areas of the social sciences as well as his fluency in many languages and cultures have not only tied me to him on a personal level but also led me to have my work appear in a series edited under John's intellectual guidance and professional aegis.

It was through John that I got to know Micah Kleit, our editor. I owe Micah much gratitude for his enthusiasm for our project—enthusiasm that he voiced with confidence well before he had actually seen any of our work on paper (or on his computer screen). Gary Kramer's insights were always appreciated. Peggy Gordon guided the production process with expertise and efficiency. Our exchanges increased in their cordiality and warmth once Peggy informed me of her love for dogs and her practice of adopting rescued strays. I also want to thank the detailed comments that the two anonymous reviewers offered on our manuscript. Their insights and knowledge have certainly improved the final product immensely. Greg Cairns and Mark Rozny deserve much praise and warm thanks for their fine work as our research assistants. I would like to single out Joanne Gerstner among our wonderful subjects; without her this study simply would not have happened. After interviewing Joanne for the book, we developed a friendship that has enriched me in many ways.

As always, I owe my greatest debt to my dear wife Kiki, who remains my rock. Together with our darling Cody, she makes my life a daily joy. And I would like to dedicate this book to my great mentor, teacher, coauthor, colleague, and friend Karl W. Deutsch, whose birthday's centenary we celebrate in 2012; and to my beloved father, the late Ludwig Markovits, to whom I owe everything, including my love of sports and thus this book's very essence and soul.

Andrei S. Markovits

Ann Arbor, Michigan

There is no other way to start than by thanking Andy Markovits. I came to Andy in November 2010 asking for work as a research assistant, and we walked away less than a year later with a finished book. This result was a product of Andy's believing in me, trusting me, and most of all teaching me. Surely, I learned from Andy as a student in his class, but even after I was given the honor of coauthoring this book, I continued to learn from him every day, in every one of our interactions, from his incredible experiences and inspiring intellect. I am inexplicably grateful to Andy for giving me this opportunity.

For Mom and Dad, for finding the perfect balance between telling me what I want to hear and telling me what I need to hear. Thank you, I love you.

For Nicky, Teddy, my cousins, and neighbors, for always letting me play, sometimes as Tails, disappearing when Andy (not Markovits) sped ahead as Sonic, but equal times as all-time QB. I love you all.

For all my roommates at 341 E. Jefferson, for letting me into the club and making me a real sportista. Thank you all for giving me confidence in my sports savvy and for supporting me in this project as its coauthor and cosubject.

Emily Albertson

Ann Arbor, Michigan

Introduction

ports matter. Their marquee events—the Olympics, various world championships, most prominently the World Cup in soccer, the Super Bowl, the World Series, the UEFA Champions League Final, the NBA and NHL finals, the Rugby World Cup, the four slams in tennis, the four majors in golf, the Ashes in cricket, the America's Cup in sailing, and the Grand Prix, Indy, and NASCAR auto racing, to mention just a few—have become global icons known to and loved by billions across the globe. These events regularly furnish among the most watched television shows on earth. Other than the final episode of *M*A*S*H*, clocking in at number three and the final installment of *Cheers*, at number nine, all of the top ten most watched television shows in U.S. history have been Super Bowls.[1] And just like the formerly all-American Super Bowl has become a global television event watched by 130 million viewers around the world, so, too, has the semi-annual (occasionally even more frequent) intra-Spanish showdown between soccer greats Real Madrid and FC Barcelona mutated into a global event watched by more than 100 million people fully conversant with the term "El Clasico," barely known outside the world of Spanish soccer a few years ago.

In terms of both teams and individuals, the purveyors of sports have become national and global icons, rivaling the fame of movie stars and politicians.

---

[1]Lindsay Powers, "10 Most Watched TV Shows Ever," *The Hollywood Reporter*, February 7, 2011, available at http://www.hollywoodreporter.com/blogs/live-feed/10-watched-tv-shows-97180 (accessed August 22, 2011).

Manchester United, FC Barcelona, the New York Yankees, and the Los Angeles Lakers are but a few of a bevy of teams that invoke passion and command knowledge to a degree virtually unthinkable barely two decades ago. The same is true for individuals such as Wayne Rooney, Lionel Messi, Derek Jeter, and Kobe Bryant, to stick with star representatives of the aforementioned teams. Moreover, athletes performing as individuals, such as Usain Bolt, Michael Phelps, Serena Williams, and Tiger Woods, have also become household names across the globe. There can be no doubt about the immense importance and ubiquitous presence of sports consumption.

The same pertains to sports production. More people are actively engaged in playing sports today than at any other time in human history. In a formally organized manner as well as in myriad informal, spontaneous, and ad hoc manifestations, sports have become more than ever central to people's leisure time activities. Here, too, their ubiquity is remarkable.

In two earlier works, Markovits has attributed this development to what he called "the second globalization."[2] In particular, he emphasized sports' emancipatory and democratizing powers in that both their production and their consumption have constantly included hitherto excluded social groups. Borrowing Kwame Anthony Appiah's term, Markovits labeled sports' positive contributions "cosmopolitan." Yet, his work also concentrated on sports' darker side, on their tribal, exclusionary, and discriminatory dimensions, which he, again borrowing from Appiah, called "countercosmopolitan." In both of these books, Markovits devoted attention to how women have come to relate to sports and how issues of gender are played out in the arena of sports, to stick with sports-related imagery. While the topic of gender and women in sports received respectable consideration in Markovits's previous work, it did not receive the thought, care, presentation, and analysis that an issue of such importance so richly deserves. Our current book, we hope, remedies the previous neglect.

Here is its central concern: Sports fandom has been a remarkable vehicle for including the most varied and disparate social groups into a common whole. While the inherently agonistic and competitive nature of sports necessarily leads to partisanship and thus division, even animosity and hatred, the equally inherent meritocratic dimensions and wide intelligibility have given sports a power of inclusion and participation that is second to none. Indeed, by dint of their inclusiveness and ubiquity, sports have created ties across class, ethnic, regional, cultural, religious, and age lines that few, if any, other forces

---

[2]Andrei S. Markovits and Lars Rensmann, *Gaming the World: How Sports Are Reshaping Global Politics and Culture* (Princeton: Princeton University Press, 2010); and Andrei S. Markovits, *Sport: Motor und Impulssystem für Emanzipation und Diskriminierung* (Vienna: Picus Verlag, 2011).

could even approximate. By virtue of their inclusive qualities, we have come to view sports as powerful agents of democratization.

Note that we did not list gender in our aforementioned array of categories, which, we claim, sports include and integrate. This is precisely our point. There is one clearly marked social group that sports have not fully integrated on either their production or their consumption side, and that is women. Women, as our book argues and demonstrates, have made enormous strides in the construct "sports" over the past four decades. Still, they remain second-class citizens. What makes this obvious discrimination all the more interesting, although also shocking, and certainly unique, is the fact that, even in the liberal democracies of the advanced industrial societies, which form the sole empirical and theoretical framework of our work, this inequality is openly accepted, indeed officially sanctioned and—shockingly—barely contested. Sports furnish the sole public construct in these societies, where the concept of "separate but equal" continues to be alive and well. And as Eileen McDonagh and Laura Pappano's excellent study demonstrates, separate in sports, as in so many other realms of life, is anything but equal.[3] Our book focuses on women's experiences in their constant contestation to attain equal inclusion in our extant sports space.

While women had been present in this space since the Middle Ages, if not before, and while they certainly participated in what we have come to know as sports, constituted at the end of the eighteenth and throughout much of the nineteenth century, we really time women's meaningful contestation of and participation in this construct since the late 1960s and early 1970s. In other words, it was the power of the second wave of feminism, with all its institutional and societal reforms and their immense cultural ramifications—Title IX as a convenient marker—that changed virtually every aspect of public life in America, sports included. This milieu informs the core of our book.

In the process of writing and researching this book, we tried to provide some—though far from exhaustive—responses to the following questions: How have sports included women? In what way has sports production (i.e., the doing of sports) differed from sports consumption (i.e., the following of sports) in terms of women's incorporation into sports? In what way have men and women remained so different in terms of their following of sports? How and why do women continue to "speak" sports so differently from men?

To be sure, there have been superb studies on women in sports. First and foremost, there is Jennifer Hargreaves's pioneering and comprehensive book,

---

[3]Eileen McDonagh and Laura Pappano, *Playing with the Boys: Why Separate Is Not Equal in Sports* (New York: Oxford University Press, 2008). See also Andrei S. Markovits, "The Last Legitimate Bastion of 'Separate but Equal,'" available at http://www.huffingtonpost.com/andrei-markovits/the-last-legitimate-basti_b_544059.html.

which includes virtually all aspects of women's sports and women in sports in a richly detailed historical analysis that features mainly the British situation, though also provides valuable insights into its American counterpart as well as issues pertaining to women and sports everywhere.[4] Then, Allen Guttmann, the eminent sports historian and theoretician who has enriched us with a number of crucial books on various aspects of sport, also weighed in on women's sports, their history, and their condition in the last two decades of the twentieth century.[5] And Jean O'Reilly and Susan K. Cahn's edited volume on crucial aspects of women and sports in the United States—from competing body images to sexuality, from institutional biases to important legal and equity matters pertaining to Title IX—constitutes an indispensable collection of texts for any scholar working on the complex issue of women and sports as well as women's sports.[6] In the German-speaking world, we would be remiss not to mention the prolific writings of Gertrud Pfister on many aspects of women and sports as well as the fine anthology compiled by Eva Kreisky and Georg Spitaler on the gendered nature of soccer in Europe and beyond.[7]

However, none of these authors, and few, if any scholars to our knowledge, have devoted their major attention to a study and analysis of women as sports fans, in other words, primarily, if not indeed solely, to women as sports consumers, in particular, how women follow sports, and specifically, what Markovits has come to call "hegemonic sports," in other words, those very few (quite possibly no more than seven) team-anchored contests involving some kind of ball-like contraption (pace hockey puck) that have come to comprise a cultural preoccupation bordering on obsession way beyond the actual contests produced on the field, arena, or rink. This phenomenon developed a global ubiquity in the course of the twentieth century, with few comparable parallels. A defining part of this ubiquity has been its predominantly, de facto virtually exclusively, male nature. It was the rare but growing presence of women that interested us and forms the core of our study. With both of us being much more involved and interested in the following of sports instead of their doing, we were particularly eager to shed light on that still rare but steadily growing

[4]Jennifer Hargreaves, *Sporting Females: Critical Issues in the History and Sociology of Women's Sports* (New York: Routledge, 1994).

[5]Allen Guttmann, *Women's Sports: A History* (New York: Columbia University Press, 1994). Two of Guttmann's other important books on sports are *From Ritual to Record: The Nature of Modern Sports* (New York: Columbia University Press, 2004); and *A Whole New Ballgame: An Interpretation of American Sports* (Chapel Hill: University of North Carolina Press, 1988).

[6]Jean O'Reilly and Susan K. Cahn (eds.) *Women and Sports in the United States: A Documentary Reader* (Boston: Northeastern University Press, 2007).

[7]Eva Kreisky and Georg Spitaler (eds.), *Arena der Maennlichkeit: Ueber das Verhaeltnis von Fussball und Geschlecht* (Frankfurt: Campus Verlag, 2006).

phenomenon of the female sports fan. What constitutes such? How, if at all, is her fandom different from a man's? Above all, what kinds of female sports fans and experts exist? How do they construct their fandom and expertise vis-à-vis other women and men? In particular, we were most interested in analyzing the world of the female sports fanatic as well as connoisseur: the woman who not only loves her sports but also knows them; the woman who distinguishes herself from most of her world by being immensely passionate and knowledgeable about sports. It is such a person whom we named "sportista" in an analogy to the well-known word "fashionista," indicating a person who regards fashion—what she wears—as a crucial part of her identity and therefore worthy of both knowledge and passion of the highest order.

Just as the "fashionista" knows fashion's minute details in terms of its designers, models, fabrics, patterns, accessories, players, and—crucially—its history and culture, and derives tremendous pleasure from using this knowledge to enhance her passion and appreciation for fashion, the sportista does the same with sports: She knows their minute details in terms of their teams, players, coaches, standings, trades, statistics, and—crucially, here, too—their history and culture, and all of these enhance her passion and appreciation for a great jump shot, a well-delivered fastball, a forty-yard run off left tackle, a sixty-yard cross into the box, a tight pennant race, the competition for batting and pitching prowess in baseball denoted by their many already extant and still developing metrics, and their actual equivalents and conceptual counterparts in basketball, football, and hockey among the North American Big Four team sports, which, of course, have their parallel markers in the hegemonic sports cultures of most countries in the world, be it soccer in all of Europe and Latin America; cricket in India, Pakistan, Australia, New Zealand, and South Africa; or rugby in the latter three.

While we have a bevy of convincing, if only anecdotal, evidence that the phenomenon of sportistas in the United States has its counterpart in the cultures of comparable advanced industrial democracies of Western Europe, Canada, Australia, and New Zealand, and while our study will periodically include examples from Germany, in particular, our efforts remain largely confined to describing and analyzing the world of female sport fandom in the United States during the first two decades of the twenty-first century. As Markovits repeatedly told Albertson throughout the duration of the project: This book is about explaining her to the world.

Relevant research has confirmed our assumption that women's relationship to sports commences at an early age. Analyzing how early childhood and adolescent experiences set a powerful path for how girls see themselves in connection with sports, which—as it turns out unsurprisingly—is closely linked to these girls' differing perception of their world compared with boys', forms the core of Chapter 1. Not interested in, or able to, resolve the age-old question as to whether gender differences at an early age hail from nature or nurture, and very much agreeing with Peggy Orenstein that "at issue, then, is not nature or nurture but how nurture becomes nature: the environment in which children play and grow can encourage a range of aptitudes or foreclose them,"[8] we present how the foundation for interests and preferences that in later years are conducive to making one a devout sports fan, both in knowledge and passion, emerge early in life: Boys are more competitive than girls, boys are more combative than girls, boys are more result-oriented than girls, and boys are more action-centered than girls. All of these factors, probably mainly the result of nurture rather than nature, which, however, does not render them any less potent in the culture of advanced industrial democracies, constitute essential ingredients for any success in both the doing and the following of sports. Michael A. Messner has aptly characterized the issue at hand:

> The most fruitful approach is not to ask why boys and girls are so different but rather to ask how and under what conditions boys and girls constitute themselves as separate, oppositional groups. Sociologists need not debate whether gender is 'there'—clearly gender is always there, built as it is into structures, situations, cultures, and consciousness of children and adults. The key issue is under what conditions gender is activated as a salient organizing principle in social life and under what conditions it may be less salient.[9]

In sports, we argue, gender is a particularly salient organizing principle on all levels: that of production and consumption, on the part of athletes and of fans.

For important historical reasons, boys are drawn more to sports than are girls. But surely there are many other areas of life that are massively gendered in favor of men apart from sports. For us to understand the special nature of sports' gendered character, we had to investigate a few other fields in which

---

[8]Peggy Orenstein, "Should the World of Toys Be Gender-Free?," *New York Times*, December 30, 2011. Orenstein states, "As any developmental psychologist will tell you . . . toy choices among young children is the Big Kahuna of sex differences, one of the largest across the life span. It transcends not only culture but also species: in two separate studies of primates, in 2002 and 2006, researchers found that males gravitated toward stereotypically masculine toys (like cars and balls), while females went ape for dolls. Both sexes, incidentally, appreciated stuffed animals and books. Human boys and girls not only tend to play differently from one another—with girls typically clustering in pairs and trios, chatting together more than boys and playing more cooperatively—but, when given a choice, usually prefer hanging with their own kind."

[9]Michael A. Messner, "Barbie Girls Versus Sea Monsters: Children Constructing Gender" in *The Sport and Society Reader*, ed. David Karen and Robert E. Washington (New York: Routledge, 2010), 191.

women have traditionally been woefully small and consistently discriminated and disadvantaged minorities. We do so in Chapter 2. The still extant paucity of women in the so-called STEM fields (science, technology, engineering, mathematics)—and chess—hails from a number of sources, none more salient than the much smaller talent pool, which, in turn, is due to major barriers of entry based on conventional and traditional mechanisms of selection and exclusion that discourage girls from choosing such fields. But we found that those women who do gain access to these male-dominated fields have an invaluable ally in the mechanism of credentialing.

It is this mechanism—and this alone—that lends these women the legitimacy and authenticity that they need to enter these fields, but, more important still, to survive in them and even be accepted as peers by the male majority. Thus, male members of a physics laboratory or an engineering company may actually believe that men make better physicists or engineers than women. They may even behave this way in their daily demeanor on the job. However, regardless of their attitudes toward women, when the new female colleague enters the premises with a bachelor's degree from MIT and a Ph.D. from Cal Tech, she has the formal credentials that define her as a bona fide physicist or engineer whom one needs to take into consideration and who deserves professional and collegial courtesy, even if one believes that men make better physicists or engineers than women. As we discuss the mechanism of credentialing at some length in Chapter 2, we make it amply clear that this in no way alleviates long-held prejudices and that the latter continue to flourish in various other guises, couched either in secrecy or in various codes of informality. Thus, credentialing in and of itself does not create equality. But it does accord a formal ticket of admission to a formerly closed world and therefore lowers— but clearly does not abolish—the barriers of entry. We mention and study credentialing in a few male-dominated realms because we believe that its absence in the world of sports fandom makes the barrier of entry for women into that domain totally arbitrary, ever changeable, and thus murky and ultimately virtually insurmountable.

Briefly put, precisely because the language of sports is so much more ubiquitous and facile and thus more accessible and democratic than that of physics, many more men are fluent in the former than they are in the latter. But because there exists no credentialing in the proficiency of sports fandom, on its dimension of either knowledge or affect, because sports fandom provides a democratic inclusion for men that bridges otherwise virtually insurmountable social differences, such as class and race, and because entry into this world remains purely arbitrary, with no validating degrees that bestow immediate legitimacy on any newcomer, the already included participants—that is, men (of many otherwise incompatible collective identities)—remain this world's self-made guardians, which allows them to keep the entrance requirements murky, arbitrary, and ultimately exclusionary toward any potential entrants, mainly women. We are arguing that the democratic and uncredentialed nature of sports fandom that has been so essential to male identity throughout the twentieth century in the advanced industrial world continues to pose an immense barrier of entry for women, including sportistas, who, we will present, have all of the "formal" prerequisites to enter into this male world and succeed it in brilliantly and on fully equal terms, yet are prevented from doing so by many implicit and explicit forces that we will discuss in detail.

One of this book's main themes is to delineate the different worlds of being an athlete and being a fan, what we call "doing" as opposed to "following" sports. We discuss the complexity of this relationship in detail throughout the book, highlighting how one might not have anything to do with the other, how indeed there is ample evidence that—most certainly among men, and thus hegemonic sports culture—the most avid fans might indeed be the least active athletes, that being a diehard fan almost exacts the accompanying identity of couch potato and nerd rather than committed athlete on an amateur, let alone professional, level. Indeed, quite frequently, males with the highest quantity of social capital by way of their sports *following* are often those whose actual *doing* of sports is not of central importance to them or to their prowess and standing as sophisticated sports fans amidst their peers. However, the two need not preclude each other. Indeed, there is ample evidence that having played sports, even at their most rudimentary level, does in fact lead to a committed interest in, knowledge of, and passion for them, in other words that "doing" and "following" sports are solidly connected for men.

However, our research reveals that this connection has a much greater salience for women than it does for men. Whereas we encountered the occasional sportista who was not athletic by any stretch of that term, and rarely, if ever, played sports in any meaningful way in her youth or as an adult, the link between having been an athlete (i.e., "doing" sports) and developing a love for following them remains quite crucial for women. To be sure, just like for men, these two worlds operate on different axial principles for women as well, and there need not be much interaction between them. Still, we thought the world of women's athletics sufficiently important to devote Chapter 3 to its development and existence. Because unlike in the area of sports consumption and fandom—our concerns in later chapters—the tremendous gains that women have attained in this area since the late 1960s and early 1970s are nothing short of phenomenal, indeed revolutionary. Examples abound, and we will not bore the reader with too many at this juncture. Just a quick glance at the Olympic disciplines will reveal that women have attained a virtual parity with men in terms of the sports in which they compete and the number of athletes present at the games. Moreover, women compete in events that not so long ago were deemed the sole prerogatives of men: Women's boxing became a medal sport at the 2012 Olympics, with wrestling having been one since 2004; the marathon run was added to track and field in the 1980s, the women's pole vault and weightlifting events were added in 2000, and women will compete in rugby sevens along with the men at the 2016 Olympic Games in Rio de Janeiro and will make their debut next to men in Olympic ski jumping at the 2014 Olympic Winter Games in Sochi (they are notably still excluded from Olympic competition in the 1500-meter swim, even though they compete in the event at non-Olympic races). At our very own University of Michigan, there are now well over three hundred female varsity student athletes at virtual parity with men. There were de jure none as late as 1970.

While women have long ago attained prominence, even stardom, in a number of individual sports, such as figure skating, tennis, downhill skiing, and gymnastics, they now have also come to the fore in team sports. Thus, the University of Connecticut's ninety-game win streak in Division I college basketball over nearly three full seasons garnered national attention that was unimaginable barely a few years before. While as late as the early 1980s, women's basketball was not even recognized by the NCAA and women played their games in small and dingy gymnasiums, completely unnoticed by a disinterested public, ESPN, the national and international behemoth in sports broadcasting and self-proclaimed "worldwide leader in sports" shows every game of the women's national championship to solid, if not spectacular, ratings. And just like on the men's side, where team sports have long produced major individual stars, so, too, has Maya Moore, the Lady Huskies' sensational player, attained stardom hitherto unparalleled on the women's, with the sole and telling exception of soccer, where Mia Hamm confirmed her crossover stardom by appearing in commercials with none other than Michael Jordan. Indeed, as we discuss in this chapter, women's soccer's key events, such as the World Cup and the Olympics, have garnered a degree of popularity both in the stadiums and on television that—at least in the United States—often surpass the men's and have thus created the most watched event of any kind in which women are the sole protagonists.

Women's phenomenal advancement in the production of sports deserves special accolades because it has occurred in a constantly contested cultural tug-of-war between the male-dominated dictates of culturally hegemonic notions of femininity and beauty on the one hand and the equally male-dominated exigencies of the super-masculine world of top-level competitive sports on the other. Thus, as we will demonstrate with examples from the world of top-level female team sports in the United States and Germany, conflicting issues deeply related to identity and sexuality beset female athletes to an extent completely unknown to their male counterparts. Tout court, women do not only have to win on the playing field; they have to look good doing so, meaning that they are structurally (if not explicitly) expected to remain physically and sexually appealing to men by conforming to the hegemonic notions of conventional femininity.

Despite these constant contradictory demands and other hurdles specific to their gender's participation in the world of sports, the tally on women's recent advances as athletes, on sports' production side, is truly remarkable and, we argue, of great social significance. Yet, we remain skeptical whether these gains on the production side have any commensurate effects on sports' consumption. Maybe women do not much care if and when they do. Maybe women will never care to follow sports, to "speak sports," the way men do. Maybe there are institutional and cultural impediments willfully imposed by or structurally inherent to male-dominated hegemonic sports cultures that render such massive transformation in the world of female sports fandom impossible. Maybe women have established alternate means of communication that serve as the functional equivalents to men's sports speak. Maybe these are much more diversified and far richer than the relative one-dimensionality of the male-dominated discourse of the typical sports fan. Whatever the case, the immensely rich trials and diverse tribulations of female fandom in contemporary America comprise the remaining three chapters of our book.

Chapter 4 offers a detailed presentation of contemporary America's "regular" female sports consumer or sports' "normal" female fan. In this chapter, we delineate the similarities and differences as to how women consume sports in contrast to men, how they "speak" sports in their own voices, which are markedly distinct from men's. We analyze how, for women, attending a sports event in a stadium or watching it at home on television is much more a social occasion than a passionately partisan, deeply emotional but also significantly cognitive and intellectually challenging one, as it is for the typical male fan. We discuss how stories are much more important to women sports fans than are results, which constitute the very raison d'etre of any sport's attraction to men. We analyze how sports fandom compares with its analogies in areas such as music and note how, in our culture, we have come to differentiate between a "connoisseur," an aficionado, and an "expert," which we associate with high-brow culture—nobody speaks of a Bach or a Goethe "fan"—as opposed to "fan," often considered the sometimes wild and certainly uncouth "other" devoted to items that we categorize as low brow, with popular sports comprising any hegemonic sports culture squarely among them. We discuss the field of fandom along the axes of passion or affect and knowledge and argue that one needs to excel on both to be considered a genuine fan, or what we term a "superfan," but how to men—in marked contrast to women—no legitimacy as a bona fide sports fan can be accorded to anybody without some factual knowledge about the sport, with the exact quantity and quality of such remaining vague. The depth and breadth of the knowledge of a sport's history, strategies, tactics, players, and statistics remain indeterminate, but it is clear that to most men who call themselves sports fans a certain mastery of facts remains a sine qua non for being accorded legitimacy as a sports fan. Loving a team, a player, a sport, or a league—or all of these—still marks the cultural world of the normal female sports fan in the United States and the rest of the advanced industrial world. It is perfectly acceptable for a woman who just loves the Lakers, the Yankees, or Manchester United, as well as basketball, baseball, or soccer—without any details or knowledge—to view herself (and be so viewed by her social circles) a fan. But this has begun to change with the issue of knowledge becoming more salient to a growing number of women as well.

We then proceed in our quest to search for, describe, and analyze precisely such women in Chapters 5 and 6. In the former, we concentrate on women sports journalists, in other words, women who made their expertise in and knowledge of sport their livelihood. Here we discuss the trials and tribulations of the professional sportista as it were: the woman who has made her sports expertise into her very vocation, her livelihood. Based on interviews that we conducted for this study, as well as others amassed by Gillian Warmflash for her senior honors thesis written under Markovits's supervision and submitted to the Committee on Degrees in Social Studies at Harvard University in 2004, we obtained what we believe constitutes a fine picture as to how these professionally successful women construct their sports world. We present their paths to sports journalism, look at their experiences performing in this environment, and analyze the travails, hurdles, and also fulfillment that their choice of profession accords them.

One of our main concerns, of course, is how these accomplished women negotiate their existence in a world that—more than any other areas of contemporary journalism—remains massively male. Indeed, the hegemony of maleness reaches well beyond the newsroom since all of the players whose performances and product are the very reason that these journalists exist are male, as are the coaches, managers, general managers, virtually all owners, and—still—most fans. To paraphrase one of our interviewee's astute assessments of this issue: With the possible exception of the Vatican, there exist no more male-dominated structures in modern society than the sports that constitute all hegemonic sports cultures, in other words, the sports about which people, disproportionately of the male variety, truly care 24/7. In the course of our research, we found that many of these accomplished journalists who know their sports details inside and out and whose sports knowledge rivals any male expert's do not exhibit an emotional involvement to sports anywhere near commensurate with their high level of knowledge.

Indeed, when Albertson attended the 2011 annual convention of the Association for Women in Sports Media (AWSM), where, it is safe to say, each participant possessed a degree of sports knowledge miles above that of the average American female and quite possibly many a male, she was struck by how little, if any, sports schmoozing occurred among the participants in the hotel's hallways, cafés, bars, and restaurants. Sports remained confined to the professional (and knowledge) world of the convention's public domain, but did not spill over into the hobby (and passion) world of its private sphere. And in this chapter, just like in Chapter 3, we will once again revisit the issue of beauty and sexuality, which, though very different on some level from the travails imposed by society and culture on female athletes, also pose major impediments to the professional lives of these accomplished experts and knowledgeable journalists. We will discuss the multifaceted roles that physical attractiveness and appearance play in the experiences of women in sports media. Here we will focus on the issues of sexuality, beauty, and a mixing of the two sexes in a venue that was previously sacred and exclusive to one.

In search of a final synthesis between passion and knowledge, we turn our attention in Chapter 6 to a group of young women who, by virtue of their self-definition and by having fulfilled all of the criteria that we set as a minimum to be considered a genuine sports fan, we believe embody the prototypical amateur sportista for whom knowing, loving, and following sports is not a vocation but a hobby. In analyzing the essence of this identity, we pay special attention to these amateur sportistas' standing in the male world of sports fandom. We describe their insecurities and rivalries and show how tenuous they believe their position to be in relation to all relevant constituencies: male fans, regular female fans, and women in general. It is clear how aware these hobby sportistas remain about their lack of legitimacy and credibility in the sports discourse in which—possibly more than in anything else—the simple ascription of maleness still overrides virtually any achievement attained by virtually any woman.

In our brief Conclusion, we speculate as to whether and, if so, under what circumstances, this might change in the future.

Youth

The Origins of Gender Difference in Sport

S ports fandom is not only a man's domain—as it turns out, it is also a boy's. The gendered imbalance of sports fans, research shows, may be a phenomenon that begins before young boys and girls are even aware of any conscious choice to pursue or abandon venues for entertainment and enrichment.[1] To understand better why adult women do not live sports fandom to the same degree and in the same manner as their male counterparts, we need an examination into how and when the first sign of this partition, both real and self-perceived, enters the social sphere of young boys and girls.

Living Proof

In early spring 2011, we took a walk through Burns Park, a small park adjacent to an Ann Arbor elementary school's playground area. The playground space offered an array of different options for the Burns Park Elementary School recess participants, with basketball courts, tetherball posts, four-square areas, jungle gyms, swings, a field for soccer, and both grassy and paved patches on which the children could sit or stand. At first glance, we were convinced that, given our current immersion in research in young children's behavior, we were simply projecting our expectations onto what we were seeing, but a closer look

---

[1]Jacquelynne Eccles, Allan Wigfield, Rena D. Harold, and Phyllis Blumenfeld, "Age and Gender Differences in Children's Self- and Task Perceptions during Elementary School," *Child Development* 64, no. 3 (June 1993): 830–847.

at the division of activities on the playground led us to realize that we were not imagining things.

Of all the groupings, ranging from a single student wandering the play space without an immediately discernible reason or purpose, to a group of ten to twelve boys playing an organized game of basketball, we saw only one instance of gender mixing. One girl, probably about ten years old, had chosen to participate in a game of soccer on one of the grassy patches, making herself the only girl in a game of around ten total students. That one girl's choice to spend her recess among a group of boys represented the only deviation from the otherwise strict gender segregation that we could see.

In addition to the physical separation of play among boys and girl, the types of activities pursued by each gender group varied significantly. First, there was the difference in the size of the groups partaking in each activity. Overall, we noticed the boys playing in much larger groups, often ten or more of them split into multiple teams and playing organized games. Of a total group of approximately eighty children, we could only spot a handful of boys in groups of three or fewer. The games that these boys played were already created, their rules known by everyone who decided to play, as opposed to being any local and spontaneous invention by the boys themselves. They played basketball, soccer, and baseball, all games that would be easily recognized and named by any onlooker, activities that had become deeply institutionalized in the quotidian culture of contemporary American life.

It was not a warm day, and we wore warm jackets for the walk, but most of the boys had, since recess started, tied their coats around their waists or abandoned them in a heap on the ground. The boys' activities were fast-paced and physically demanding enough to compel them to ditch their jackets and roll up their sleeves, while most of the girls were wandering the area and wearing parkas and gloves.

After a close scouring of the playground, we found that most of the girls were divided into groups of two to three (in no cases do we recall a group of more than five). There was a lot of walking and talking between these small groups, with no clear "activities" or "games" being pursued. In some cases, the group would be on the swings or the jungle gym, but the activity or physical hardware seemed to serve as a backdrop to the primary purpose: talking to the others in the group. Often the girls would be sitting on a bench or on the ground; there was not one instance that day of any large group of girls splitting into distinctive teams or pursuing any detectable "goals," save the principal one of chatting and socializing with each other.

We did not venture close enough to any of these young females' conversations to glean their primary themes or topics (Gossip? Role-playing? Individual story telling?), nor did we get to witness the original formation of the boys' teams or decipher much of the levels of competition between them, but the visuals we *did* garner that day served as shockingly blatant representations of those principles of young children's activities about which we had previously only read from scholarly sources.

Playground Dynamics

Research suggests that the gendered gestalt of a Burns Park Elementary School lunch recess is not an anomaly in contemporary America, nor, for that matter, in comparable contexts in other advanced industrial democracies, such as Austria and Germany, first-hand familiar to Markovits. It usually requires just a glance at any typical elementary school's playground to discover that children are aware of their gender. Boys and girls—beginning at ages as young as preschool (three or four years old)—are almost completely segregated as far as their social group composition. Furthermore, the activities in which each gender group tends to participate are highly aligned with the most stereotypical behaviors and preferences that hegemonic culture expects of them as they continue through adolescence (when awareness of gender difference is often most heightened) all the way to adulthood.[2]

The nature of boys' play is aggressive, competitive, and often combative. There are "sides," there are "good guys" and "bad guys," seemingly impossible percentages of participants "die," and most importantly, there are almost always winners and losers.[3] Research done by Elizabeth Grugeon shows that boys' activities are relatively chaotic and occur on some type of wide-open athletic field, while the girls' play is characterized by a theme of "closeness and intimacy," featuring role-playing (often in the positions of members of a typical family), collectivity (commonly seen through unison songs, chants, and clapping rhythms), and gossip, all activities that share a "universality of their sociability and friendliness."[4]

The above distinctions might not be particularly surprising, especially considering the crucially formative role that one commonly accords "nurture" in shaping an individual's development (and the concomitant discounting of variations between boys' and girls' behavior as the direct results of innate biological differences between them). Research conducted by Beverly I. Fagot,

---

[2]Elizabeth Grugeon, "Gender Implications of Children's Playground Culture," in *Gender and Ethnicity in Schools: Ethnographic Accounts*, ed. Peter Woods and Martyn Hammersley (London: Routledge, 1993), 11–24; and Barrie Thorne, *Gender Play: Girls and Boys in School* (New Brunswick, NJ: Rutgers University Press, 2008), 29–49.

[3]Ibid.

[4]Ibid., 12.

Richard Hagan, Mary Driver Leinbach, and Sandra Kronsberg has shown that the stereotyped *expectations* that adults (parents, teachers, playground supervisors) place on children actually affect the way that a particular act by a child will be perceived by those adults.[5] That is, if an individual adult or a group of adults *expects* that a boy, for example, will display more aggressive behavior than his female peer, then any remotely aggressive acts on his part will be more closely and more often noted. Even relatively nonaggressive acts are more likely to be interpreted as aggressive when there is an underlying expectation that a child is, by nature, going to be more aggressive. This pattern, Fagot et al. find, often has the consequence of eventually contributing not only to the adults' genuine view of that boy as a relatively more aggressive child, but also to the boy's own perception of *himself* as comparatively aggressive. That is, the boy will internalize the preconceived expectations that are placed on him and will be more likely to perceive himself as reflecting those expectations.

While a young girl may actually be acting very similarly to that particular boy, the adults' expectation that she comport herself more passively results more often in ignorance, neglect or even active suppression or denial of any demonstrated aggression on her part. Fagot et al. further show that, in a sort of a self-fulfilling prophecy, the boy's belief in and perception of himself as an aggressive child often translates to him actually *becoming* one by more frequently carrying out aggressive acts. In other words, he begins to see himself as an individual who is reprimanded for this type of behavior more often than others, and so, even if he did not originally exhibit such behavior, he begins to pursue the very acts that he has come to believe are characteristic—and tacitly expected—of him.[6]

The important concept within this hypothetical example is that expectations and assumptions placed on young children do have the power to have real consequences in terms of the way a child develops his or her character and identity. In a process that involves adults' socially and culturally conditioned perception of children's behavior and the corresponding ways that children are praised or disciplined in response to their behavior, children can end up internalizing the stereotypes under which they operate in a manner in which they grow up to truly embody them. In this way, the widespread fulfillment of stereotypes should not be seen as a proof of their objective truth, but rather as a reflection of their strength in shaping our self-perceptions.

---

[5]Beverly I. Fagot, Richard Hagan, Mary Driver Leinbach, and Sandra Kronsberg, "Differential Reactions to Assertive and Communicative Acts of Toddler Boys and Girls," *Child Development* 56, no. 6 (December 1985): 1499–1505.

[6]Ibid.

Collectivity Versus Chaos, This Time on Paper

The types of play that research has found that girls and boys prefer—girls centered on collectivity and family-themed role-playing, and boys on competition and chaos—seem perhaps to be more than just a preference in activity. Instead, these markedly different preferences appear to reflect a way in which boys and girls construct their worlds. Research conducted in 2008 by Ageliki Nicolopoulou looked at three- to five-year-old boys and girls in Massachusetts and their distinctive "forms of narrative coherence" in storytelling.[7] Nicolopoulou observed her subjects for a couple of years, throughout which they were invited, at certain times of the day, to dictate a story, any story they wished, to their teacher. There were no "rules" as far as theme, characters, or length of the stories, no requirement that any given child produce a quota of material, and no prompting at any specific moment to generate an idea.[8] After being transcribed by a classroom adult, all stories were eventually read aloud by that adult to the entire class while the child author selected a cast of peers (only, of course, if the story required multiple actors) to act out the story in front of the rest of the class.

Nicolopoulou's research objectives included examining the "narrative purposes and intentions" that the children were aiming to achieve, as well as their "handling of events and event structures" and the methods they employed in their portrayals of "characters and the relations between characters."[9] After years of plot lines (or a lack thereof), characters, and performances, this research found significant differences in the narratives produced by the boys and those produced by the girls (interestingly and notably, differences that correspond closely to those delineated by research into playground behavior). "Although the children's stories were shared with the entire class every day, they divided systematically along gender line," Nicolopoulou writes.[10]

To best organize the categories of responses, Nicolopoulou delineated two main genres: the female-favored "family genre" and the more male-leaning "heroic-agonistic genre." These genres differed along several dimensions, including their foundational images of (dis)order, their portrayal and focus on interpersonal (or, in some cases, inter-creature) relationships, and their presentation of the story's broad social context.[11]

---

[7]Ageliki Nicolopoulou, "The Elementary Forms of Narrative Coherence in Young Children's Storytelling," *Narrative Inquiry* 18, no. 2 (2008): 299–325.

[8]Ibid., 310.

[9]Ibid., 300.

[10]Ibid., 310.

[11]Ibid.

The girls' stories, Nicolopoulou notes, were far more stable than those of their male classmates, in terms of both the relationship networks in which their characters were embedded (and remained until the story's end) and the specific settings and activities in which their stories were played out. Family was a popular theme in these girls' stories, with the typical (even benign) routines of family and home life often serving as the foundation for the characters' relationships as well as the plot. Even when drawing upon images and characters from external pop culture influences (e.g., movies, fairy tales, and television), the girls pulled various princesses, princes, kings, and queens into their stories, effectively incorporating an element of fantasy into an otherwise domestically conventional narrative.[12]

The girls' stories often started with an introduction of the group of characters and a recognition of their relationships to each other (that would remain stable throughout the story). Rarely did the female storytellers center their pieces on an individual protagonist; it was overwhelmingly about the (family) group.[13]

"Once there was a little girl and she lived with her Mom and Dad and her big sister," one girl wrote.[14] "Once upon a time there was a princess, a prince, a queen and a maid," another wrote, and again in a setup focused on familial ties, another girl wrote, "Once upon a time there was a beautiful little princess. Then a prince came . . ."[15]

The girls also employed the frameworks provided by the characters' established relationships to drive the story's plot forward, allowing them room to introduce more complicated plot components while maintaining order within their original band of characters' connections. The characters remained linked, and, in the case of most of the girls' stories, returned "home" as a final conclusion to the story.

"And then [the little girl, her Mom and Dad, and her big sister and their grandma] went for another little walk and they came home again," one girl concludes. The story about the princess, prince, queen, and maid continued when they went on a walk on which they "met a unicorn and brought her back . . . met a tiger and a bear . . . went back home and took the bear but not the tiger home," went to sleep, woke up, had breakfast, and "went to the mall [while] the unicorn and the bear guarded the house," where the princess "bought something and she bought a new gown." The story concludes, "They went back home. The end."[16]

---

[12]Ibid., 311.

[13]Ibid., 314.

[14]Ibid., 315.

[15]Ibid.

[16]Ibid.

The boys, Nicolopoulou found, were more comfortable in the heroic-agonistic genre, often beginning their stories with an individual protagonist whose character was a product of his actions as opposed to his relationships and who was usually immediately faced with a specific problem to which the solution was quickly determined to be some sort of conflict, most often a physical fight.[17] Where the girls' stories often featured ordinary characters ("moms," "sisters," "friends," etc.), the boys preferred "big and powerful animals, real or mythical (e.g., wild horses, growling bears, T-Rex, Godzilla, huge monsters), or else superheroes . . . drawn from pop culture (e.g., Batman, Superman, Captain Hook, etc.)."[18] These boys' stories invariably featured some sort of conflict. Specifically, their stories were eager to determine which character was "the best" and who was the "winner" (a title often awarded by default to any character still alive at the end of the story). The boys' stories depended on aggressive violence, chaotic destruction, and active conflict, and were virtually devoid of consistent relationships (or even an initial recognition of any relationship of any kind, except perhaps one of animosity between "rivals" or "enemies") between characters. The characters in these stories, Nicolopoulou describes, "functioned as little more than vehicles for action and movement."[19]

> A Batman came. He got the policeman dead. And Robin came. He can shoot the monsters. A wolf comes. A knight comes. The dragon killed the princess. The knight killed the dragon. The wolf bites the dragon. The end.[20]

The variations in these stories can be seen as reflective of important differences that young boys and girls start to exhibit at very young ages, most notably the girls' propensity for group identification, relationships, and collectivity over the male tendency toward the glorification of individual dominance and authority. Beyond those specific characteristics, though, is the simple fact that, even after only three years on earth, and probably only one in social settings with peers, there is a distinct and consistent line drawn between how girls see the world and are prepared to recount it as opposed to how boys do both. That is, before many adults would even credit them with having an understanding of the world, these children, through their stories, are displaying the influence of "socially constructed patterns bound up with the formation of gendered

---

[17]Ibid., 312.

[18]Ibid.

[19]Ibid., 318.

[20]Ibid.

subcultures and the sociocultural dynamics of the children's peer group life."[21] All of these patterns are beautifully borne out in Messner's research of the soccer lives of four- and five-year-old boys and girls in an American Youth Soccer Organization community in Southern California. The girls chose sweet and cutesy team names, such as "Blue Butterflies," "Beanie Babes," "Sunflowers," "Pink Flamingos," and "Barbie Girls." The boys, in contrast, opted for power names, such as "Shooting Stars," "Killer Whales," "Shark Attack," "Raptor Attack," and "Sea Monsters."[22] While the boys across all age categories (four to seventeen) were much more prone to choose power names for their teams as opposed to any from the cutesy or even neutral categories (such as "Galaxy," "Pink Panthers," "Little Tigers," "Flower Power," or "Blue Ice"), this was particularly pronounced among the youngest group. Messner noticed an interesting progression on the girls' side: Whereas the youngest among them opted in great proportion for teams with cutesy names, by the time the girls reached fourteen to seventeen, such team names all but disappeared. But even at this age, a higher segment of the girls chose neutral or paradoxical team names than did the boys.[23]

Messner also demonstrates that both girls and boys picked up on the different gender roles that their parents expect them to assume and in which they revel: "'They are SO [sic] different!' exclaims one smiling mother approvingly. . . . In the entire subsequent season of weekly games and practices, I never once saw adults point to a moment in which boy and girl soccer players were doing the *same* thing and exclaim to each other, 'Look at them! They are *so similar!*'"[24]

Differentiation in Self-Perceptions of Competencies

Given these tenets of the "self-fulfilling prophecy" in the case of the overly aggressive boy as well as the evidence of the practical differences in boys' and girls' internalization of their social worlds, let the discussion now turn to another significant component in the question of the developmental gaps between young boys and girls: the differences in their self-evaluations of their competencies in different realms of academia and society.

---

[21]Ibid., 311.

[22]Michael A. Messner, "Barbie Girls Versus Sea Monsters: Children Constructing Gender" in *The Sport and Society Reader*, ed. David Karen and Robert E. Washington (New York: Routledge, 2010), 187.

[23]Ibid., 188

[24]Ibid., 184, 185, emphasis in original.

Research into this area has shown that, in much the same way that adults' expectations transform a child's behavior, so too can that child's beliefs about his or her competencies.[25] The foundation for those self-evaluations most likely is provided by society's wider gendered expectations (which are then transmitted through the child's parents), but the consequences in terms of perpetuation of those norms can nonetheless be ignored. That is, as Sociology 101 may have once preached, just because a phenomenon is "socially constructed" does not mean that its effect is not very much real.

Several relevant studies conducted with children as their subjects strengthen the notion that the expectations under which a child operates can and do have real consequences in terms of their identities and abilities. First, of course, we must mention the renowned "Pygmalion in the Classroom" experiment, carried out by Robert Rosenthal and Lenore Jacobson in 1965, research that opened social scientists' and educators' eyes in terms of the power vested in their own expectations. In this study, Rosenthal and Jacobson informed teachers at an elementary school that, based on a (fictional) "Harvard Test of Inflected Acquisition," certain students in their classrooms should be expected to be what they coined "growth spurters." Teachers were to be ready to see high academic performances and intellectual growth from these students, although, of course, these "growth spurters" were identified at random and, as far as the researchers could tell, were not significantly different as a group from those students not thus identified.[26]

The results of the experiment reflected what psychology calls the "observer-expectancy effect," a phenomenon in which an observer's or evaluator's biased and often unconscious expectations shape the behaviors of those they are observing (in this case, the students). Those students who were marked "growth spurters" were, in fact, recognized by teachers as outperforming their peers, even in situations when researchers determined that there were no significant differences between them and the rest. Teachers were found to recognize early and then celebrate disproportionately the successes of the "spurters," only to make these children eventually gain the confidence to truly, objectively outperform their peers. The children who were not initially labeled as "spurters," meanwhile, were not fostered and did not have their success facilitated in the same ways, and consequently, the study concludes, began actually to perform at objectively lower levels. James Rhem, in

[25]Janis E. Jacobs, Stephanie Lanza, D. Wayne Osgood, Jacquelynne S. Eccles, and Allan Wigfield, "Changes in Children's Self-Competence and Values: Gender and Domain Differences across Grades One through Twelve," *Child Development* 73, no. 2 (March–April 2002): 509–527.

[26]Robert Rosenthal and Lenore Jacobson, "Pygmalion in the Classroom," *The Urban Review* 3, no. 1 (August 20, 1968): 16–20.

an article for the National Teaching and Learning Foundation, put it simply when he explained, "When teachers expect students to do well and show intellectual growth, they do; when teachers do not have such expectations, performance and growth are not so encouraged and may in fact be discouraged in a variety of ways."[27]

Expectancy-Value Theory and the Achievement-Choice Model

Achievement motivation and all of its component parts constitute a crucial concept in this discussion of childhood and adolescent development. Theories within the study of achievement motivation aim to elucidate individuals' "choice of achievement tasks, persistence on those tasks, vigor in carrying them out, and performance on them."[28] There are a number of different models and variations within the topic of achievement motivation, the most useful for our presentation at this juncture and our book's overall argument being the *expectancy-value* theory, a detailed model of which was developed and tested by Jacquelynne Eccles, Allan Wigfield, and their colleagues in the early 1980s. First employed by Eccles and Wigfield in studies on achievement in mathematics, the model has since been employed in a wide variety of achievement domains, sports included.[29] The core concept within all iterations of expectancy-value theory is that, as explained by Wigfield and Eccles themselves, "individuals' choice, persistence, and performance can be explained by their beliefs about how well they will do on the activity and the extent to which they value the activity."[30] This model asserts that both one's belief in one's own ability and one's conception of an activity's intrinsic value play a part in determining one's choice to pursue (and the degree to which one pursues) a given activity.[31]

The influence of gender role stereotypes on children's perception of activity stereotypes and gender roles, and eventually on their interpretations of their experiences is a path that precisely addresses the processes addressed previously in this chapter. Sticking with this model while moving forward in

---

[27]James Rhem, "Pygmalion in the Classroom," *The National Teaching & Learning Forum* 8, no. 2 (1999): 1–4.

[28]Allan Wigfield and Jacquelynne S. Eccles, "Expectancy-Value Theory of Achievement Motivation," *Contemporary Educational Psychology* 25 (2000): 68–81 (quote from p. 68).

[29]Ibid.

[30]Ibid., 68.

[31]Ibid., 69.

this discussion, we now focus on "expectancies for success" and "subjective task value" (consisting of importance, interest, utility, and cost of an activity) to "achievement-related choices and performance."[32] This specific part of the broad theory of achievement motivation will help in an understanding of how and why men and women eventually find themselves miles apart when it comes to following sports. That is, a survey of several studies on achievement motivation, broadly defined, will demonstrate the factors that lead to a child's opinion of an activity and the degree to which the child chooses to pursue it.

A 2002 study by Janice E. Jacobs, Stephanie Lanza, D. Wayne Osgood, Jacquelynne S. Eccles, and Allan Wigfield followed the changes in self-beliefs in competencies as well as subject valuation (how much value a respondent placed on each domain) among 761 boys and girls from first through twelfth grade. The basis for this longitudinal study came from previous research on the connection between self-beliefs concerning one's competencies and one's actual achievement, a relationship that past research had positively identified.[33] The study by Jacobs et al. meant to build on previous research that showed positive correlations between an individual child's belief in his or her abilities, the child's consequent achievement motivation and self-esteem, and the child's eventual objective performance in a given domain. Jacobs et al. hoped to explain the differences in young boys' and girls' preferences as well as their respective pursuits and areas of relative success. The aforementioned work by Fagot et al. highlighted the ways in which the vertical imposition of expectations from parents and teachers to children often results in the fulfillment of anticipated behaviors; in contrast, the research by Jacobs et al. attempted to focus more closely on the intermediate process by which children begin to discover and develop differing beliefs about their abilities and, eventually, about the objective value that certain abilities and activities possess in general.[34]

Jacobs et al. delineated three domains of interest: math, language arts (or reading), and sport. The researchers first employed "competence belief items" to determine each individual's self-perceptions of her or his own abilities in each domain.[35] A set of "subjective task value items" (questions that addressed how subjects felt toward each activity in terms of being "interesting/fun," useful, and important to possess skills in) was then used to determine the value placed on the respective domains.[36] Lastly, the scholars designed an actual

---

[32]Ibid.

[33]Jacobs et al., "Children's Self-Competence and Values."

[34]Fagot et al., "Toddler Boys and Girls."

[35]Jacobs et al., "Children's Self-Competence and Values," 513.

[36]Ibid.

evaluation of performance to determine the subjects' objective abilities in each of the three domains of interest.

Self-Perceptions

In the case of the subjects' beliefs in their math competence, first-grade males ranked higher than females, but both groups steadily declined until they finished the study as twelfth graders for whom gender did not affect their self-evaluation (they finish high school with equal beliefs in their math competence).[37] Language arts competence began with first-grade boys and girls evaluating themselves the same, but very quickly split, with females displaying more beliefs in their competence all throughout the study. Sports competence, at any temporal point in the study, featured the largest gap between the boys' and girls' beliefs in their respective competence, with males possessing significantly more confidence in their ability than females. Both groups, however, reported a steady decline in the perception of their competence throughout the duration of the study, meaning that the aging process seemed to have a humbling effect on both genders' self-perception of their respective athletic abilities.[38]

Attributed Value

The significance of these findings becomes clearer when they are paired with the differences in valuation across gender groups. After all, the purpose of the study was to determine if there existed any influence from subjective task value to competence beliefs.

When controlling for competence beliefs (splitting gender groups into "with ability"/"without ability," based on subjects' responses), females "without ability" began in first grade, and would remain thus throughout twelfth, to grant the lowest attributed valuation to sports.[39] This group recognized "sports competence" as possessing the least amount of general value among all subsets of the survey population.

However, around tenth grade, females with perceived ability surpassed all other groups in terms of the value that they placed on sports.[40] That is, it appears as though, in the course of their high school years, the girls experi-

---

[37]Ibid., 516.

[38]Ibid., 517.

[39]Ibid., 519.

[40]Ibid.

enced a huge split in terms of their own belief in their competence between those "with ability" and those "without ability" in terms of the value they recognized in sport. As a unified gender group (regardless of "ability"), women's valuation of sport declined in the elementary school years, but during middle school, those females with a recognition of their own ability began to place a steadily increasing value on sport, until the end of high school, when they valued it even more than all of the study's males.[41]

Throughout the respondents' time in high school (ninth to twelfth grade), all males (both with and without "ability") valued sports about the same, while females "with ability" rapidly increased their evaluation of sports and females "without ability" remained sports' most underwhelmed or modest appraisers.[42]

Ability ≠ Appreciation

What this research may be showing is that (albeit self-perceived) confidence in one's competence may be more important for females than for males in terms of the value that is ascribed to that specific activity. That is, a female's own ability to do well in sports may play a large role in the value that she attributes to sport in general as well as her involvement with it on any level, whether consumer or producer. In contrast, her male peers may be less concerned with their individual capacities when deciding where a particular pursuit's value lies, with sport being an especially salient case in point. If one is to split up both gender's populations into subgroups "with" and "without [self-perceived] ability," the two female groups show larger differences from each other than do the two male subgroups. That is, for girls, there is a huge difference between those with a belief in their ability and those without it in terms of the kind of value they attribute to sport.[43] This suggests that, as a girl, one's ability—or perhaps more accurately one's confidence in one's ability—matters more than it might for a boy when it comes to recognizing the value in sports.

It seems, then, that compared with boys, for a girl to see value in a domain, it is more important that she see herself as being "with ability" in it. Drawing from a study conducted by Jacquelynne S. Eccles and Rena D. Harold, we find that a girl's belief that she is "with ability" is subject to many other forces.[44] In this study, Eccles and Harold created a model for activity choice for children, with the two main mediators of choice being expectancies for suc-

[41]Ibid.

[42]Ibid.

[43]Jacobs et al., "Children's Self-Competence and Values," 520.

[44]Jacquelynne S. Eccles and Rena D. Harold, "Gender Differences in Sport Involvement: Applying the Eccles' Expectancy-Value Model," *Journal of Applied Sport Psychology* 3 (1991): 7–35.

cess (undoubtedly linked to the recognition of one's ability) and values. The component parts of "expectancies" included, among other things, gender role stereotypes. "Gender differences in children's attitudes toward sport are quite strong and emerge at a very young age," Eccles and Harold explain.[45] These gender differences seem to be a consequence more of gender role socialization than of "'natural' aptitudinal differences."[46]

Gendered differences exist from the earliest stages of social interaction, but they are less likely to be reflections of actual ability and are more probably consequences of the ways that stereotyped expectations are internalized at an early age. This furnishes an example of the "continuing strong and early role of gender role stereotypes on observed gender differences. Even before they have much experience with different activities in more formal evaluative settings such as school, boys' and girls' competence beliefs and subjective task values differ."[47]

The stereotyped expectations placed on a young girl (specifically, in this case, that which suggests that she will be less athletically inclined) inform her internalized understanding of herself and eventually her actual level of self-competence in that domain. Having a lower level of self-competence, or falling under the heading "without ability," we can conclude, constitutes a huge detriment to a girl's appreciation or recognition of value in a certain area. In terms of finding value and enjoyment in sports as a general institution, it is more of a deterrent for a female not to see herself as being individually competent in the production of sports than it is for a male. And, as our later chapters argue, this gendered valuation of self-competence as a source of interest in and involvement with sports obtains a fortiori to the world of consuming and following of sports as well.

Eccles and Harold's research shows that perceived value, as much as performance expectations or belief in one's own ability, is a strong mediator of children's choices of activities. The authors' main puzzle in their childhood development study was to entangle "how . . . children develop their ideas about whom they would like to be, and about how specific activities fit their self-schema."[48] Eccles and her research team created a theoretical model for understanding and analyzing the factors and motivations—focusing on achievement

---

[45]Ibid., 7.

[46]Ibid.

[47]Allan Wigfield, Jacquelynne S. Eccles, Kwang Suk Yoon, Rena D. Harold, Amy J. Arbreton, Carol Freedman-Doan, and Phyllis C. Blumenfeld, "Change in Children's Competence Beliefs and Subjective Task Values across the Elementary School Years: A 3-Year Study," *Journal of Educational Psychology* 89, no. 3 (September 1997): 451–469.

[48]Eccles and Harold, "Gender Differences in Sport Involvement," 17.

motivation and competence beliefs—that underlie the choices that individuals make. Certainly, culture and life experiences inform children's definitions and evaluations of some activities, as Eccles and Harold recognize, but "what is important, then," they continue, "is to understand the meshing of children's views of the activity with their view of themselves, and the extent to which they see the task or activity as either being instrumental or counter-productive to reinforcing their self-views."[49] In other words, the choices that children, and all individuals, make are not determined simply by an isolated, impersonal evaluation of the options as they exist to everyone, but are partially determined by individuals' view of themselves and their abilities.

Significant shifts in evaluating one's standing in the world of sports production usually center on high school, when competition "bottlenecks" force less exceptional athletes and students to pursue alternative tracks.[50] Without controlling for ability, the average high school boy awards more value to sports than does the average high school girl, but as was mentioned earlier, accounting for ability sends the two groups of females to opposite evaluative poles. Whereas this process may deter those females who are unable to "make the team" (and are therefore losing much of their self-perceived ability) from further according "sport" with value, it seems as though the boys are more likely to keep their subscriptions to *Sports Illustrated*, continue watching SportsCenter, and still dream of season tickets, regardless of whether they are starting on the varsity team or were cut from the freshman team.

Furthermore, Jacobs et al. point out that the timing for the decline of "competence beliefs" and "task values" for boys followed a relatively linear pattern, suggesting that the boys' beliefs in their own abilities in a given area

---

[49]Ibid.

[50]Jacobs et al. ("Children's Self-Competence and Values") offer an explanation for the overall decline in reported self-perceptions of competence in sport, by pointing out that throughout school, children move into situations in which there are more interested individuals than there are available slots on increasingly competitive teams (p. 522). While in elementary school, there is more room for all children to play a variety of sports, but "as [they] get older sport activities become more selective and competitive, and fewer children are selected to be on competitive teams" (p. 522). Hilary Levey, in her research on contemporary America's unprecedented levels of competition at increasingly younger ages, finds that the pool of children at the elementary stages of virtually any valued endeavor has grown incredibly large. She sees this as a result of parents' desire to get their children involved in as many activities as possible so as to increase their curricular capital and hopefully train them to reach the level of exceptionality that is seemingly required in this newly über-competitive culture. The large numbers of children at low levels of competition have actually moved the "bottlenecks" that Jacobs described to earlier places on the developmental timeline way before the former high school threshold. (Hilary Levey, Lecture in the Department of Sociology, University of Michigan, January 11, 2011; see also Hilary Levey, "Congratulations on Your New Credential!," Playing to Win, entry posted February 10, 2011, available at http://hilaryleveyfriedman. blogspot.com/2011/02/congratulations-on-your-new-credential.html [accessed March 13, 2011].)

may have something to do with the overall importance that they recognize the domain as possessing. In contrast, the females in the study reflected a "decline in self-competence concentrated in the high school years and a decline in values concentrated in the elementary school years."[51] This research shows that these girls maintained their confidence in their own sports competence through high school, but had begun to devalue sports competency in general at a much earlier stage in life. Thus, the separation of "doing" sports and "following" them receives an added dimension in the lives of girls that simply does not have any parallels in boys'.

There seems to be an interaction at play between gendered expectations, individual understandings of competencies, and eventual differences in assigned value. If this is in fact the case, as the results suggest it is, then this body of research, combining Eccles and Harold with Jacobs et al., offers a significant explanation for the gendered gap in the salience of sports fandom among adults. In particular, this scholarship provides helpful insights that the kinds of connections that may initiate and foster a woman's interest in sport as a fan (i.e., possessing an individual aptitude for—or at least having experience with—a given sport) may not be nearly as important a contributor to a male's (much more ardent) fandom.

In essence, Eccles and Harold tell us that how one sees oneself (i.e., one's self-perception) matters in terms of one's actual performance. Thus, if one sees oneself as incapable of success, one will have a much harder time finding it. Girls more so than boys think that they have many fewer capabilities in sports, which means that there will be fewer opportunities to stimulate and maintain girls' interest in sports, which also means that this world will offer girls fewer rewards than it does boys.

Jacobs et al. argue that a negative self-perception in sports matters more for girls than for boys. Being "good" at sports, or seeing oneself as such, is more important in a girl's evaluation of whether sports are a worthy way to invest time than it is for boys. Interpreting the results of Jacobs et al., it becomes apparent that the gap between "with" and "without" ability is bigger for girls than for boys. The timing as to when this happens is essential, given what we glean from Eccles and Harold: When females start to see themselves as bad at sports in high school (when sports get truly competitive), they abandon sports altogether as a worthwhile pursuit. This abandonment of "doing" sports, of sports production, has massive ramifications for "following" sports (i.e., sports consumption) for girls who stop being interested in any and all of the many dimensions of sports.

As a rule, most girls like sports less than most boys. Both boys and girls have to go through competition bottlenecks. The consequences of the bot-

---

[51]Jacobs et al., "Children's Self-Competence and Values," 521.

tlenecks (the possibility that individuals may lower their competence beliefs) are more detrimental to girls' following sports than to boys' because the girls attach "doing" and "following" much more than boys, for whom these two realms remain much more discrete and separate. Girls will not stick around sports if their production of them is not of the quality to make them part of the team or a larger whole that rewards their effort. If boys do not make the team, if their sports production remains deficient, this does not alienate them from sports at all and does not have any detrimental effects on their being avid sports consumers. Indeed, quite the contrary may be the case. Many a male sports expert and aficionado became such precisely because of his shortcomings as an athlete. With men, failure in doing sports might very well lead to the compensatory mechanism of becoming an expert in following them.

A Formula for Fandom

In a study preceding the Jacobs et al. publication, Jacquelynne Eccles, Allan Wigfield, Rena D. Harold, and Phyllis Blumenfeld looked into the differences that seven- to ten-year-old elementary schoolchildren express in their self- and task perceptions of sport, music, reading, and math.[52] Significantly, this work finds that differences in children's self-evaluations with regard to specific domains begin to appear before children actually commence participating in activities featuring such domains, contesting the widely held assumptions of allegedly gendered differences in innate ability. Thus, for example, female babies are widely alleged to have more favorable language skills than their male counterparts, even in the face of evidence that demonstrates the inherent abilities of both to be essentially the same in this domain.

In a comparable conceptual process by which boys are attributed to have an innate penchant for excessive aggression, the *expectations* that adults (those with the power to recognize and celebrate achievement) place on children often dictate the *reality* of those children's actual behaviors. Research shows that adults' expectations and perceptions, including the expected differences based on gender, are easily internalized by young children. Thus, children's gender-differentiated beliefs about themselves as individuals easily precede actual differences that manifest themselves in actual behavior in the real world.[53] That is, children often act in gendered ways, or understand their competencies in a gendered scheme, anticipatorily, so to speak, as a result of the expectations

---

[52]Jacquelynne Eccles, Allan Wigfield, Rena D. Harold, and Phyllis Blumenfeld, "Age and Gender Differences in Children's Self- and Task Perceptions during Elementary School," *Child Development* 64, no. 3 (June 1993): 830–847.

[53]Ibid.

placed on them by adults (as opposed to any consequence of their actual gender, which may have allowed more time for individual development).

Eccles et al. found that the gaps between boys' and girls' respective competence beliefs are significantly higher in the realm of sport than in any of the other domains that they studied.[54] Substantially enhancing the qualitative salience of this difference is the fact that evaluations of girls' and boys' actual athletic abilities by a bevy of metrics yield only negligible, if any, differences. Crucially, however, the reality of the virtual parity in tangible sporting skills between the genders is markedly less important than an individual child's *belief* about his or her athletic ability, leading ultimately to a situation in which, as Eccles et al. found, "it is likely that children will select those tasks at which they feel relatively more competent."[55]

This pattern, combined with the results of the research by Jacobs et al. indicating that females have a relatively durable psychological connection between their individual athletic competence and their valuation of sport in general, makes the paucity of female sports fans in adolescence and adulthood appear increasingly inevitable. To simplify, if women need more individual athletic ability than they actually have to valorize sport as an institution (which constitutes arguably a sine qua non to be a bona fide sports fan), and if their perceived athletic ability—regardless of reality—is less than that of males (due in part to socialization practices employed by their parents and teachers), then the outcome appears to be rather overdetermined and unsurprising, fully confirming the current situation in the United States and all countries of the advanced industrial world: It is relatively simple to understand how thus far a small minority of women among an overwhelming majority of men finds the way to sports fandom.

A fascinating study conducted by scholars in the Department of Sports-Sciences at the University of Goettingen in Germany corroborates these findings in a different country and social setting. In a large study on how four- to six-year-old children establish their body image and their kinetic movements, and how gender-specific both might be, researchers conducted in-depth interviews with sixty-one children in five kindergartens in the university town of Goettingen, which is comparable in size, milieu, and atmosphere to our very own Ann Arbor. Not surprisingly, here, too, children take their cues from adults, particularly their parents. And as one of the reports from the study shows, children reproduce their mothers' and fathers' deeply gendered world not only in their actual comportment and behavior but also in their knowl-

---

[54]Ibid., 841.

[55]Ibid.

edge and preferences. This report demonstrates how the children's parents very much expect their youngsters to conform to conventional gender behavior and image and how the kids pick up on these expectations, even if the parents do not verbalize or demand them in any visible manner.[56] In a companion report, Maika Bepperling presents powerful evidence on how boys in the study are deeply involved with and impressively knowledgeable about sports, in this case, soccer, of course, Germany's hegemonic equivalent to the Big Four of baseball, basketball, football, and ice hockey in North America.

These four- to six-year-old boys not only know the various teams' names, the colors of their jerseys, and the names and numbers of their key players but also the different strategies played by different teams, as well as the historical dimension of games that happened when these boys were much younger and could not possibly remember in an active way or even preceded their birth, occasionally by a good number of years. In other words, these boys got to know their soccer by listening to their dads and their (presumably male) friends and by participating in these collective conversations. Reinforcing the gendered nature of sports talk as an intragender bonding experience, Bepperling reports that when she and other women spoke to the boys about soccer, the boys responded curtly by offering the bare minimum that was asked of them, nothing more. But when the interviewers were male, the boys became much more animated and volunteered all kinds of information beyond merely stating the facts that the question required. In other words, the boys clearly used sports—in this case, soccer—as a medium to connect with their male interviewers on a much deeper level than they did with the female researchers whom they simply assumed not to be sufficiently knowledgeable about the topic at hand and whom they uncomfortably perceived as outsiders to this world (which, by Bepperling's admission to Markovits, they decidedly were). The boys talked about sports to the interviewers, among themselves, and to their general surroundings. The girls, in contrast, showed absolutely no interest in talking about sports and seemed totally unperturbed about not knowing any facts that seemed so important to the boys. Instead, the girls offered detailed responses about varied aspects of daily life, both theirs and their surroundings', provided elaborate descriptions of the colors and contents of their (and their friends') school bags, and revealed a surprisingly rich knowledge about physical appearance.[57]

[56]Steffen Loick, "Geschlechtsspezifische Koerper-und Bewegungssozialisation in der fruehen Kindheit—Qualitative Teilstudie mit Eltern" (unpublished paper, University of Goettingen, Goettingen, May 2011).

[57]Maika Bepperling, "Jungen sprechen ueber Sport!—Und Maedchen?" (unpublished paper, University of Goettingen, Goettingen, July 2011). The title translates as "Boys talk about sports—and girls?"

So far, this discussion of the processes by which male and female children commence and continue their gradual social severance can be seen as having several components: (1) the (unintentional) biased identification and encouragement of specific behaviors on the part of adult supervisors; (2) the appearance of gendered differentiation with regard to young peoples' self-evaluations of their competencies in specific arenas; and (3) the differences across gender (and perceived ability) in the value granted to different activities and domains. Put more simply, boys are assumed to like sports and are encouraged and rewarded for athletic pursuits, they then understand themselves to be athletically competent and to associate sports with an affirmation of their success, and eventually they determine that sports in general are of great importance in the world. With the comprehensive goal of discerning the mechanisms that contribute to the reality of low levels of sports fandom among females, a logical next step is to look into the social capital that sports offer young boys and girls.

Social Capital

Research by Joel Thirer and Stephen D. Wright focuses on the way that involvement in sport affects the social standing of adolescents. Their study found that, among a number of options given as possible criteria for ranking popularity, both male and female respondents chose to "be an athlete" as their top priority for boys.[58] That is, more so than, for example, being on the honor roll, or being a leader in social or cultural activities, to be an athlete was the single most important evaluative piece when determining a young boy's popularity with both genders.

For girls, however, the story looked different: For them, to "be in the leading crowd" sat atop all other options. Once again, both male and female respondents placed this available category as the most socially rewarding for girls. In short, whether one asks the boys or the girls, the unanimous results show that association with sport is more important socially for boys than any other factor, while association with the "in crowd" carries the most social capital for their female peers.[59] This may not seem much of a surprise to the reader, but, given that young children were the subject of this research, the results offer us important insights into a proper understanding of the deeply gendered nature of virtually all aspects of our contemporary sports world among adults.

---

[58]Joel Thirer and Stephen D. Wright, "Sport and Social Status for Adolescent Males and Females," *Sociology of Sport Journal* 2 (1985): 164–171.

[59]Ibid., 167.

More specifically, for our purposes, these results frame the main focus of our book: the gender-deviant woman who lives as an ardent sports fan.

Typologies of Girls: Conformity and Deviance

So far in this presentation, the assignations "boys" and "girls" have been used to represent the majority members of these groups. While social science research inevitably must make use of generalizations, averages, and broad groupings, it is also significant for the purposes of this book to take a look at those outliers who are less accurately represented by their larger group. Research into young children's attitudes toward gender deviation, specifically, a girl's rejection of her femininity, will add to the explanation of why adolescent and adult women do not end up following sport—a decidedly manly realm—in the same way that men do.

In Diane Reay's study of the cultures of femininity in elementary school classrooms, we meet a self-proclaimed (and proud) "tomboy" named Jodie.[60] "Tomboy" was one of the four typologies developed by Reay to group the girls she observed, the remaining three being "girlies," "spice girls," and "nice girls."[61] To briefly outline the characteristics of Reay's categories, the "girlies" participate in the display of pronounced femininity and rely on "boyfriend/girlfriend" scenarios to provide much of their identity.[62] The "spice girls" also participate in boyfriend/girlfriend games, but approach their social world with an attitude and willingness to use their femininity as a means of challenging (and gaining) power. In this way, "spice girls" are more often identified as exhibiting bad behavior than their counterparts. The "nice girls" are high achieving and well behaved, heavily informed by the model of "mature girls and immature boys."[63]

The "tomboys" fall into a unique position among their male and female peers. In this study, only Jodie identified herself as a full-fledged tomboy (notably, her words were, "I'm not a girl; I'm a tomboy").[64] Her attitude was that the girls in her class are "stupid and girlie," and that their activities and preferences do not in any way reflect her own.[65] Reay, in this study, found that the

---

[60]Diane Reay, "'Spice Girls,' 'Nice Girls,' 'Girlies,' and 'Tomboys': Gender Discourses, Girls' Cultures and Femininities in the Primary Classroom," *Gender and Education* 13, no. 2 (2001): 153–166.

[61]Ibid., 158.

[62]Ibid., 159.

[63]Ibid., 158.

[64]Ibid., 162.

[65]Ibid., 161.

young boys unanimously considered it more favorable to be male as opposed to female.[66] Citing such factors as "you get to do much better things," and the fact that "it's boring being a girl," the boys maintained that they had been dealt the biological upper hand, that "maleness, if not a superior subject positioning, was a more desirable one."[67] The boys upheld this powerful claim against all three groups of girls *except* the tomboys. The girls, in turn, dismissed the boys' claims and defended the value of their femininity. "In particular the 'spice girls,' but also at various times both the 'girlies' and the 'nice girls' defended girlhood against such [the boys' dismissive] claims."[68] However, these girls' opinion was "routinely undermined by the position adopted by the tomboys," who, with Jodie as their spokesperson, decided, "Girls are crap, all the girls in this class act all stupid and girlie."[69] The tomboys represented the only faction of the entire mixed-gender population that recognized the *other* gender as decidedly superior or more desirable than one's own.

Perhaps not surprisingly, the attitude that many of the girls held with regard to tomboys was that they were traitors to their gender, that their decision to pursue the lifestyle of the boys suggests and affirms that things are not good enough among the girls. At the same time, though, Jodie's position afforded her respect and friendship from the boys, a result that may have been the impetus behind the tomboy phases attempted by many of the other girls.[70] Where the "spice girls" took advantage of their femininity to gain power, Jodie was able to find power in a departure from her traditional gender because she was granted respect from the boys that the other girls could not earn.

Jodie did have to earn this respect, though, by doing maintenance work to reaffirm her similarity to the boys. She often participated in making fun of traditionally girly-girls' activities as well as her peers who engaged in them, thereby joining the boys in what Madeleine Arnot, cited by Reay, describes as the maintenance of males' superior place on the social hierarchy by way of "maintain[ing] the hierarchy of social superiority of masculinity by devaluing the female world," a practice that we will see repeated as these "tomboys" attempt to continue to toe the line between the gender-segregated realms of sports fandom and non-fandom.[71]

---

[66]Ibid., 156.

[67]Ibid., 161.

[68]Ibid.

[69]Ibid.

[70]Ibid., 162.

[71]Madeleine Arnot, "Male Hegemony, Social Class and Women's Education," *Journal of Education* 16 (1982): 164.

Jodie illustrates several important processes that will be echoed through-out our story, most notably, the experience of resentment from females in re-sponse to gender deviation, a unique respect and friendship (and therefore power) awarded in exchange for a commitment to enhance masculinity by way of denigrating traditional femininity. Of greatest significance in this example is the fact that Jodie's changing of teams and rejection of "girliness" eventually gave her special power and reaffirmed the notion that "malehood" is, in fact, understood as superior to being female. In short, the individual empowerment that Jodie achieved through gender deviation may have sealed another pane in the glass ceiling for her female counterparts.

Conclusion

In this chapter, we focused on children as a means of recognizing that there *are* marked differences between boys and girls. This is not something that we are looking to refute or about which we mean to express frustration; we under-stand that, for better or worse, and as a result of either "nature or nurture" as it were—more likely a complex, constant, and intertwined interaction between the two—boys and girls generally are significantly different participants in society. It is important, though, for our project, to understand the way that such differences are fostered, even at the earliest stages of development.

Our book's main subject is the girl who somehow makes her way into a realm of interest toward which the large majority of her female counterparts never venture. The process of steering individuals toward sport—or any do-main of interest—starts at a very young age and is a combination of a number of different "real" and "imagined" assumptions, motivations, self-perceptions, and choices. Illustrating the world in which our subject grows and operates, in which this gender-bending, sports-following girl first conceives of her sense of identity and her place in society's specific milieu of sports fandom, is essential if we are to understand the important differences that she embodies as well as the nature of her deviance.

Had our minds not been immersed in the topic of our book, had we as individuals and as a collective not been deeply interested in studying, ana-lyzing, perhaps explaining, but certainly admiring the rare woman who is an avid sports connoisseur as well as aficionado, one equally knowledgeable of and passionate about the hegemonic sports languages informing our quotidian culture, our walk through Burns Park might not have incited any fascination whatsoever. After all, there was nothing at all unusual about the scene. Its deep gender segregation bespoke the norm of pretty much every coeducational insti-tution's recess in contemporary America. But it was precisely the pedestrian—

indeed, expected—normalcy of this heavily gender-segregated situation that piqued our interest as two individuals preoccupied with exploring the origins of such a pronounced difference between genders in the world of sports. Reflecting back on that playground scene after having educated ourselves at least a tiny bit by the rich scholarship on childhood development has helped us immensely in contextualizing the magnitude of a sportista's deviance from the norm. We were keen on studying, analyzing, and feting the (still) few women who became fluent sportspeakers in their lives, thus rendering their passion for, and knowledge of, sports as a major marker of their very identity.

To find initial—and then maintain—deep interest in the following of sports requires that a girl endure a large number of pressures, be it from adults, peers, one's own self-perception, larger social forces, or any combination of these. Making matters more challenging still is the fact that the gravity, propensity, and normal modus operandi of each and every one of these powerful demands consists in steering such a girl away from sports fandom. The little girl who was playing soccer with the boys may very well end up, like many women, as a highly skilled athlete with little to no interest in the *following* of soccer, let alone other popular sports.

Let us consider, for a moment, though, that, in addition to being a fine soccer player and thus a proficient sports producer, she also developed a strong interest in the consumption of sports, she loved to follow them in various venues; in other words, she was well on her way to becoming a veritable sportista. There are a number of breaks with, detours, and deviations from the norm that this imaginary young woman will have to have actively sought and overcome to reach this stage: First, she had to separate herself from her peer group by playing soccer with the boys. Next, she augmented the distance from her peer group's norm by excelling at soccer and playing as well as the boys. This means that she had to have maintained a sufficiently high level of confidence in her athletic ability to put herself on the field and compete on level terms with the boys, a group that most likely possesses a much higher degree of "competence beliefs" when it comes to its soccer ability or any athletic prowess than our prototypical girl is likely to have had. By this stage, her ability to *play* herself might be maintained, and so too would her interest in sports in general. Whatever combination and interaction of influences in her life have thus far informed her opinion of herself and of the benefits of sport for her life might just leave enough room for her to hold on to the value that she now sees in sports throughout her high school years, regardless of whether she ever makes the varsity team.

Nearly every boy on the Burns Park playground that day was playing an organized sport. Boys, as a gender group, already value sport more than their female peers, and will likely continue to do so throughout their time in school.

Tryouts, "A" and "B" teams, and cuts will also be in their future as the competition of organized sport increases exponentially as they age, with the clear certainty that only an ever-diminishing minority will "make the team." It is clear, though, that the boys' appreciation for and interest in sport has a much greater chance of surviving the disappointing but near-certain experience of being cut from some team than is the case with the girls. But our sportista constitutes a decided outlier. Even though she, like her male teammates, has been more than likely to experience disappointments by not making it to the next level of the competitive scale, she will have internalized the idea that it's okay to play with the boys. She will perceive the value in sport and in her own ability to play it. Hopefully, she will be able to hold on to this. Still, what will this acquisition of skill and immersion in passion—this process of becoming conversant with a culture whose main protagonists remain, if not openly hostile, then most decidedly suspicious of her—mean for her future in the world of sports, their production and consumption?

Having explored the origins of gender differences in young boys and girls, we now turn to an examination of the ways that these differences become pronounced as women enter professional realms in society that—just like sports— have by and large remained heavily dominated by males. We have shown how different forces and influences in society tend to pilot boys and girls in specific directions, and will now, in Chapter 2, examine the experiences of women whose professional tracks lead them to positions not typically occupied by members of their gender group.

2

Women in Men's Worlds

Process of Exclusion and Suppression of Females in Male-Dominated Realms Other Than Sport

Beginning in the earliest stages of a child's development, young boys and girls are often steered in what have been deemed gender-appropriate directions in terms of their preferences and activities. This practice of (often unintentional) gendered guidance translates into real differences in young boys' and girls' perceptions about their abilities in certain academic areas, which in turn supports the production of professional realms that are clearly dominated by one gender group. Domination, however, does not entail complete exclusion; men and women exist who, like Jodie, the representative "tomboy" from Chapter 1, as will be recalled, consciously choose to pursue paths on which they remain in the disempowered minority, perhaps for a bounded period, perhaps for life.

Before narrowing the focus to the domain of sports fandom, we will conduct a broader examination of the common processes of exclusion and suppression of females within male-dominated areas. We will introduce the concept of *credentialing* and use it to compare the relative difficulty with which a disempowered individual can advance him- or herself by way of "proving" her or his worth or ability. We argue that the salience of credentialing for successful entry of disempowered groups to realms of power, prestige, and social value that remained previously closed to them constitutes one of the most equitable forces in the creation of fairness in modern liberal democracies. Alas, we also know that such important mechanisms of procedural as well as contextual access to valued structures in no way alleviate the relative ease with which arbitrary discrimination and other measures of exclusion continue to protect the power of the status quo.

We will subsequently examine women's experiences in such fields as science and engineering, information technology, ROTC programs, coaching, and investment banking, with special focus on the shared practices and strategies that contribute to the comparative challenges that these women face in gaining acceptance and advancement.

Credentialing

One need not invoke the work of the great Max Weber to argue persuasively that a system adhering to legal-rational rather than charismatic and traditional criteria of authority and legitimation of public action is more favorable for the inclusion and advancement of a larger group of people, particularly the disempowered. Selection mechanisms mainly based on universalistic and impersonal measures constitute a fairer and more inclusive—thus democratic—system than those featuring particularistic ones. Even if it is patently clear that all universalistic criteria are not only subject to steady undermining and circumventing in practice but also are, of course, in and of themselves creations of erstwhile particularisms, such formal and procedural matters should not be underestimated as important legitimizing agents for the increased participation and inclusion of the formerly weak, disempowered, and excluded.

The practice of strict exclusion is easily carried out when rigid requirements for entry are in place. Young folks are effectively kept out of decidedly racy films when an age requirement is established and can be validated with a government-issued identification card; individuals without the equivalent of a high school degree are excluded from the college admission process by virtue of that one tangible requirement not being met; any denim-clad individual will face expulsion from any private country club practicing blue jean prohibitions. With strict and concrete requirements for entry (or grounds for exclusion), the presiding group has only to refer to its own, seemingly objective, regulations if it wishes to exclude any newcomer. Notably, too, under solid rules governing entry, *any* individual, regardless of additional characteristics that he or she might possess, would be excluded based on the uniformly applicable criteria that furnish the sole measure for entry. That is, not meeting the very criteria that are expressly delineated would preclude entry for each individual in an identical manner. Of course, the other side of this coin is that the *fulfillment* of such objective credentials should serve as a way of giving an equal chance to all individuals, regardless of any additional characteristics that they might possess. Credentials are an evaluative tool that can be used successfully to exclude individuals or large groups, but also can be seen to help integrate the excluded and the weak.

While strict credentials are effective in excluding those who do *not* possess them, they are equally as helpful for the individual who *does* meet the requirements and who otherwise may not have been granted entry. If a degree is all that is required to apply for a particular job, for example, the individual without a degree is successfully banned. However, an otherwise disempowered individual *with* the degree would be able at least to apply for entry, a chance that he or she may not have been afforded if the requirements were based on any number of other (legal) factors.

Let us make clearer this process by way of a simple hypothetical scenario. A candidate wishes to apply for a new job, the base requirement for which is the possession of a college degree. The candidate does not see him- or herself as a standout candidate, but is extremely excited because he or she possesses precisely such a college degree; therefore, the candidate is able, at a minimum, to apply for this job because of having fulfilled this first and formal requirement. The presence of the degree is undeniable and is all that is required at this first stage of the application process. The hiring committee cannot, if the only requirement is the degree, discriminate against the candidate based on gender, age, or race (and any other non "bona fide occupational qualification"[1]), so, in effect, the candidate has successfully entered his or her application into the pool by tangibly meeting the formal requirement. This brief scenario illustrates why there exists formal "equality" in many of the extant and established realms that remain male-dominated purviews. That is, when objective requirements are delineated and fulfilled (gender not legally being among them), discrimination based on gender has no place.

This formal "equality" is deceiving, though. After all, it is characterized by numerical parity, but should not be considered as providing functional equality in terms of opportunities, treatment, evaluation, and other crucial ingredients affirming the nature and value of this good. The gap between parity and

---

[1]The Civil Rights Act of 1964 outlines this foundational component of U.S. labor and employment law. Title VII of the Civil Rights Act states:

> It shall not be an unlawful employment practice for an employer to hire and employ employees, for an employment agency to classify, or refer for employment any individual, for a labor organization to classify its membership or to classify or refer for employment any individual, or for an employer, labor organization, or joint labor-management committee controlling apprenticeship or other training or retraining programs to admit or employ any individual in any such program, on the basis of his religion, sex, or national origin in those certain instances where religion, sex, or national origin is a bona fide occupational qualification reasonably necessary to the normal operation of that particular business or enterprise. (Civil Rights Act of 1964, *U.S. Code*, vol. 42 SEC. 2000e-2 *[Section 703] (e)*).

equality, as it were, lies in the use of loose (and often informal and intangible) credentials. That is, after entry is achieved by way of meeting objective credentials, discrepancies in treatment (and therefore advancement) arise as the credentials employed and "required" are less tangible and more subjectively identified and evaluated. The point is, even if a candidate "proves" by objective, often numerically assessed means, his or her worth, as it turns out, the candidate still may not be meeting certain criteria that are systematically beyond him or her. Nonquantifiable, inexplicit, and informal selection mechanisms often prove the most obdurate and powerful. The softest criteria make for the hardest glass ceilings.

Still, the concept of credentialing facilitates a situation in which the more concrete the requirements for entry and success are, the more difficult the practice of discrimination and exclusion based on arbitrary factors often related to particularistic characteristics and mostly not directly related to the required field, task, or domain becomes. By way of this process, relatively powerless groups and individuals have been able to achieve entry into previously exclusive domains, including those of science and engineering, to a brief discussion of which we now turn.

Women in Male Domains: Subjective Criteria Make for Easy Justification of Exclusion

Science

Of all of the scientists and engineers having a doctorate in the United States in 1973, a mere 8.7% were women.[2] Since then, the female presence in the sciences has grown significantly (although it remains far from that of men); in 2003, women accounted for 29.8% of the doctorates among scientists and engineers in academic institutions in the United States.[3] The sciences, much like most skilled professions that require high levels of education, began as virtually exclusively male domains. Whether by dint of volition or prohibition, women, as a whole, did not attend school to obtain the degrees necessary to work in so-called STEM fields (science, technology, engineering, and mathematics). Of course, larger-scale female advancement and empowerment, specifically, the proliferation of the notion that women's choices were not limited

---

[2]Gerhard Sonnert, "Women in Science and Engineering: Advances, Challenges, and Solutions," *Annals of the New York Academy of Sciences* 869, no. 1 (1999): 34–57.

[3]Academe Online, "Percentage of Women Doctoral Scientists and Engineers in Academic Institutions by Field and Rank in 2003," American Association of University Professors, available at http://www.aaup.org/AAUP/pubsres/academe/2009/MJ/Feat/rossertab2.htm (accessed April 10, 2011).

to the household, would eventually pose a challenge to the previous pattern of exclusion from the sciences (and, arguably, all other realms). In the course of the past three to four decades, women would make their way into what were once completely male worlds, and, in the face of resistance, would be able to do so in good part because of the rigidity and impersonal nature of the requirements to enter those worlds. With a degree, a piece of tangible "proof" of her professional credential and clout, a woman could successfully fulfill the requirements and at least formally evade the prejudice that had previously kept her out of such male domains.

Formalizing entry requirements represents merely the very first and most elementary step in the democratic inclusion of formerly excluded groups. However, one's professional journey does not end upon entry, and some sort of advancement is arguably just as desirable as the original job offer. It is once she has gained access, once her solid degrees and curriculum vitae have brought her to the point at which the lab's or firm's number of women scientists could increase by one, that she begins to be subjected to new types of prejudicial criteria that in fact may retard or impede her advancement, not to mention eliminate her passion for her professional life.

Without the option to simply reject or deny the existence of a woman's equivalent degree (or other form of objective credential), men circumvent the presence of equal scientific (directly relevant) credentials and turn to less relevant criteria to deem women less capable. Research into this subject reveals that while women are granted entry (and in many cases are even heavily recruited), their advancement within the field is stifled by the injection of various post hoc subjective criteria, designed specifically to demonstrate the women's weaknesses and inferiority. In other words, newly construed, often ad hoc subjective criteria that govern the quotidian interaction of the male-dominated workplace serve as informal, but powerful, barriers to women's advancement, professional development, and fulfillment in these labs and firms.

Thus, for example, Sandra L. Hanson and Rebecca S. Kraus, in their research on women in male domains, found that the male scientists in their study employed these kinds of subjective and murky criteria in their evaluations of their female counterparts.[4] The men, overall, identified a "lack of self-confidence, achievement-motivation, independence and androgyny" in the women with whom they worked, all characteristics that the men perceived as prime evidence that the women were less capable of strong scientific work.[5] Immediately notable in this case is the target of these criticisms, or the nature

---

[4]Sandra L. Hanson and Rebecca S. Kraus, "Women in Male Domains: Sport and Science," *Sociology of Sport Journal* 16 (1999): 92–110.

[5]Ibid., 96.

of the criteria that these men had identified as not being met by the women. The men in the study did not venture to discredit any of the hard skills or more tangible professional credentials of their female counterparts. Tellingly, they did not claim that the female scientists were actually any less qualified at science, or were in possession of fewer cognitive skills than the men. Instead, the men introduced their own new criteria for judgment that rendered the women inferior.

These factors—"self-confidence, achievement-motivation, independence and androgyny"—are notable for two main reasons. First, the criteria are not immediately relevant to the job of the women scientists whom the males are supposedly evaluating. (A male scientist, one would think, would not cite any ascendancy in "androgyny," for example, as a means of demonstrating his prowess as a scientist.) Second, the fulfillment of any one of these criteria is not objectively determinable—the presence or absence of "achievement-motivation," for example, is surely open to some degree of individual interpretation. These men could not deny the existence of the women's degrees, but they had control over the assessment of "soft," subjective traits that they used to illustrate the alleged relative weakness and professional inferiority of the women with whom they worked.

Fiona Devine's research on this topic found that "some employers still preferred men to women irrespective of their educational credentials."[6] So while a man and a woman may possess equal credentials with regard to their actual scientific prowess, a number of justifications were made to defend the preference of men over women. These included the recognition of the fact that high-level jobs in the industry "had always been men's," the conviction that technical competence is innately higher in men, and the assumption that women will possess low career commitment because they will undoubtedly have "childcare responsibilities" in the future.[7] Once again, in the face of undeniable equivalency in terms of "hard" credentials, or those that speak directly to one's capacity in a specific area, the insiders invoke unmeasurable and often unsubstantiated criteria and claims that clearly disadvantage the successful minority of recently admitted outsiders to maintain the marginal presence of the underrepresented group.

Women scientists and engineers interviewed as a part of Devine's research expressed that they did not believe that the criteria for promotion within the workplace were solely based on actual performance or potential, and that

---

[6]Fiona Devine, "Gender Segregation in the Engineering and Science Professions: A Case of Continuity and Change," *Work, Employment & Society* 6, no. 4 (December 1992): 557–575 (quote from p. 565).

[7]Ibid.

intangible factors (with evaluations over which they had no control) often became the basis for advancement.[8] There was a general understanding that discrimination against them as women could come from "a variety of other formal and informal factors,"[9] meaning that their job performance was constantly being evaluated in terms of factors that they were often unaware of and, in some cases, could not control. It seems that, for these women, fulfilling the requirements of one's job was not a guaranteed way to be recognized positively for doing so, for at any moment new "requirements," perhaps impossible to accomplish, could emerge with no warning for the affected.

There may be no better gift for a man seeking validation of his opinion that his female counterparts are inferior than an actual exhibition of a disparity in technically relevant aptitude—an operative difference to serve as proof for what was once just prejudice. Devine's research highlights some of the ways that credentialing subjectively, or excluding or devaluing based on ambiguous criteria, can actually bring about relevant differences in professional ability and capacity, differences that are then used to justify the initial notion of women's inferiority.

One way that this is played out in the engineering company in Devine's research is in the institution of "sponsorships," unofficial guiding partnerships between company executives and younger employees. The beneficiaries of these sponsorships were privy to "invaluable advice, providing them with the appropriate experience for promotion and advertising their skills to other managers."[10] The possession of this "advice" alone could easily constitute a tangible, observable gap between those with it and those without, providing "proof" of the latter's inferiority and therefore diminishing their chances of being promoted or even recognized on an equitable basis. Not surprisingly, the women in Devine's study reported that it is only their male coworkers who are ever taken under the wings of any senior employee.

One encounters this pattern throughout many different professional realms, and research has found that one of the primary justifications on the part of the "sponsors" is that they "see themselves" in their younger counterparts, that they recognize their potential because they remember being in their shoes and doing things similarly.[11] In this powerful but rather narcissistic case, in which senior experts assume the tutorship of junior colleagues whom they regard as embodiments of themselves in their younger years, "soft" or

---

[8]Ibid., 568.

[9]Ibid.

[10]Ibid.

[11]Ibid.

ambiguous credential requirements, namely, mirroring some sort of reflection of one's professional superior as well as subordinate, serve to exclude women from equal recognition and its corresponding professional advantages. Even one of the male managers Devine interviewed admitted, "For a woman to be promoted into a manager's job would still be a bit of a struggle. You do need to have a senior manager who will back you and who will argue your corner for you. When I look at the higher levels in the company, the women aren't there."[12] So, promotion requires a "sponsorship" (a relatively objective criterion—you either have one or you don't), or at least the benefits of a sponsorship, but to "earn" a sponsor, one must meet a set of more subjective criteria (save, apparently, the rather rigid requirement that one be male).

The case of discriminatory mentoring often mutates into (or consequentially creates) *real* differences in aptitude and performance, at which point the professional stagnation of women becomes extremely easy to demonstrate for the powers that be. Beyond just losing out on precious advice, the women in Devine's study described having less access to and support in the educational tools within the company that presumably increase one's professional and technical capital. As one woman explained, "If you're a woman you really do have to push and say, 'Have you any courses?'" Courses are the tools that the engineers use to acquire and practice new skills.[13] She proceeded to explain how a series of lies from those in charge of the course programs led her to conclude that she was being systematically kept from the courses as a means of ensuring that her skill set would not grow. The widespread assumption, Devine finds, is that women are "less likely than men to pursue an exclusively technical career," and they instead prefer to move to the "softer" side of engineering, a presumption that surely does not help women to gain easy access to courses meant to bolster their technical skill.[14]

The fact is that, if a woman is effectively kept away from those courses, in the same way (and with compounding consequences) that she is excluded from one of her superior's sponsorships, palpable and relevant gaps in achievement and ability *will* arise, and will indeed serve as evidence of her failure to fulfill "hard" credentials. That is, by inhibiting *opportunities* via imposing "soft" subjective credentials (e.g., an individual's degree of perceived similarity to her or his potential sponsor or an assumed affinity toward a different area of expertise), genuine differences in terms of "hard" credentials (e.g., not having an executive "in your corner" or not possessing the updated skills that would

---

[12]Ibid.

[13]Ibid.

[14]Ibid.

have been obtained via a "course") arise, which make for easier justification of exclusion and discrimination.

Let the following fictional quote from a frustrated female scientist illustrate this process:

> Well, yeah, *now* I actually *am* worse at science, because nobody took me under his or her wing! Don't let *my* position hurt the new women coming in, though—that is, don't assume that they too are worse at science and try to use *my* case as "proof" of it. Given *actually* equal opportunities, we all could have been as good, but when you decide that I'm "just not well suited for the inner circle," or whatever bogus criteria you decide I don't meet, of course I'm not going to be able to perform at the same levels as you.

By inhibiting opportunities via soft credentials, one creates disparities in the hard credentials, which then justify exclusion and discrimination based on objective criteria. The problem is that, in the case of genuine differences in skill and aptitude, choosing the more accomplished candidate in no way constitutes discrimination, but rather the reasonable and rational practice of selecting the best person for the job, the one with the strongest relevant credentials. What often gets masked, though, are the soft credentials that do not appear as relevant criteria in any prima facie selection and evaluation, yet linger sub rosa to emerge as powerful forces in the informal but potent judging of reluctantly admitted newcomers.

A third study on this topic, conducted by Gerhard Sonnert, makes use of Long and Fox's model for the "breeding grounds of discrimination" in the natural sciences.[15] As cited in Sonnert's research, J. Scott Long and Mary Frank Fox outlined four ways by which women's career advancement in the sciences is hindered.[16] First, they cite the widespread "absence of information on individual's scientific qualifications" as a practice that allows men in authority positions essentially to "play dumb" to the fact that a female with stronger scientific credentials may not advance as much as a relatively less qualified male.[17] Second, they identify the "ambiguity of evaluation standards for scientific performance," a clear case of *credentialing*, as a method by which women are left behind.[18] This item speaks directly to the concept of credentialing, as it alludes

---

[15]Sonnert, "Women in Science and Engineering," 43.

[16]J. Scott Long and Mary Frank Fox, "Scientific Careers: Universalism and Particularism," *Annual Review of Sociology* 21 (1995): 45–71.

[17]Sonnert, "Women in Science and Engineering," 43.

[18]Ibid.

to the fact that the more room there is for subjective evaluation, the easier time an evaluator will have in arbitrarily devaluing a person's performance. The third item refers to the "low degree of consensus about the basic theories and methods in a discipline," also possibly representing another area in which the "right" and "wrong," or "best" scientific results may not be concrete, therefore leaving room for soft credentials to aid in the advancement of one group (i.e., males) over another. The last of the four patterns delineates the "low consensus about basic theories and methods in a discipline" and the "secrecy about decision making" that is characteristic in the labs included in the study.[19]

ROTC Programs

Research into other male-dominated realms showed similar patterns of introducing more subjective criteria for success when the presence of equal credentials seems to have mitigated the dominant group's built-in advantage. In Jennifer Silva's study on the self-reportedly gender-neutral ROTC, we have a case of exceptionally objective evaluative criteria for the men and women involved.[20] In physical training sessions, max-out benchmarks are delineated and represent the ultimate goal that men and women have for their respective physical performances. Although the program's (and most of this country's military units') aim is to come as close to gender neutrality as possible, biological differences in strength are accounted for in the determination of max-out values for men versus those of women.[21] As mentioned earlier, the existence of these rigid markers of "success"—numbers that draw a clear line between meeting and not meeting a task—should result in completely objective evaluations upon their being met or not. "Did you max-out?" should be a simple yes-or-no question.

What Silva found, interestingly, is that, even given a general acceptance of a biological gap in strength between the two sexes, most male and female ROTC students do not consider a female who reaches her max-out values to have truly achieved the peak of performance that a male reaches when *he* maxes out.[22] That is, it is not until a female can reach the *male* max-out values that she is credited with having achieved success in this task. "Did you max-out?"—when asked of a woman who just met the female requirements—might, as it turns

---

[19]Ibid.

[20]Jennifer M. Silva, "A New Generation of Women? How Female ROTC Cadets Negotiate the Tension between Masculine Military Culture and Traditional Femininity," *Social Forces* 87, no. 2 (2008): 937–958.

[21]Ibid., 943.

[22]Ibid., 946.

out, not be such a simple matter. Perhaps this norm is in pursuit of unadulterated gender equality, but it seems to confirm yet again the overwhelming research results on the experiences of women in male-dominated domains: Females are automatically and incessantly called upon to "prove themselves," and to do so they need not just perform as well as their male counterparts, but must indeed outperform them, effectively showing that they are *better* than the males alongside whom they work.

What renders this ROTC example very convincing, though a tad different from the sciences, business, and chess that we will discuss in the ensuing sections, is the fact that the most decisive measure of ultimate acceptance as an insider in this military world pertains to bodily strength rather than intellectual capabilities. As such, it much resembles the world of sports where, too, the differences in men's and women's bodies necessitate a different metric gauging their output and achievements. But, to the federal government's credit—and possibly to sports' shame—it has been much more eager and successful than sports in creating an institution in which the two genders coexist and operate according to uniform, universalistic gender-neutral criteria.

Interestingly, however, sports' male-dominated judgment criteria constituting what insiders and outsiders consider the real worth as well as the ultimate measures of quality and legitimacy—as opposed to the government-mandated metrics of a formally required equality, which, as Silva demonstrates, lack legitimacy, even among the very subjects whose achievement they are to gauge, let alone in the larger outside world—remain solely and solidly the men's as opposed to the women's numbers. Just as Silva informs us that the women's maxing out at their numbers is simply not regarded as legitimate, even though it is, of course, officially mandated and fully approved, because their targets are below the men's, so, too, one always encounters a genuine resistance on the part of many men to see women's sports on their own terms rather than in a constant comparison with men's or gauged solely by the criteria defining the men's. "The 150th ranked male tennis player could easily beat any of the Grand Slam–winning top-ranked female players," one often hears. Or, "a good high school basketball team could easily beat the women's Division One NCAA champions, most of whose players cannot even dunk the ball." Further, as Markovits constantly heard during women's World Cup soccer tournaments in the United States and Germany, "a third- or fourth-division men's squad could and would easily beat the top women's sides, such as Germany's, Brazil's, Sweden's, Japan's, and, of course, the United States'." Excepting perhaps childbearing and rearing, virtually all of women's achievements—well beyond the worlds of the physical, such as the military and sports—continue to be gauged in comparison with men's and almost never on their own terms.

Business

Joy A. Schneer and Frieda Reitman's research into the longitudinal professional experiences of male and female MBAs in business confirms this pattern.[23] It seems as though, as in the sciences, men and women are brought to entry in virtually identical numbers (with women even being specifically recruited). There are no reported differences in the males' and females' experiences upon entry, as hard credentials, such as objective (enumerated) performance in school, as well as status as an MBA recipient, are the primary criteria with which all candidates are evaluated for hire. This research shows that throughout the first four to five years on the job, the salaries of male and female MBAs did not show significant differences based on gender.[24] One would think, based on these data, that women and men are equally as likely to achieve the same levels of success in these business-dominated careers.

Yet Schneer and Reitman found that it is after the four- to five-year honeymoon period that gender begins to separate the experiences of the MBAs.[25] It seems that as men and women move farther away from the hard credentials that had initially granted them virtually equal entry into this male-dominated world, on-the-job evaluations of the MBAs become subject to increasingly subjective criteria. It is at this point that senior males begin to integrate younger ones into support systems and professional "old boys' networks" that allow men to rise and surpass the women. By midcareer, the study reports, "the work environment is less supportive of women . . . whether one considers income or more subjective measures of treatment such as satisfaction, boss appreciation or discrimination."[26] This lack of support, not surprisingly, leads many women to seek employment elsewhere, where frustrations about being left behind are perhaps less pronounced. Again, in this case, even in the face of equal performance, and most certainly equal potential and abilities, the structure of business seems to be arranged so as to unofficially but most decidedly boost the success of males, while leaving females to fend for themselves as underequipped, undersupported versions of their male peers. It seems that after a few years in business, a woman's credentials make it quite difficult, if not impossible, for her to overcome the power of informal

---

[23]Joy A. Schneer and Frieda Reitman, "The Importance of Gender in Mid-Career: A Longitudinal Study of MBAs," *Journal of Organizational Behavior* 15 (1994): 199–207.

[24]Ibid., 200.

[25]Ibid., 205.

[26]Ibid., 204.

male networks, which are neither challenged nor matched by any comparable female construct.

The support systems for women, the study finds, are significantly weaker than those for men, because women are rarely incorporated into the male-run networks. Moreover, according to women in these fields, there exist insufficient women role models in this industry to constitute potent and effective role model networks for younger women. Female managers are held back from advancement and consequently do not constitute a critical mass at top levels to help younger women succeed in the same way that males can and do.

Tracey Rowe and Anne Crafford conducted a similar study, this time narrowing the focus to women in investment banking firms.[27] Their study highlights even more the power of support structures and networks in terms of advancing one's career, specifically illustrating how a woman's exclusion from informal networks proves detrimental to her career and solidly trumps her stellar individual performance. Again, it seems as though the investment banking industry seeks actively to "bring on board young female graduates and to develop them into senior executive positions."[28] As the authors find, though, "the fruits of these initiatives are still a long way off, and the barriers (real and perceived) challenging other women today still remain a reality for these graduates."[29]

Recognition of one's work by senior employees seems to be of paramount importance in working one's way up in this industry. However, female respondents in the study identify a lack of precisely such recognition as a major detriment to their ascension. In the face of immense pressure to succeed and to prove oneself, "nobody's actually there to help you prove yourself and if you shout and ask for help you are considered a silly woman."[30] The general female understanding is that while the men are waiting for the women to prove themselves, the men's desired outcome is that women will not be able to do so, thus not being able to amass sufficient evidence of their worth. The men require that women prove themselves, but, in what one might be tempted to call a conflict of interest (but perhaps may represent a perfect alignment of interests), the men also get to withhold valuable tools and advantages that would most likely help women advance, as well as dictate the details and terms of what "proving oneself" even looks like.

---

[27]Tracey Rowe and Anne Crafford, "A Study of Barriers to Career Advancement for Professional Women in Investment Banking," *Journal of Human Resource Management* 1, no. 2 (2003): 21–27.

[28]Ibid., 21.

[29]Ibid., 22.

[30]Ibid., 23.

Survey respondents in this study reported that, as females, they feel more pressure to prove themselves and their professional worth than men do. "There seems to be less pressure on men to prove themselves," one respondent said. "Women are forced to keep driving forward whereas it is far easier for men in this industry. It is more difficult for women to make an impression."[31] The idea of *making an impression* does not so much entail the attaining of a clearly measurable goal as it does the valorization of some sort of intangible "it factor," comprising ill-defined criteria of judgment. It is at this point that the systematic exclusion of women becomes easiest, be it intentional or not.

The invincibility of the "old boys' clubs" in business, this research shows, has been recognized and accepted by many females who brave entry into it. "Many of the participants believe," the study explains, "it is not worth making an issue of this as it may potentially lead to sacrificing one's career to try to prove a point."[32] Credentialing, in this example, seems to come into play most directly in terms of providing access to these valuable (but still unofficial and informal) professional networks. Objective credentials, such as degrees, allow for entry into the investment banking firm at the lowest levels, but induction into this world's loose but very powerful networks and support systems is based on intangibles that heavily favor the insiders, meaning men. "Men in authority positions over women often underrate them," explains Christine Williams, "because they evaluate them on masculinity, a standard women can never measure up to."[33] So the world of investment banking does not seem that different from the worlds of the ROTC and sports. "For these women who acquire the necessary 'human capital' to enter the technical professions," Devine explains, "the labor market is only partially open."[34] Let us now proceed to this book's main concern, the world of sports and its female fans and on the way discuss the gendered nature of chess, which, by some measures and categorizations, qualifies as a sport.

Chess

As an interesting intersection of intellectual pursuit and competitive sport, the game of competitive chess serves as an interesting example of a male-dominated realm. Of all of the world's current Grandmasters, a title that is granted

---

[31]Ibid., 24.

[32]Ibid.

[33]Christine Williams, *Gender Differences at Work: Women and Men in Non-Traditional Occupations* (Berkeley: University of California Press, 1991), 69.

[34]Devine, "Gender Segregation," 571.

to any player, male or female, who earns an Elo rating[35] of 2,500 or more, only 1 percent are women.[36] Women do, however, make up 100 percent of another chess ranking: Woman Grandmaster (a title that requires an Elo rating significantly lower than that of the Grandmaster, and even lower than the "second place" title of International Master). Even considering chess's largely nonphysical nature, separate women-only titles are available for women who choose to compete in tournaments restricted to women. There is no male counterpart—there are no "men-only" tournaments—both men and women are welcome to compete for the general titles (a woman would need to take part in coed tournament play to earn a non-female title), and the Elo rating system remains the same throughout all play. The Elo rating is a relative ranking, however, and it is notable that one's Elo rating that was earned through play in women-only tournaments would not, even if sufficiently high, attain a woman a non-restricted title.[37]

Several curiosities arise with regard to the organization of international chess. Why, first of all, would segregated titles have a place in an activity or "sport" that is not primarily physical?[38] Does the fact that a Woman Grand-

---

[35]Named after Arpad Elo, the Elo rating is used in chess as a means of rating the relative skill of all players. Elo ratings are employed by both the World Chess Federation—FIDE—and the U.S. Chess Federation to grant titles such as grandmaster. A grandmaster must earn, at some point, an Elo rating of at least 2,500. Once attained, the title is maintained for life. Other lesser titles, such as International Master and Candidate Master, are obtained by way of earning Elo ratings near 2,400 and 2,200, respectively.

[36]Christopher F. Chabris and Mark E. Glickman, "Sex Differences in Intellectual Performance: Analysis of a Large Cohort of Competitive Chess Players," *Psychological Science* 17, no. 12 (2006): 1040–1046.

[37]Mark E. Glickman, "A Comprehensive Guide to Chess Ratings," *American Chess Journal* 3 (1995): 59–102.

[38]The debate about chess being a sport has raged for decades, if not longer.

Indeed, the World Chess Federation has been lobbying the International Olympic Committee for years to include chess in the Games. As part of its efforts, the federation even instituted drug testing to bring chess into compliance with the committee's rules. (Players have grumbled about this, pointing out that aside from caffeine, there are no drugs that can plausibly help them play better.) In making a case for chess, Kirsan Ilyumzhinov, the president of the federation, has said that curling is essentially "chess on ice." Chess has its own Olympiad every two years. And in 2006 and 2010, chess competitions were added to the Asian Games, an Olympic-style event that also includes basketball, boxing and wrestling. The Olympic committee has granted the federation status as a Recognized International Sports Federation, but that may be as far as things progress, some chess officials acknowledge. In an interview published a few days ago on Chessbase, a chess news Web site, Ilya Levitov, the head of the Russian Chess Federation, said that in the Winter Olympics, "there are ground rules: ice or snow. Chess has none of these." Referring to the Olympic slogan of "faster, higher, stronger," Levitov added, "It's not in any way related to chess." (Dylan Loeb McClain, "Making the Case for Chess as an Olympic Sport," *New York Times*, December 18, 2011)

master need obtain a lower Elo rating than a nonrestricted Grandmaster not suggest prima facie that women are deemed less intellectually capable than men, an assertion that one would think (and hope) would cause a significant stir in the twenty-first century? Furthermore, how would a response to that question help explain the fact that only 1 percent of all Grandmasters, a title that is earned by way of objective Elo ratings, which are totally gender neutral, are women?

Research on this disparity has produced a number of explanations, including some based on biological differences between men and women, as well as others that simply point to the gap between the genders hailing from the massive differences in terms of the sheer numbers of male and female participants at the initial stages of competitive chess.[39] While clearly several processes may be at work in the production of this stark gender imbalance in top-level chess, a synthesis of research seems to point to theories on stereotyping and, specifically, stereotype threat, as a solidly plausible means of explaining how, even under a relatively objective rating system (Elo rankings) and an understanding that women are not less intelligent than men (surely not the case, as evidenced by the 1 percent female presence among Grandmasters), women seem to be underrepresented at the top of this male-dominated realm.

Chess's origins are ancient, with the earliest versions of the game believed to have been developed in India as early as the sixth century of the Common Era. By the thirteenth century, versions of the game had made it to Europe and were continually modified there, but by the late fifteenth century, the game looked very similar to the way it does today.[40] By the nineteenth century, chess developed into a major part of social life, with chess clubs serving as popular social outlets for men. Women's participation in the game began early. However, it did not assume the same place in their lives as it did in men's. In the

---

[39]Merim Bilalić, Kieran Smallbone, Peter McLeod, and Fernand Gobet, "Why Are (the Best) Women so Good at Chess? Participation Rates and Gender Differences in Intellectual Domains," *Proceedings of the Royal Society* 276 (1009): 1161–1165. *Participation-rate hypothesis* is one of many presented by Bilalić, Smallbone, McLeod, and Gobet to attempt to explain the absence of women at the highest levels of competitive chess. It is a simple model, outlining that the women are not there at the top because they never entered in the same numbers at the bottom. This research shows that, while the performance of the best 100 German male chess players is better than that of the best 100 German women, "96 percent of the observed difference would be expected given the much greater number of men who play chess" (p. 1161). While this explanation and process are easy to understand, its consequences may be somewhat more veiled. The absence of über-successful female chess players can be seen as bolstering the stereotypical notion that women are not as capable of playing chess as well. The statistics of top-ranked female chess players (being reflective of a glaring lopsidedness in favor of males) may serve as "proof," consciously or not, that women are, by dint of their gender, simply not as good at chess. The consequences of this stereotype are outlined in detail by way of our discussion of Claude M. Steele's *stereotype threat* later in this chapter.

[40]Harold J. Murray, *History of Chess* (Northampton, MA: Benjamin Press, 1986).

course of history, men construed women to be less capable in many essential areas of the game. To wit: this excerpt from the April 1906 issue of *Lasker's Chess Magazine*:

> A careful examination of the games of players whom the world recognizes as great reveals the fact that the faculties and qualities of concentration, comprehensiveness, impartiality and, above all, a spark of originality, are to be found in combination and in varying degrees. The absence of these qualities in women explains why no member of the feminine sex has occupied any high position as a chessplayer.[41]

Even considering the notion that women were viewed as unfit for the game, ladies-only chess clubs made their way into the social sphere and provided a space for women to maintain their femininity while still pursuing the intellectual excitement of chess. Already at this time, though, chess's strict gender segregation was apparent and troubling to some, such as the author of this immensely prognostic observation from that same issue of *Lasker's Chess Magazine*:

> The existence of "ladies' chess clubs" is a means of perpetuating mediocrity among its members. Of course, if exclusiveness is more important to them than improved play, they will continue in this way. If any women have any idea or ambition of holding a high position in the chess world apart and independent of sex, they will endeavor to meet all-comers in practice and so pave the way to take part in general tournaments. No player has ever existed who has been more than a shade superior to his contemporaries, and if women continue to play only with women the best of them cannot hold their own in a general tournament, because of the poor standard of the play they have been engaged in.[42]

During this period of chess's rise in social prominence, women were neither completely excluded from play nor understood as being incapable of playing the game.[43] That is, it was not the game of chess that was itself deemed

---

[41]Edward Winter, "Chess and Women," chesshistory.com, available at http://www.chesshistory.com/winter/extra/women.html (accessed May 19, 2011).

[42]Ibid.

[43]A satirical excerpt from "A Scientific Hint for Women Players," an article in the September 1897 issue of *American Chess Magazine*, reflects an early recognition of the unreasonable understanding of men as more capable chess players than women:

> Many conservative men (a fair correspondent avers they are brutes more or less) have strongly contested the claim that a woman could play a consistently good game at

inappropriate for women to play. Rather, it was the larger issue of women competing directly with men, explicitly perceived as the more capable gender at the time, which caused the problem. In fact, women were in many ways encouraged to participate in the game. Many publications from the time praise the positive effects that women might find in playing chess with other ladies. "Experience vouches its value as a domestic charm," reads an 1881 article entitled "Chess and the Fair Sex," "and every young lady will do wisely in acquiring the power of adding its fascination to the attractions of Home."[44]

Competitive chess was, by dint of society's understanding of women's intellectual capacities as well as the appropriate realms in which they were to operate and recreate, segregated at its outset. Similar to the other male-dominated realms visited in this chapter, the initial exclusion of women began as a fairly accepted reflection of the appropriate places for men and women to operate. Notable in the case of chess, though, is that women were participating, just in segregated spaces, playing only against other women. As early as 1927, the Women's World Chess Championship was established.[45] Compare this with a hypothetical situation in which positions in science, engineering, and medicine, to name but a few of our society's occupational areas enjoying high status and much prestige, were equally as available to women throughout their histories as was chess, provided women were willing to work in a gender-segregated all-female setting featuring only women scientists, engineers, and doctors. This comparison reflects the fact that chess was not viewed as something

---

chess. They persistently declare that, though the play of this or that woman may be, at times, of a fair order, it is inevitably erratic, and subject to those illogical aberrations which science, as exemplified in chess, most severely frowns upon. Now, if there is any foundation for this charge, it is evident that the women's game must be affected by some extraneous cause that does not influence the men, and there has been much puzzled inquiry as to what that cause can be. It has remained for the *Troy Times* to solve the great mystery. It declares, on the authority of "a great scientist"—what a pity we do not know his name—that the cause of the present intellectual activity of our women-folk is due to the use of wire hair-pins. He explains the matter in a charmingly lucid manner which, as so often happens with scientific explanations, leaves the unscientific reader in rather more of a muddled entanglement than ever, but when "boiled down" it amounts to this: that the wire hair-pins excite "counter-currents of electricity," whatever they may be, and so bewilder the wearer's brain with strange vagaries, and lead them to do whimsical things. Now, it would be well for players to take note of this, for the "wire hair-pin" theory explains many things. It is evident that when a woman wears a handful of wire hair-pins there is an amount of electrical disturbance going on around her scalp that puts good chess out of the question. When she wears shell contrivances her head is clear and cool, and she plays the fine, winning game her friends admire. So, in future tournaments, one of the rules governing the play should be: "All ladies-players are requested to wear shell hair-pins."

[44]Winter, "Chess and Women," excerpt from *Chess Player's Chronicle*, March 15, 1881.

[45]Mark Weeks, "World Chess Championship for Women," *Chess for All Ages*, available at http://www.mark-weeks.com/aboutcom/aa04c20.htm (accessed May 19, 2011).

that women were incapable of *doing*, but rather that women were seen as incapable of doing it as well as men and were best off doing it on their own, apart from men. In this way, chess more closely reflects competitive sports (or the military, remembering our ROTC example), which are understood to be performed by definition at a higher level by men by dint of their biologically determined bodies that make men swifter, allow them to reach greater heights, and provide them with more strength: citius, altius, fortius, as the credo of the Olympic Games so succinctly puts it. While, as mentioned earlier, Ilya Levitov, the head of the board of the Russian Chess Federation, may in fact be prima facie correct in arguing that the Olympic slogan "is not in any way related to chess," thus properly excluding chess from becoming a bona fide Olympic sport, the gender segregation—as well as the concomitant primacy accorded to the male contests—in virtually all Olympic disciplines constitutes a crucial commonality that sports competitions share with chess.[46]

Should chess, though, not have long ago discarded its gender segregation, in full accordance with the notion of women being fully capable of competing against men on an intellectual level? Why has society preserved the (less prestigious) female-only titles and thus perpetuated gender segregation in a realm that features strength of mind and not of body? Perhaps the words of Jennifer Shahade, female chess champion of the United States, explain the situation without condoning it: "The category of women's chess does not refer to some intrinsically female way of playing chess but rather to being a minority in the chess world, which can affect the way a woman plays."[47]

Research has shown that the notions of women being by nature inferior to men at chess have not yet left the psyche of players. Simply knowing that one is playing against a woman might change a player's choice of strategies. Christer Gerdes and Patrik Gränsmark show that "both men and women seem to change strategy when they face a female opponent,"[48] specifically, that they are "more inclined to choose a risky strategy . . . on occasions when the [female] opponent is superior by means of their respective Elo ratings."[49] This response, to play more aggressively when matched with a more skilled female, reflects theories of stereotyping and stereotype threat, which purport that "judgment

---

[46]Ilya Levitov, as quoted in Dylan Loeb McClain, "Making the Case for Chess as an Olympic Sport," *New York Times*, December 18, 2011.

[47]Jennifer Shahade, *Chess Bitch: Women in the Ultimate Intellectual Sport* (Los Angeles: Siles Press, 2005), 6.

[48]Christer Gerdes and Patrik Gränsmark, "Strategic Behavior across Gender: A Comparison of Female and Male Expert Chess Players," Discussion paper no. 4793, February 2010, for the Institute for the Study of Labor (Forschungsinstitut zur Zukunft der Arbeit), 18.

[49]Ibid., 20.

can become more stereotypic under cognitive load."[50] Let the increase in cognitive load be represented by the presence of a skilled female opponent, and more stereotypic framing can easily, "manifest itself through the selective judgment of evidence, for example regarding another person's intelligence."[51]

In short, when opponents feel threatened, which might be the case when a man or woman discovers that he or she is facing a female opponent with a higher Elo rating, they might increasingly rely on stereotypic evaluations of the opponent, viewing her as less intelligent, an archaic, but perhaps, in this case, useful stereotype. This will incite, research shows, men especially to employ increasingly aggressive strategies, which, in turn, might result in a surplus of confidence on their part, yielding a double combination of helpful attributes in chess competitions, enhancing the prospects of success.

Recalling our topic in Chapter 1, this pattern also pertains to children chess players in that one's expectations can turn into real results, thus confirming a self-fulfilling prophesy. Concretely, a male's understanding of himself as superior and more aggressive and a female's corresponding view of herself as weaker and as an "underdog" most likely influences the actual outcome of real chess competitions and serves to "prove" to men that they are in fact superior chess players. Put concisely by Anne Maass, Claudio D'Ettole, and Mara Cadinu, "The difficulty encountered by female chess players may mainly reside in their awareness that others expect them to perform poorly in a predominantly male domain."[52]

These three scholars selected forty-two male-female pairs over the Internet to play against each other. The pairs were always matched for ability in terms of their Elo rating, but the researchers controlled for the participants' awareness of the sex of their opponents. The results reflect the power that a person's awareness of his or her expected performance (based on gender) can have on play. In cases where both players were unaware of their opponent's gender, women and men performed at approximately equal levels. However, female contestants showed a significant decline in performance when they were informed that they were playing against a man. Notably, when female players were told that they were playing against a woman (which was, by design, never the case), they performed at a level perfectly on par with their (male)

---

[50]C. Neil Macrae and Galen V. Bodenhausen, "Social Cognition: Thinking Categorically about Others," *Annual Review of Psychology* 51 (2000): 105.

[51]Gerdes and Gränsmark, "Expert Chess Players," 20, citing James L. Hilton and William von Hippel, "Stereotypes," *Annual Review of Psychology* 47 (1996): 237–271.

[52]Anne Maass, Claudio D'Ettole, and Mara Cadinu, "Checkmate? The Role of Gender Stereotypes in the Ultimate Intellectual Sport," *European Journal of Social Psychology* 38 (2008): 231–245 (quote from p. 233).

opponents. It seems that women experienced a clear a lack of confidence in their chess playing abilities when they knew that they were facing a male opponent, which, of course, offers a possible and plausible explanation for the continuation of female-only chess competitions. Women may simply prefer not to play against men because they do not perform at their best when matched with an opponent whom they subjectively perceive as being superior in his abilities compared with theirs, which then may, in fact, create a situation in which men objectively outperform women. Instead of fighting against this stereotypic expectation and effectively reinforcing it by performing poorly against males, female players may instead choose to compete only against other females so as to eliminate such a tangible threat to their confidence.

Stereotype Threat

Claude Steele's groundbreaking work on *stereotype threat* is of crucial importance in understanding the gaps in achievement in men and women when it comes to competitive chess, among other domains in which any group is subject to a stereotypical "inferiority." The idea behind Steele's concept is that apprehension produced by one's awareness of widespread negative stereotypes about a certain dimension of one's identity (race, sex, class, or any other collective marker) might cause sufficient psychological distress to disrupt one's actual performance. That is, one's knowledge that one is "supposed to"—according to stereotypical categories under which one falls—perform poorly, or at least less successfully than one's opponent, can easily translate into an actually poor performance that is far below one's real ability.[53]

Steele's original study on this phenomenon involved African American and European American college students taking a relatively challenging verbal section of the Graduate Record Examination. The students participated in the study knowing that the test was meant to be a measure of intellectual performance (the instructions for the exam explicitly said as much). The results of the test mirrored national averages, with the black students garnering a lower average score than the white students. In the second iteration of the exam, the instructions were changed. This time, nothing in the instructions or in the proctoring of the exam implied that the test was a measurement of intellect. After this change was implemented, Steele noticed that the gap in performance shrank significantly. The black students performed better on the exact same exam when the test was not presented as an evaluation of intelligence, in other words, when the stereotype threat was removed. When the black students were

---

[53]Claude M. Steele and Joshua Aronson, "Stereotype Threat and the Intellectual Test Performance of African Americans," *Journal of Personality and Social Psychology* 69, no. 5 (1995): 797–811.

aware that the test was a measure of intelligence, an area in which black people, according to stereotype, are "supposed to be" less proficient than white people, their actual performance suffered.

Similarly dramatic results emerged from a large number of other studies on stereotype threat, including the one mentioned earlier about competitive online chess performance. Sometimes, such as in the case of women performing below their abilities on mathematics exams, an individual's awareness of a prevalent stereotype constituted the source of the stereotype threat. Other studies show that the way a task is framed (as an intelligence test, as a test of athletic ability, or even simply as a fun exercise) can invoke stereotype threat and have effects on individuals' performance. In a study by Michael Inzlicht and Talia Ben-Zeev, men and women were divided into groups of three, in all possible gender combinations, and asked to complete difficult verbal or math tests.[54] Female test subjects who were in the minority within their group (two males, one female) produced performance deficiencies on the math exams, while males did not show any difference in performance between the two exam types when they were in the minority. The study found that the mere presence of a male within her group (even if it was only one man) resulted in poorer-than-expected performance in math for the female subjects.

The simple presentation of a particular task can change the way in which individuals understand their desire for and construct their confidence in participating in the task. Vishal K. Gupta and Nachiket M. Bhawe found that when the stereotypical notion of entrepreneurship as being a male pursuit was emphasized (or simply mentioned), the women displayed significantly less interest in pursuing entrepreneurship, while the males' reported interest increased.[55] When the stereotype threat was removed ("entrepreneurship" was presented as a gender-neutral domain), the expressed levels of interest were the same between the male and female subject groups. Even the game of golf can be reframed in specific ways to reveal the power of stereotype threat. A study by Jeff Stone, Christian Lynch, Mike Sjomeling, and John Darley had black and white men participate in a golf task, first framing it as "diagnostic of 'sports intelligence'" and then as a test of "natural athletic ability."[56] The latter framing

---

[54]Michael Inzlicht and Talia Ben-Zeev, "A Threatening Intellectual Environment: Why Females Are Susceptible to Experiencing Problem-Solving Deficits in the Presence of Males," *Psychological Science* 11, no. 5 (2000): 365–371.

[55]Vishal K. Gupta and Nachiket M. Bhawe, "The Influence of Proactive Personality and Stereotype Threat on Women's Entrepreneurial Intentions," *Journal of Leadership & Organizational Studies* 13, no. 4 (2007): 73–85.

[56]Jeff Stone, Christian Lynch, Mike Sjomeling, and John Darley, "Stereotype Threat Effects on Black and White Athletic Performance," *Journal of Personality and Social Psychology* 77, no. 6 (1999): 1213–1227.

garnered better results from the black subjects, whereas the former witnessed a superior performance by the white participants. Even a task at which both populations were equally capable (as can safely be presumed by the fact that they both outdid the other), the evoking of negative stereotypes—the introduction of stereotype threat—for both populations seemed to have had real consequences on their actual performance.

Margaret Shih, Todd Pittinsky, and Nalini Ambady echo this pattern.[57] In their experiment, Asian American women were selected to take a quantitative exam, before which they were to fill out a questionnaire. To make specific dimensions of the subjects' identities more salient, one group's questionnaire was focused on race (the "Asian-identity-salient" group), one on gender (the "female-identity-salient" group), and one on topics unrelated to race or gender (the "no-identity-salient" group). The "female-identity-salient" group—fully conforming to theories of stereotype threat and the widely held stereotype that women are not proficient at quantitative tasks—performed poorly compared with the control group. The "Asian-identity-salient" group also exhibited features of the expected stereotype threat (or, perhaps more accurately, stereotype boost), as its members' performance surpassed that of the control group, solidly reflecting the common cultural stereotype that Asians have "superior quantitative skills compared with other ethnic groups."[58]

Stereotype threat is absolutely vital in illustrating the experience of the (intangible) unfairness that women face in manifestly fair and equitable contexts. Not only are objectively equivalent performances evaluated differently (via "soft," malleable criteria), but there are also quieter disadvantaging forces at work, such as a woman's own awareness that she is expected to do worse than a man. The expectations and stereotypes that women know exist about their gender group (whether such stereotypes are explicitly subscribed to and openly articulated by a woman's work environment is almost immaterial) have real effects on the way that women perform. A subpar performance and the ensuing lack of advancement only strengthen the stereotype, sometimes to a degree at which "stereotype" does not appear to some to be the right word anymore, perhaps best replaced by "fact."

When a woman, for example, performs worse than a man, she is providing "proof" of her gender's stereotypical inferiority, making the power of stereotype threat in the future that much stronger. Even seemingly objective criteria, such as standardized tests designed to represent a level playing field for individuals of all backgrounds and circumstances, lose some of their alleged objec-

---

[57]Margaret Shih, Todd L. Pittinsky, and Nalini Ambady, "Stereotype Susceptibility: Identity Salience and Shifts in Quantitative Performance," *Psychological Science* 10, no. 1 (1999): 80–83.

[58]Ibid., 80.

tivity as an individual's internalization of his or her collective's stereotypes might adversely affect performance, although—as we saw with the example of the Asian American subjects—there are certain occasions where stereotype threats mutate into stereotype boosts.

At the outset of the seminal 1998 article by Steele et al.[59] reporting their research on stereotype threat, the authors included a quote from Rodney Ellis, an African American member of the Texas legislature who expresses this phenomenon fittingly: "For some reason I didn't score well on tests. Maybe I was just nervous. There's a lot of pressure on you, knowing that if you fail, you fail your race."[60] Ellis recognized that, by way of bolstering the potency of the negative stereotype, an individual failure on his part might bespeak a much larger failure for the community of African Americans.

These results mirror those mentioned in our previous section on chess, insofar as the stereotyped expectations (that African Americans will perform worse on intelligence tests, men are better at math, and women are worse at chess) have real-life consequences for the performance of individuals holding such expectations. These stereotypical framings of the world, and of the populations and individuals within it, are powerful and have the clout to change a person's perception of her or his experiences. Stereotypes, regardless of their applicability or accuracy in a specific situation, have significant influence over a person's internalization and interpretation of experiences and abilities—and then real influence over their actual performance.

And Vice Versa? Men in Female Domains

Might the experiences of women in male-dominated realms simply be a reflection of minority dynamics in general? That is, could their experiences of exclusion and resistance be explained in terms of their being a minority, instead of their gender? To clarify this matter, we now turn to an examination of men's experiences as minorities in female-dominated realms.

Research into men's experiences working as members of female-dominated fields, such as social work, elementary school teaching, nursing, and library science, reveals some similarities with the aforementioned phenomena in this chapter, but also highlights some very interesting and telling patterns that differ greatly from the situation of women working in predominantly male environments. The most prominent similarity is the issue of compliance or

---

[59]Joshua Aronson, Claude M. Steele, M. F. Salinas, and M. J. Lustina, "The Effects of Stereotype Threat on the Standardized Test Performance of College Students," in *Readings about the Social Animal*, ed. Elliot Aronson (9th edition, New York: Worth Publishers, 2003), 415–430.

[60]Originally from a 1997 interview.

assertion of one's gender norms—of "doing gender"[61] correctly. This seems to be a bigger issue for men working in traditionally and predominantly female areas than for women working in male-dominated realms. That is, the concern about asserting one's masculinity in the eyes of outsiders (by embracing and demonstrating traditionally masculine values and behaviors) while operating in such a feminized context seems to be a primary concern and an actual deterrent to entry for men working in female-dominated jobs.[62] The display of one's gender surely arises as a concern for women in male domains, but it is usually resolved by a move toward downplaying one's femininity so as to attempt to blend in, to minimize one's gender difference (and its consequent visibility), and to become "one of the boys" as much as possible.[63] In Simon Cross and Barbara Bagilhole's study, the exact opposite of this was shown to be at play for men, with "some of the men in the present study articulat[ing] their identity as workers in terms of a different professional role to that of women colleagues." Citing Christine Williams's studies,[64] Cross and Bagilhole explain that Williams, by way of "qualitative, in-depth interviews with men nurses, elementary school teachers, social workers and librarians," found that these men "embed

---

[61]Candace West and Don H. Zimmerman, "Doing Gender," *Gender and Society* 1, no. 2. (June 1987): 125–151. West and Zimmerman's concept of "doing gender" is now an essential concept within gender studies in which one takes part actively (and in contextually variable ways) in the reproduction of one' gender group's norms. It is "the activity of managing situated conduct in light of normative conceptions of attitudes and activities appropriate for one's sex category" (West and Zimmerman, 127). Page 126 of their original article explains:

> Our purpose in this article is to propose an ethnomethodologically informed, and therefore distinctively sociological, understanding of gender as a routine, methodical, and recurring accomplishment. We contend that the "doing" of gender is undertaken by women and men whose competence as members of society is hostage to its production. Doing gender involves a complex of socially guided perceptual, interactional, and micropolitical activities that cast particular pursuits as expressions of masculine and feminine "natures."
>
> When we view gender as an accomplishment, an achieved property of situated conduct, our attention shifts from matters internal to the individual and focuses on interactional and, ultimately, institutional arenas. In one sense, of course, it is individuals who "do" gender. But it is a situated doing, carried out in the virtual or real presence of others who are presumed to be oriented to its production. Rather than as a property of individuals, we conceive of gender as an emergent feature of social situations: both as an outcome of and a rationale for various social arrangements and as a means of legitimating one of the most fundamental divisions of society.

[62]Simon Cross and Barbara Bagilhole, "Girls' Jobs for the Boys? Men, Masculinity and Non-Traditional Occupations," *Gender, Work and Organization* 9, no. 2 (April 2002): 204–226.

[63]Nancy Theberge, "The Construction of Gender in Sport: Women, Coaching and the Naturalization of Difference," *Social Problems* 40, no. 3 (August 1993): 301–313.

[64]Christine Williams, *Still a Man's World: Men Who Do Women's Work* (Berkeley: University of California Press, 1995).

their gender identity as 'men' principally through gender-differentiated work place activities." For example, Cross and Bagilhole continue, citing Williams's study, "men nurses report distinguishing what they do *as nurses* from traditional conceptions of nursing tasks (such as caring)."[65] These men, it seems, do not see value in assimilating to the (female) culture in which they now work, but instead seek to find a place within it that is their own. This suggests that their gender does *not* serve as a barrier to their success or grounds for discrimination (as is shown to be the case for women in male domains), but perhaps as an advantageous tool. While the women in traditionally male domains attempt to mitigate or camouflage their gender difference, men in corresponding female fields exaggerate theirs. At the end of the day, after all, he is still a man, and even "the female dominant workplace is not necessarily a 'natural' setting for contestation, negotiation and change in gender relations."[66]

Importantly, masculine gender affirmation is presented here as a deterrent to males' entry into these female realms; it is men's *own* insecurities and tentativeness that are the most significant obstacles to their entry into these female-dominated realms. When compared with the challenges that women face in attempting to get hired for a position within a male-dominated area, the aforementioned discussion highlights a significant difference in terms of the "benefits" that minority status affords men as opposed to women.

Once a man overcomes anxieties about the preservation of his heterosexual masculine identity and decides to enter a female-dominated realm, what additional barriers might impede his success? It seems as if this question, although providing the potential for a concise parallel to women's experiences in male domains, is largely moot for men. That is, their gender does not appear to be a barrier at all, but rather an advantage. To use Christine Williams's apt metaphor, these men are not running into glass ceilings, they are riding on glass escalators.[67]

Compared with women, whose minority percentages are even further dwindling as they move closer to the top of an industry, the men in female-dominated professions are actually disproportionately overrepresented at top-level administrative and executive positions within such professions. "Men may be under-represented in the occupation, but they are frequently overrepresented in the senior and managerial grades so that pronounced gender-based vertical segregation is observed even in female-dominated parts of the economy," explained the European Commission's analysis of men and gender

---

[65]Cross and Bagilhole, "Girls' Jobs for the Boys," 217.

[66]Ibid., 223.

[67]Williams, *Still a Man's World*, 87.

equality.[68] This "gender-based vertical segregation," along with an individual's "token" status, has very different, in fact opposite, meanings for men working as minorities as opposed to women.[69] As Christine Williams explains, "some groups (like women) suffer because of their minority status; other groups (like men) do not."[70]

Conclusion

We digressed in this chapter from the issue at hand—namely, the world of women in sports, their consumption, in particular—for one simple but compelling reason: Just like in the instances elaborated here, in sports, too, women have not only been recent latecomers but also continue to occupy minoritarian and subordinate positions in virtually all of sports' decisive domains. Here, too, objectively measured credentialing criteria have helped women, at least to some degree, gain invaluable access to structures that, until recently—and for far too long—remained forbidden territory for them. But as later chapters in our book will show, areas in sports to which hard credentialing mechanisms do not pertain—most notably, that of the sports consumer or fan—continue to discriminate against women by essentially not taking them seriously or not even wanting their presence. While male scientists might not really want any female scientists around them, and while they might not regard women as men's equals, all recognize and respect hard credentials: B.A. (MIT), Ph.D. (Cal Tech); case closed. Legitimization, at least on the formal level, accomplished.

Alas, there are no degree-granting institutions in sports fandom. Membership in this world, as well as expertise in it, are totally fluid, unmarked, with no boundaries or any definable characteristics. Of course, there exists no formal credentialing to attain and maintain membership, let alone one with the pedigree and legitimacy that the insiders might confer upon any newcomer. With entrance criteria remaining forever murky, women have had a hard time gaining access to this world, let alone flourishing in it. While the realm of sports fandom has proven to be immensely democratic for men by dint of its very

---

[68]European Commission's Men and Gender Equality Analysis Note: Employment, Social Affairs and Equal Opportunities, "Men and Gender Equality—Tackling Segregated Family Roles and Social Care Jobs" (March 2010): 30–46.

[69]An additional barrier to men's entry mentioned in the report, it should be noted, is that "female" jobs are simply less desirable and frankly "not worth entering." The report expressed that the understanding that "many female-dominated occupations are low paid, have limited job security, benefits or training opportunities and offer restricted career ladder progression," as well as the likelihood that "female-oriented" jobs will have fewer available full-time positions, have served as significant deterrents to male's entry into these realms (European Commission, "Men and Gender Equality," 33).

[70]Williams, *Still a Man's World*, 21.

low and fluid entrance requirements and completely unstructured criteria for membership status, it was precisely these very forces that have constituted such an unwelcoming—and thus profoundly undemocratic—world for women as sports consumers. But before we undertake a detailed discussion of women's trying existence as sports fans, we must, in this next chapter, present their rapidly and successfully changed world as athletes.

3

Women as Sports Producers

Progress and Problems

While sports following and fandom—consumption—may be a realm scarcely inhabited by women, the *production* side of sports features relative gender parity at all levels of organized play. The advances made by female athletes since the Victorian era—and specifically since the advent of the so-called second wave of feminism of the late 1960s and early 1970s that indelibly changed private and public mores in all advanced industrial democracies—have been nothing short of enormous, indeed, revolutionary. The phenomenal increase in women as serious sports producers (i.e., of their "doing" sports at the highest competitive levels) that commenced in the late 1960s and early 1970s in virtually all advanced industrial democracies has no equivalent, either in quantity or quality, to women as sports consumers (i.e., their "following" sports). We argue that these two worlds have, on the whole, remained quite separate, that being a committed female athlete has not, on the whole, translated into being a committed female fan, what we have termed a "sportista." Indeed, we argue that the latter remains separate not only from the former but also from the vast majority of "normal" female sports fans, never mind the continued hegemony of the male sports world, with its myriad outlets, from the playing field to the press box, from television studios to law firms, from hospital wards to government offices, and from the White House to every county in the land. The fact that many of the most well-versed sports experts continue to be male couch potatoes of the nerdy variety, most of whom, it is safe to say, never excelled as athletes, highlights the fact that producing sports, on the one hand, and being an expert follower and passionate consumer, on the other, may in fact have a rather tenuous relationship at best. We now turn to a brief survey of the progression of female athletics.

The Victorian Woman

Victorian notions of women were informed by a perceived symbolic alignment with "nature," a connection that required that their identity be provided by their roles in reproduction, child rearing, and other matters of keeping house (in contrast to males' roles and identities, which centered on their work and activities outside the home).[1] The nineteenth-century woman (as well as, in many ways, her twenty-first-century counterpart) was understood to be emotional, passive, and, as a result, most definitely unfit for physically challenging and competitive activity. As Jennifer Hargreaves concisely writes in her important book *Sporting Females*, "The Victorians maximized cultural differences between the sexes and used biological explanations to justify them."[2]

According to the prevalent norms of Victorian culture, women's procreative duties required such energy and resources that there was not to be any expenditure of effort in the name of any other pursuits, whether intellectual, physical, or competitive.[3] However, in the latter half of the nineteenth century, certain specific types of exercise and physical activity for women gained both medical, thus "scientific," legitimation, as well as social acceptance. Decidedly *gentle* forms of physical activity, performed with moderate frequency and minimal intensity, not only came to be viewed as safe for women but also attained a clear functionality: potentially to "aid women's health and ability to bear healthy children."[4]

Included in the corpus of the earliest acceptable activities for women were gymnastics, tennis, cycling, golf, croquet, and archery. Gymnastics was seen as safe and was even adopted as a medical treatment by many physicians because it did not corrupt the rounded form of a woman, which, according to the predominant view at the time, "must not be transformed into angularity or nodosity such as in a man."[5] However, in addition to this male perspective, gymnastics also became a popular form of both medical therapy and physical activity for fit Victorian women on account of feminist efforts that agitated for

---

[1] Jennifer Hargreaves, *Sporting Females: Critical Issues in the History and Sociology of Women's Sports* (New York: Routledge, 1994), 43.

[2] Ibid.

[3] Ibid., 45.

[4] Ibid., 48.

[5] Ibid.

the physical education of women.[6] Women responded to the newfound concern for the maintenance of their physical health by embracing types of calisthenics, massage, domestic activities such as sweeping, and simple exercises such as walking. Thus, women had begun to move toward physical pursuits for the sake of their health. However, the execution of such pursuits remained limited to their proscribed domestic sphere.[7]

This development coincided with the firm institutionalization and solid foundation of the modern male sporting world on both sides of the Atlantic. While females were not included as players and had to pursue their sports production in a rigidly segregated and thus marginalized world—think of Bennets' of London and the Dick, Kerr Ladies' of Lancashire soccer teams in England and the Senda-Berenson-created Basket Ball for women[8]—women's presence in the ballpark (baseball and college football in the United States, Association and Rugby football in Britain) eventually became part of the game, as they were called upon to be "spectators and moral guardians . . . to bear on the crowds and ensure social order."[9] Albeit tepid and marginal, women's entry as spectators into the public space of the almost exclusively male-dominated world of public sporting activity contributed perhaps a tad to the social and cultural developments that would later bring female athletes out of the domestic realm. Thus, for example, by establishing something called "Ladies Days," certain baseball teams went beyond merely encouraging women's spectatorship at the ballpark as an added source of revenue to actively welcoming it as a calming and sobering agent on an often unruly male crowd.[10]

Indeed, as we know, men have repeatedly engaged women as (their) civilizing agents. We also know that men often have not taken kindly to such developments, experiencing them as emasculating and threatening to their manhood—recall Huck Finn's departure from home to escape women who wanted to "sivilize [sic] him." On the one hand, men welcomed women as civilizing agents, but on the other hand, they often perceived them in this role as restricting and confining and thus responded to such measures by receding

---

[6]Women's Sports Foundation, "Women's Pre-Title IX Sports History in the United States," published April 26, 2001, available at http://www.womenssportsfoundation.org/content/articles/issues/history/w/womens-pretitle-IX-sports-history-in-the-united-states.aspx (accessed March 27, 2011).

[7]Ibid.

[8]For the English examples, see Jean Williams, "The Fastest Growing Sport? Women's Football in England," in *Soccer, Women, Sexual Liberation: Kicking off a New Era*, ed. Fan Hong and J. A. Mangan (London: Frank Cass, 2004), 112–127; for Senda Berenson, see *Basket Ball for Women* (Park Place, NY: American Sports Publishing Company, 1903).

[9]Women's Sports Foundation, "Pre-Title IX Sports History."

[10]Debra Shattuck, "Women's Baseball in the 1860s: Reestablishing a Historical Memory," *NINE: A Journal of Baseball History and Culture* 19, no. 2 (2011): 1–26.

to male-controlled domains, such as fishing, hunting—and, of course, sports. It is not by chance that sports as an almost exclusively male bastion emerged in the Victorian age as a space for men to re-confirm their masculinity, unencumbered by women, in an epoch where men's physical strength and endurance had lost some of their salience in a rapidly industrializing and urbanizing world. Even the exacting physical nature of blue-collar factory work—let alone the physically much less demanding labor of the rapidly increasing white-collar tertiary sector that was to shape much of employment in all advanced industrial countries—appeared to feature the centrality of men's physical prowess a good deal less than did hunting and the pursuits of agricultural labor. Thus, for example, one cannot escape the feeling that in today's "humane," "social democratic," "politically correct," and "feminized" Europe, in which a powerful force that Markovits has called the "discourse of empathy" has reigned supreme since the 1970s, the soccer stadium remains the last bastion of unbridled maleness. Here, one can really behave badly—one can be racist and sexist—in other words, one can really be a man in one's element, unconstrained by the feminized discourse of empathy and civilization that many men feel to be ubiquitous, hegemonic, and, at times, constraining. It is also not by chance that such unruly male behavior exists in soccer and no other European sport since it is soccer that represents by far the most important—in many countries sole—constituent of hegemonic sports culture.[11]

In the course of the nineteenth century, particularly toward its end, the lifestyle of the middle-class Victorian family became increasingly materialistic in terms of the conspicuous displaying of one's wealth. Thus, the popularity of suitable activities, such as croquet and tennis, experienced growth commensurate with the size of the mansions built by an increasingly wealthy and burgeoning bourgeoisie. While women were, of course, never to forget their station and manners in this bourgeois world, these games became a form of mixed-gender recreation that was central to middle-class life. Surely as an unintended consequence, however, these games also proved important in integrating women into dominant leisure and culture.

In the last decades of the nineteenth century, tennis became an extremely popular sport, with "tennis parties" being one of the most celebrated facets of social life.[12] During this time, women's participation in the games was growing in frequency and acceptance. The games were often coed, but featured different rules for each gender that catered to the presumed athletic inferiority of

---

[11]Andrei S. Markovits, "Sports Fans across Borders: America from Venus, Europe from Mars," *Harvard International Review* 33, no. 2 (Summer 2011): 17–22.

[12]Hargreaves, *Sporting Females*, 54.

women. Thus, for example, women were often encouraged to stand as close to the net as they wanted when serving, and they were usually given chances to re-do shots that went into the net.[13]

As women's experience and familiarity with the game increased, so did the level of physicality featured in their play. Gradually, women's athletic participation increased in its physicality, eventually reaching a level of intensity at which women came to set aside part of their feminine poise in favor of intentionally displaying their athletic prowess.[14] The limitations placed on women's behavior were becoming less restrictive, and, even in the female domain of the home, "the 'playing of games' became an important, fashionable accomplishment for middle-class women, placed in the same category as those much admired genteel activities such as playing the piano, singing, drawing, painting, reciting poetry and doing needlework."[15]

Help from Schools: Physical Education Grows

The gradual departure from more parochially sexist views of women's limitations increased the demand for women's acquisition of a greater amount of formal education than they had been granted previously. There exists much evidence that this development was decisive in having women's sports and exercise become part of hegemonic culture.[16]

Often the underlying logic employed in the female programs differed from that of their male counterparts. Thus, for example, the former lacked team-dominated and result-oriented contests and emphasized in their stead "more avant-garde ideas about the benefits of exercise for women."[17] Still, significant shifts occurred in attitudes toward women's participation in sports to the point that medical professionals began arguing for the compulsory inclusion of physical education in any school's curriculum, including the all-female colleges that were becoming popular at the time.[18] The late decades of the nineteenth century also witnessed the increasing presence of various feminist movements that facilitated the growth of women's presence in institutions of higher education, many of which introduced female physical education programs. This formative feminism opened up additional educational opportunities for women

---

[13]Ibid., 55.

[14]Ibid., 54.

[15]Ibid., 55.

[16]Ibid.

[17]Ibid., 57.

[18]Ibid., 58.

by emphasizing sports' contribution to societal status and privilege. "As more middle-class women gained access to formal education, they took part in organized sports in increasing numbers."[19]

Beginning to Organize

Just as the formation and joining of sports clubs had enhanced men's social lives in countless ways, women, too, began to reap collective benefits by the founding of organizations devoted to competitive female athletics. By way of these clubs, as well as the growth of female populations at universities, female athletes participated in newly emerging sports such as basketball and volleyball that were new to men and had been invented in the world of YMCAs in Western Massachusetts (basketball in Springfield in 1891; volleyball in Holyoke in 1895) for the explicit didactic purposes of offering young men a proper physical component for their all-around education pursuant to the motto that encompassed a gentleman's suitable station: *mens sana in corpore sano*—a healthy mind in a healthy body. Sports such as field hockey, cycling, and tennis also experienced rapid growth in female participation in the university and club settings. Soon the collaboration of coaches and supervisors at these athletic clubs and educational organizations led to the formation of formal athletic associations and even the codification of uniform rules, both important to the further legitimization of females' pursuit of such physical activities.[20]

However, traditional fears about the relationship between excessively intense physical strength and competitive activity, on the one hand, and a resultant loss of socially demanded and expected feeble, passive, and nurturing, femininity, on the other, persisted unabated. To reconcile these two seemingly contradictory pressures and demands, a fascinating synthesis of the two emerged via a kind of "feminization" of these games that were, of course, originally designed by and for men. Concretely, modifications of the original (male) rules emerged that were to alter the very essence of these games to make them fit women better. This "feminization" of rules altered the nature of athletic competition in the early twentieth century.[21] Let us demonstrate this phenomenon with the case of basketball.

As just mentioned, in the winter of 1891, at the YMCA in Springfield, Massachusetts, Dr. James Naismith, a McGill University–trained educator, invented basketball for the explicit purpose of giving the young male students

---

[19]Ibid., 101.

[20]Women's Sports Foundation, "Pre-Title IX Sports History."

[21]Ibid.

(future missionaries and educators) a sport that could be played indoors so that their innate masculine aggression would not remain pent up through the long New England winter months. When indoor soccer proved to be an unviable option, since all of the gym's windows were shattered during a game, and gymnastics was not to these young men's liking, Naismith consciously and systematically designed an indoor ball game that he envisioned as a decided opposite to football, which, in Naismith's view, had become far too brutal and remained the purview of upper-class boys at elite colleges, where the game's increasing importance had come to undermine its original role as an appropriate physical ingredient in the well-rounded education of a modern man.

Using her perch as an educator at prestigious Smith College, an all-women's school in Western Massachusetts, the aforementioned Senda Berenson set out to "feminize" basketball by reducing the physicality of the game and tailoring it to fit the perceived frailty of women. The threat of female players suffering from adverse reactions such as "nervous fatigue," among others, was of concern to Berenson. Thus, she proceeded to make rule changes to render the game more suitable for women. As such, she became one of the most influential creators of modern basketball. Her feminizing revisions of the game had a major effect on it for nearly 80 years.

One such revision entailed the division of the court space into three sections, each one meant to contain players throughout the game. That is, of the nine players on the court, three were assigned to each section and no one was to leave her given section during any point throughout play. (This Berenson reform remained with the game until 1938, when the court was divided into two sections. It was not until 1971 that the women would play the full-court version that is used now and that informed the men's game from its very inception in 1891.)[22] Additional Berenson changes included forbidding any form of "snatching," or stealing. In addition, players could hold the ball for no more than three seconds and could dribble it no more than three times. Berenson believed that such rules prevented young women from the development of any "dangerous tendencies" or from "losing the grace and dignity and self-respect we all have her foster."[23]

Women's team sports like baseball and basketball were held back not just by the male establishment in the United States. Thus, for example, in Germany, the powerful national soccer federation—Deutscher Fussballbund—explicitly forbade women to play organized soccer between 1955 and 1970. Similar de facto, if not de jure, bans existed in many other European countries, with the Foot-

---

[22]Sally Jenkins, "History of Women's Basketball," available at http://www.wnba.com/about_us/jenkins_feature.html (accessed March 31, 2011).

[23]Ibid.

ball Association, England's soccer federation and the world's oldest, all but forbidding women to play organized soccer on an official basis in the early 1920s.

Tellingly, these de jure or de facto bans on women participating in these countries' most dominant representatives of their respective hegemonic sports cultures began to fray with the advent of the second wave of the women's movement in the late 1960s and early 1970s. Thus, in 1970, the Deutscher Fussballbund lifted its ban on women's soccer, but still insisted that it be played differently from the men's game (the women's game could last only sixty minutes, while the men's lasted ninety). The women's season commenced on March 1 and ended on October 31, lest women were to play during the inclement months in which the men played their season, which began in early August and lasted until late May. Women were not to use typical football boots with studs on their sole, but rather flat running shoes. Furthermore, due to the "female anatomy," no advertising or any kind of lettering was allowed on women's jerseys lest it attract the spectators' prurient attention and thus become a distraction from the game. Only females were allowed to coach women's teams, and all players could begin their season only after having undergone a thorough medical examination by a specialist in sports medicine and a gynecologist. Such an exam had to be repeated within four weeks after completion of the season. Women were not allowed to use regular footballs, but were required to play their games with "youth balls," which were lighter in weight and smaller in size. Lastly, women were not to play for any championships.

In the course of the 1970s, all of these discriminating distinctions fell one by one. In the 1980s, the women's game was expanded from the previous sixty minutes to eighty, and it was not until the early 1990s that the ninety-minute duration common to men's soccer was adopted by the women's game. Notable for these gradual adaptations to the men's game was a change in the women's game's nomenclature: Formerly called "Damenfussball"—ladies' football—it mutated to the now common "Frauenfussball"—women's football. And yes, the women can now sport advertising on their jerseys, that is, if sponsors can be found to advertise their products in the meager world of women's soccer in Germany, one of the globe's most soccer-obsessed lands. Let us now return to the story of women's basketball in the United States.

Basketball

The first women's basketball game occurred less than a year after the women at Smith College learned the game with the help of their coach Senda Berenson. Notable, though, is the fact that this game occurred inside a locked gymnasium, off limits to men, as they were forbidden from watching such an abomination of traditional femininity. Rules at this time, as is usually the case with new sports, varied regionally and were ever-evolving, sometimes more closely matching the rules of the men's game and sometimes being heavily tailored to the perceived needs of women. Stylistic differences made their way into the official rules in some cases, as with the two-handed shot, which was deemed a foul in many instances because of its forcing of a forward incline of one's shoulders and a "consequent flattening of one's chest."[24]

Concerns and disgust abounded in response to young, proper university women's participation in such a gritty, physical game. Physical education instructors, physicians, and parents called for the abolition of the game for women, citing concerns about the negative long-term physical and psychological effects that such play could have on their young women. In 1908, the Amateur Athletic Union officially adopted the position that women were not to play the game in public.[25]

Commentators (and possibly critics) focused attention on brash ways in which the women moved on the court, the high volume at which they screamed during play, and the superbly un-ladylike practice of calling each other by nicknames, often their last names. Additional rule changes were often suggested to counter these concerns, such as the requirement of tidily combed hair and the banning of slang, chewing gum, the practice of addressing another player by her last name, and the practice of sitting or lying on the floor of the court.[26]

Still, the women's game had spread across the country, with important women's basketball centers emerging at Wellesley, Vassar, and Bryn Mawr, prestigious all-women's colleges similar to Smith. The game came to be played by women all over the world, with rules moving toward uniformity. Berenson's rules were first published in 1899, and she became the editor of A. G. Spalding's *Women's Basketball Guide* in 1901, as her version of the sport spread.[27]

Of course, the women's game lagged behind the advancement of the men's, though, as evidenced by the Women's Division of the National Amateur Athletic Federation's 1925 ban of extramural basketball for women on account of its excessive competitiveness, the game was played by women prolifically all across the country and was, in fact, quite popular. In addition to outlawing extramural competition, the Women's Division of the National Amateur Athletic Federation's resolution included "opposing gate receipts at women's

[24]Ibid.

[25]Women's Basketball Online, "Women's Basketball Timeline," available at http://womensbasketballonline.com/history/timeline1900_29.html (accessed March 31, 2011).

[26]Jenkins, "History of Women's Basketball."

[27]Ibid.

games, all travel for women's games, and all publicity of women's sports."[28] The WDNAAF's efforts throughout the 1920s saw some success in shutting down the Amateur Athletic Union's organized women's basketball tournaments, but by the end of the decade, the tournaments had garnered enough support and acceptance to be able to withstand pressures to be shut down.

Basketball continued to spread internationally, and, 40 years after the men, in 1976, the International Olympic Committee extended an invitation to women to play basketball in the Olympics. The 1970s saw a spike in the growth of the women's game, with Title IX providing grounds for an explosion of participation in the game for girls, starting at young ages. The Association for Intercollegiate Athletics for Women (AIAW) did the most significant work for women's basketball, hosting tournaments as early as 1975, and the NCAA's eventual takeover of the game further lifted women's college basketball into cultural relevance.[29]

The first NCAA-sanctioned women's basketball tournament in 1982 included thirty-four teams and drew an audience of fewer than 10,000.[30] By 1994, the tournament had grown to sixty-four teams, seeding was done by committee (the same way the men's tournament had been, and differently from the previous women's system of seeding teams so as to keep them close to home for tournament play), and games attracted more than 23,000 fans.[31] The advancement of women's basketball into national relevance is illustrative of the rise of women's sports altogether. Nowhere close to the cultural importance and societal popularity of the men's March Madness and "Bracketology"—as we will demonstrate in Chapter 4—women's basketball gained a level of respectability that three decades ago would have been unimaginable. World War II and the developments of the 1960s and 1970s furnished important precursors to this success.

Women's college basketball cannot draw the kinds of viewership that men's does, but the women's game has advanced incredibly since its first tournaments. What began as a puny game confined to small colleges and shielded from the

[28]Women's Basketball Online, "Women's Basketball Timeline."

[29]Virginia Hunt, "Governance of Women's Intercollegiate Athletics: An Historical Perspective" (Greensboro, University of North Carolina: Doctoral Dissertation; Ann Arbor, Michigan: University Microfilms, 1977), 1–319.

[30]Joanne Lannin, *A History of Basketball for Girls and Women: From Bloomers to Big Leagues* (Minneapolis: Lerner Sports, 2000), 100.

[31]Gary Brown, "Division I Women's Basketball Tournament Expansion: An Issue for Discussion," October 13, 2010, available at http://www.ncaa.org/wps/wcm/connect/public/NCAA/Resources/Latest+News/2010+news+stories/October/Division+I+womens+basketball+tournament+expansion+an+issue+for+discussion (accessed May 18, 2011).

eyes of spectators is now home to such powerhouses as Tennessee's Lady Vols and UConn's record-breaking Huskies, teams that have become popular entities in America's overall sports culture. Superstardom has been achieved by women in the game, with Sheryl Swoopes being the first woman to have Nike name a shoe after her and Maya Moore becoming a name known to any regular viewer of popular sports commentary programming. The NCAA women's tournament is given prime time coverage on ESPN stations and, especially since the championship game's move to the Tuesday after the men's championship game on its traditional Monday evening, continues to garner ever-increasing TV audiences. The 2010 women's final game featured Stanford and UConn and earned a "2.4 cable [Nielsen] rating and [increased its audience to] 3.164 million viewers, up 20% and 22%, respectively, from a 2.0 rating and 2.585 million viewers in '09."[32]

AAGBPL: Women Fill the Void by Taking to the Field

World War II propelled many women into positions that were previously exclusively male. The formation of the All-American Girls Professional Baseball League (AAGPBL) illustrates that sports were no exception to this cultural shift.[33] As was the case with women's educational advancements in the nineteenth century, their specific progress in sports mirrored women's gradual arrival in many facets of America's public sphere.

The AAGPBL was formed and funded by Philip K. Wrigley, then owner of the Chicago Cubs, in response to widespread fears that baseball, arguably not a sport but perhaps the most beloved cultural fixture in the country, would not be able to recover from an absolute hiatus while it waited for its players to return from the war. The AAGBPL was to "serve as a viable substitute and keep the interest in baseball alive."[34]

This statement alone reveals what significant strides female athleticism had made from its position a century earlier. The league was very successful, especially in the Midwest, with the women whom Wrigley recruited mainly ema-

---

[32]*Sports Business Daily*, "ESPN Sees Ratings, Viewer Increases for UConn Women's NCAA Repeat," published April 8, 2010, available at http://www.sportsbusinessdaily.com/Daily/Issues/2010/04/Issue-143/Sports-Media/ESPN-Sees-Ratings-Viewer-Increases-For-Uconn-Womens-NCAA-Repeat.aspx (accessed April 30, 2011).

[33]Mary Pratt, "The All-American Girls Professional Baseball League," in *Women in Sport: Issues and Controversies*, ed. Greta L. Cohen (Thousand Oaks, CA: Sage Publications, 1993), 49–58.

[34]Ibid., 49.

nating from already established women's amateur softball leagues that were flourishing all over the country. The women of the AAGBPL were brought in to serve as placeholders to keep baseball in the minds of Americans just enough to ensure that it was not abandoned. But the women ended up garnering large crowds of their own.

Throughout its twelve-year run, the League employed more than 500 women ball players from the United States, Canada, and Cuba, and in the late 1940s, the "Belles of the Ball Game" drew more than one million fans to their games. The actual game played on the field initially closely resembled softball (as that was the sport from which the women came), with a larger ball than a baseball thrown underhand. Eventually, though, the game evolved to look more like that which the men played, with a smaller ball and an overhand pitching style.[35]

The creators and propagators of women's baseball were committed to helping it earn a position as a legitimate professional sport, one in which the players received remuneration, advertisement proliferated, and fans paid their entry to the ballpark. Still, the fact that the game's protagonists were women always remained salient. Wrigley's teams featured such names as the Rockford Peaches, the Milwaukee Chicks, and the Fort Wayne Daisies, mascots that reinforced and reminded fans of the players' gender (and the presumed cuteness that accompanied it). While these women were embraced in many ways as bona fide athletes, there was still the expectation that they, at all times, even at the plate, would maintain their complete femininity.

Wrigley himself insisted that, even while on the field, his athletes would at all times embody what he considered "the highest ideals of womanhood."[36] The teams all had male managers in charge of lineups, drafting, and all matters relating to the actual playing of the game, as well as female chaperones whose duties revolved around making sure that the players' public images and actions were appropriately ladylike.[37] Both of these roles, though, included responsibilities related to the enforcement of the players' maintenance of their ladylike appearance and lifestyle.

On the field, this meant well-kept hair, lipstick, and makeup, and uniforms that more closely resembled tennis dresses, and were certainly ill suited for anyone looking to run between—or especially slide into—bases. The guidelines

---

[35]Encyclopædia Britannica, s.v. "All-American Girls Professional Baseball League (AAGPBL)," available at http://www.britannica.com/EBchecked/topic/15840/All-American-Girls-Professional-Baseball-League-AAGPBL (accessed April 21, 2011).

[36]Ibid.

[37]Pratt, "All-American Girls Professional Baseball League," 51.

for the women in public included such restrictions as the prohibition of shorts or slacks, rules against smoking and drinking, and even the requirement that each woman's hair be at least chin-length.[38] While compulsory charm school enrollment may be seen as a representation of the symbolic glass ceiling behind which the women of World War II–era baseball were stuck, the formation and success of the League nonetheless represents a large step forward for female athletics. More than ever before, spectators were gathering to watch females compete in what was widely regarded as a physical man's game.

While the women's baseball league was surely a sign of progress in female athletics, the situation in schools and colleges was not necessarily as enlightened, as the "sporty girl" concept was still, throughout the 1950s and 1960s, understood as a phase that would eventually give way to a girl's pursuit of motherhood. Physical education programs in institutions of learning were, at the time, segregated by gender, with the female curriculum often being devoid of comprehensive team sports, and therefore of interschool competition, instead featuring intramural activities, dance groups, and synchronized swimming guilds. The opportunities for athletic competition provided by schools and colleges were, relative to those available to men at the time, very limited; real sports *teams* for girls that were sponsored by physical education departments barely existed. Instead, girls had to make do with various intramural *clubs*.

Governance of Women's Athletics

The governance of women's college athletics has a complex history that arguably starts in 1941, when intercollegiate competition was first organized at the national level, in the form of the first national collegiate golf championship.[39] One of the earliest overseeing entities for female collegiate athletics was a tripartite committee formed in 1956 comprising the National Association for Physical Education for College Women, the National Association for Girls and Women in Sport, and the American Federation of College Women.[40] In 1957, at the request of that three-part committee, the National Joint Committee on Extramural Sports for College Women was formed and charged with the responsibility of organizing and overseeing women's collegiate athletic programs. The Division of Girls' and Women's Sports (DGWS), a subset of the American Association for Health, Physical Education and Recreation, had also previously been established, and in an attempt to consolidate the administration of women's athletics, it was granted control over women's college sports in 1965.

---

[38]Ibid.

[39]Hunt, "Women's Intercollegiate Athletics."

[40]Ibid.

The DGWS quickly created the Commission on Intercollegiate Athletics for Women in 1967, with responsibility to design and oversee women's intercollegiate play, specifically, to create and sponsor national championships. In 1969, the DGWS organized an event, the National Workshop on Intercollegiate Sports, designed for female physical education instructors and featuring discussions on the positive and negative components of different types of competitions and programs.[41] Emanating from this event, and in combination with the Women's Board of the U.S. Olympic Committee, an extremely influential development emerged for women's sports in the form of the National Institutes on Sport.

Each of these institutes focused on a few specific sports and sought to update participants on the latest developments and research in the teaching and coaching of those sports. The agreement on the part of participants was that they would, on leaving the institutes, promise to facilitate at least two additional statewide workshops so as to share their expertise and experience with other women coaches and educators. These institutes and their reverberations constituted a critical growth point for the legitimization of women's sports; instead of being viewed as a relatively leisurely venue for diversion or purely as a means of achieving physical health, the institutes "created a groundswell of interest in higher-level skill for girls and women." Sure enough, an increasing number of schools and colleges began to develop and foster women's sports programs.[42]

In 1971, the aforementioned AIAW was formed by the DGWS executive board, with the vision of being an institutional membership organization that would "lead and conduct programs for women in colleges and universities," and administer national championships.[43] The AIAW would eventually, by 1981, grow to a membership of more than 800 colleges and universities (it began in the 1971–1972 academic year, with 278 charter member institutions) and would host a total of forty-one championships for nineteen different sports (badminton, basketball, cross country, fencing, field hockey, golf, gymnastics, indoor track and field, lacrosse, rowing, skiing, soccer, softball [fast and slow pitch], swimming and diving, synchronized swimming, tennis, track and field, and volleyball).[44]

During this time, the National Collegiate Athletics Association (NCAA) was overseeing all of men's college sports, and the AIAW was deliberate in

---

[41]L. Leotus Morrison, "The AIAW: Governance by Women for Women," in *Women in Sport: Issues and Controversies*, ed. Greta L. Cohen (Thousand Oaks, CA: Sage Publications, 1993), 60–68.

[42]Ibid.

[43]Ibid.

[44]B. J. Hultstrand, "The Growth of Collegiate Women's Sports: The 1960s," *The Journal of Physical Education, Recreation, and Dance* 64, no. 3 (1993): 41–43.

its attempts to remain a separate and distinct body, solely in charge of women's sports. The AIAW did not, for example, allow full athletic scholarships or off-campus recruitment so as to impede the perceived corruption of NCAA athletics become in any way associated with the AIAW's programs.[45] In other words, great effort was made to differentiate women's collegiate sports from men's in which the former's purity was contrasted with the latter's complexity, popularity, and the accompanying alleged vices. The AIAW saw itself as representing a philosophy of sport's role in higher education that the organization perceived as markedly different from—and morally superior to—the practices of the NCAA. The two organizations coexisted, but had little interest in each other's territory, until the growing significance of women's sports could no longer be ignored.

Title IX

Dramatic change for all women's athletics came in its largest dose in 1972. Two years earlier, legislation that would eventually be known as Title IX was drafted and brought to the U.S. Congress. Title IX was not designed to affect athletics; its writer first drafted it as an effort to protect women from sex discrimination in employment at universities. Federal law already forbade employment discrimination based on sex for all federal contractors, and congresswoman Bernice Sandler brought deliberate light to the fact that, in her words, "since most universities . . . had federal contracts, they were forbidden from discriminating in employment on the basis of sex."[46] In 1970, Representative Patsy Mink of Hawaii wrote the amendment to the Civil Rights Act of 1964 known as Title IX.[47] Title IX would be passed in 1972 and would call for the requirement of gender equality in any educational program that receives federal funding. Here are Title IX's immensely weighty thirty-seven words:

> No person in the United States shall, on the basis of sex, be excluded from participation in, be denied the benefits of, or be subject to discrimination under any education program or activities receiving Federal financial assistance.[48]

---

[45]Hunt, "Women's Intercollegiate Athletics," 122–148.

[46]Iram Valentin, "Title IX: A Brief History," *Women's Educational Equity Act Resource Center Digest* (August 1997): 2, available at http://www2.edc.org/WomensEquity/pdffiles/t9digest.pdf.

[47]Betsy M. Ross, *Playing Ball with the Boys: The Rise of Women in the World of Men's Sports* (Cincinnati, OH: Clerisy Press, 2011), 37.

[48]Ibid.

In the 1971–1972 season, according to the American Association of University Women, 294,015 girls were participating in high school sports programs (compared with 3,666,917 boys), 29,972 females were competing as varsity athletes (compared with 170,384 males), scholarships for women totaled less than $100,000, and the average number of women's teams at any given university was 2.1.[49] By 1973, even though schools were given three years to become fully compliant with Title IX's requirements, there were about 1.3 million girls in high school sports programs. In the early 1970s, the average American university spent 1 percent of its athletics budget on women's sports; by 1980, that figure had increased to 16 percent.[50] In 2004, the average university athletic department offered 25 women's sports.[51] AAUW reports that in 2007–2008, the number of females in high school sports was 3,057,266 (4,372,115 for males)—a 940 percent increase—and the number of NCAA female varsity athletes had reached 166,728 (compared with 222,838 males)—a 456 percent increase.[52] That is, in 2007, girls comprised 49 percent of the high school sports population, a more than significant increase from their representation previous to Title IX.

The AIAW advanced women's college athletics to previously unreached levels by bringing about more opportunities for women to participate in sports via its support of Title IX as well as making these events featuring women athletes into legitimate spectator experiences that could be monetarily successful. The women's basketball championship tournament in 1973, for example, garnered a crowd of more than three thousand spectators and profits of about $4,500.[53] Though on a much more modest level, women's basketball was starting to get both corporate sponsorship and television contracts, much like its male counterpart had been doing for many years.

NCAA Takeover

As women's college athletics grew, so too did the NCAA's interest in incorporating them into its organization. The institution of the national championship was a profitable one for any sport under any jurisdiction, so when, in 1981, the

---

[49]The American Association of University Women (AAUW), "Title IX Athletic Statistics," available at http://www.aauw.org/act/laf/library/athleticStatistics.cfm (accessed March 21, 2011).

[50]Pamela Grundy and Susan Shackelford, *Shattering the Glass: The Remarkable History of Women's Basketball* (New York: The New Press, 2005), 148.

[51]Linda Jean Carpenter and R. Vivian Acosta, "Women in Intercollegiate Sport: A Longitudinal, National Study Thirty One Year Update," available at http://webpages.charter.net/womeninsport/2008%20Summary%20Final.pdf (accessed March 30, 2011).

[52]AAUW, "Title IX Athletic Statistics."

[53]Lannin, *A History of Basketball for Girls and Women*, 83.

NCAA proposed to host Division I championships for women's teams, there was an effort by the AIAW to stop this innovation. In response, the NCAA decided to pursue the acquisition of women's sports, the very thing in which nary a few years before this institution had absolutely zero interest until the AIAW had successfully lifted these sports into social relevance.[54]

Until the early 1980s, many schools' athletic departments allowed their women's teams to belong to the AIAW and their men's to the NCAA, but athletic programs would soon have difficulty spurning the support and resources that the NCAA offered in its attempt to woo these programs away from the AIAW. Not only was the NCAA henceforth going to host women's championships, but it was also willing to pay all of the expenses associated with any team's playing in such championships. The NCAA also promised to waive any additional fees assessed to a school to have a women's team join the Association if that institution's men's teams were already NCAA members. Additionally, the Association also offered a system of financial aid, as well as various recruitment and eligibility rules that more closely resembled those that it employed in men's athletics. Perhaps most important of all, the NCAA guaranteed women sports more television coverage. In short, with the NCAA providing much more to women's college sports than the AIAW ever did or could, the writing was on the wall. It would not take long for many schools to abandon the latter and join the former.[55]

The AIAW's efforts to oppose the NCAA's hosting of championships failed, and after the 1981 convention, an increasing number of athletic programs belonging to the AIAW began the migration of their women's teams to the NCAA. The AIAW suffered significant membership losses, with its Division I championship participation decreasing by 48 percent.[56] The final straw came when seventeen of the top twenty women's basketball teams, representing perhaps the most successful women's sports in terms of attracting the largest spectatorship, decided to enter the NCAA's tournament instead of that hosted by the AIAW.[57] In 1982, the AIAW, the organization that had done invaluable work in the advancement of women's sports, met its own demise by dint of its singular success.[58] That year, the NCAA held its first national Women's Basketball Championship.

Anson Dorrance, legendary coach of the University of North Carolina's multiple-national-championship dynasty women's soccer team and coach of

---

[54]Morrison, "The AIAW," 64.

[55]Grundy and Shackelford, *Shattering the Glass*, 179.

[56]Morrison, "The AIAW," 64.

[57]Grundy and Shackelford, *Shattering the Glass*, 180.

[58]Morrison, "The AIAW," 59.

the U.S. women's national team that won the first FIFA-sanctioned Women's World Cup in China in 1991, had nothing but praise for the AIAW and credited its open-mindedness toward soccer and its unfailing support for all women's varsity sports as the decisive agent in creating, fostering, and legitimating women's athletic activities on America's college campuses and thus in American society and culture at large.[59]

Viewership of the women's games may not compare with that of the men's, but the fact is that today the NCAA hosts forty-seven women's championships and forty-six for men throughout all three of its divisions.[60] At all levels of amateur competition, women are participating in the *doing* of sports in nearly the same numbers as men. Title IX and legislative requirements clearly helped to facilitate this parity. But the overall societal changes regarding female behavior embodied a necessary development and furnished an indispensable reason for the successful story of women's athletics.

Women Athletes as Sports Consumers, the Special Nature of Women's Soccer in the United States, and the Complicated World of Women Athletes' Beauty and Sexuality

In the last segment of this chapter, we would like to address three related issues:

First, we will discuss the fascinating phenomenon of how top-level female athletes have no problems at all performing in a team sport at the highest level yet not follow this very sport via any medium and be actually quite disengaged from its existence at that level. We will present a disconnect between producing a sport at its most advanced level accompanied by a concomitant ignorance of and disinterest in its manifestations that form this sport's main attraction to men.

Second, we will briefly delineate the case of women's soccer in the United States, which has a place all its own, in that it provided women with a unique venue of a team sport to which it lent cultural prominence and social importance beyond any sport performed by women in the United States, indeed globally, perhaps precisely because women excelled at this sport that has remained so secondary to the main denizens of the American sports space: men.

Third, we will end this chapter by looking briefly at the hopelessly fraught overlap between women's athleticism and their sexuality as well as sexualization.

---

[59]Anson Dorrance, *The Vision of a Champion: Advice and Inspiration from the World's Most Successful Soccer Coach* (Ann Arbor, MI: Huron River Press, 2002), 4.

[60]www.ncaa.org/wps/wcm/connect/public/ncaa/championships.

Since sport entails, almost by definition, a bodily endeavor, and since sport constitutes, at its most basic level, some sort of physical competition, and since its practitioners at the top rung—both male and female—represent arguably the most attractive, healthy, youthful, well trained, and esthetically beautiful bodies in society, admiring (but also objectifying) them is almost unavoidable. Yet, here, too, women face a completely different reality than men. As we will see, beauty and looks remain center stage for women athletes to a degree unimaginable for men. This phenomenon further exacerbates the salience of gender differences in sport on all levels, from the playing field to the couch in front of the television set in the family den.

The Gap between *Playing* and *Following* Sports

Most interesting in this exploration of women's participation in and production of sports has been an accompanying engagement in their consumption of sports. A study by Andrei Markovits and David Smith shows clearly that an individual's *playing* of sports does not seem to have any compelling relationship with his or her consumption of them.[61] The research results demonstrate that the student athletes at Michigan are, in fact, less conversant with, less ardent fans of popular sports than many non-athletes, particularly a cluster of men whom one could safely categorize as sport savants, or sport know-it-alls, by dint of their being *sports omnivores*, who passionately follow and know a bevy of the most diverse sports. Thus, our previously presented story of the near-meteoric advancement of women in athletics since the early 1970s constitutes a vital part of our larger concern because there seems to be no concurrent and analogous development in women athletes' following of hegemonic sports.

For the purpose of our study, we had a leading member of the University of Michigan's varsity women's soccer team keep a daily diary of her and her teammates' sports consumption for an entire semester, from January to April 2011. She noted the ways her teammates talked about sports, how the players watched them, if in fact they did, and the general role that sports talk assumed in the quotidian social exchanges between her and the women on the team. The members of this group clearly represent immensely accomplished Division I athletes, and their sport takes up enormous amounts of their time and assumes an absolutely central part of their identity. They are completely im-

---

[61] Andrei S. Markovits and David T. Smith, "Sports Culture among Undergraduates: A Study of Student-Athletes and Students at the University of Michigan," *The Michigan Journal of Political Science* II, issue 9 (2008): 1–58; reprinted in *Sports and Society in Comparative Perspective*, ed. David Karen and Robert E. Washington (New York: Routledge, 2010).

mersed in playing sports—soccer, in this case—as are many of their friends who are not on the team. Courtney's account of her team's sports talk and activities reinforced our presumed gap between doing and following sports, as these soccer players' consumption practices—despite their being totally devoted and talented athletes—did not appear to be any more enthusiastic or knowledgeable than a typical person's who was neither an athlete nor a fan.

The players all watched the big games, meaning events whose social and cultural relevance reaches well beyond the confines of the actual contest. Courtney noted that "every single girl on [the] team had watched the NCAA championship football game."[62] They tune in more often to sports when the games are part of the playoffs or a championship tournament, Courtney observed. "Some girls noted that they had not watched a single game during the college basketball regular season, yet when March Madness started, they followed much more." As college students, they never miss rivalry games between Michigan and Ohio State, even in basketball, and even considering Courtney's observation that "the Big Ten Tournament was the first time that a majority of my teammates watched a Michigan basketball game." The whole team watched the Super Bowl, but "many girls hadn't watched even one regular season NFL game." In the same vein (that being a pattern of watching only the big games that are actually social events and that everyone—fan or non-fan—will most likely use as a reference), the Michigan women's varsity soccer players talk about stars when they discuss sports. "We talk about big names such as Ben Roethlisberger, Brett Favre, Troy Polamalu, Tom Brady, etc. These are the names that the girls heard on the news, saw on the Internet and in newspapers, and heard other people talking about." It is not so much that these accomplished varsity athletes are following sports out of love for them, but rather as a means of not being left out of what are sure to be universal topics of conversation in their social milieu.

Courtney admits that they, as a team, do not possess much "specialized knowledge" about the major sports that they discuss, and that their "conversations are much more generalized" than those that might be held among genuine sports experts. Sometimes, the sports conversation becomes "absolutely non-sports-related," with topics such as the relative attractiveness of players and the types of athletic jerseys that look best on men. Much of the conversation, Courtney described, turns into "gossip about players that [is] usually unrelated to their sport."

The gap between playing and following in the world of these elite athletes and soccer players becomes even more pronounced in soccer, a sport

---

[62]Courtney Mercier, 2011.

about which they surely *do* possess the highest levels of "specialized knowledge" and, presumably, one in which they are interested. "Even though we are soccer players at a very high level," Courtney describes, "we absolutely do not follow men's and women's professional soccer!" Even in the case of the very sport that constitutes a huge part of these young women's lives, they are not interested in watching or following it being played at its top levels by men and women. To be sure, these Michigan soccer players are more likely to watch big soccer events, such as the World Cup and Olympic matches (events that the whole world, regardless of soccer skill, seems to follow). But their interest does not seem to extend to following games in the Union of European Football Associations Champions League, featuring the very best club teams in the world competing at arguably the highest level of the sport. Moreover, Courtney's teammates are more likely to watch one of the Big Four North American sports' big games than they are soccer's, illustrating that the sports that one plays, even when they are played at high levels, do not necessarily inform one's consumption habits of sports as a whole. "We talk more about the actual playing and doing of our sport rather than the following of other sports teams," Courtney explains, "be they in our own sport of soccer or any other, for that matter."[63]

It seems that even when the topic of other (popular) sports does arise, it is not necessarily a technical discussion about the playing of the sport, but rather gossip about celebrities. "When it came out that the Phoenix Suns' point guard Steve Nash and his wife had a baby, but the baby was black because Nash's wife had cheated on him with one of his teammates," Courtney reported that the girls on her team were very excited to talk about this controversy. Never addressing the fact that Steve Nash is a seven-time NBA All-Star and that he won the League's MVP honors two consecutive years, the discussion was relevant to the team's players because of the human interest controversy, the baby-daddy drama, and not because of the effects that this might have on Nash's production on the basketball court. Indeed, "the girls had absolutely no idea who Steve Nash was," Courtney shared, "but they found much enjoyment in talking about this story."

Courtney's account that her teammates did not engage in any discussion about, and did not have any interest in, any matters of soccer outside their own immediate world of being prepared for their own competition received virtually verbatim confirmation from Liz Elsner, who was a mainstay of the Division I University of Michigan varsity softball team between 2000 and 2003. In her interview with us in the summer of 2011, Liz recounted how she and her

---

[63]Mercier, 2011.

teammates did not pay any attention to the baseball world around them and that, other than watching some World Series games—and even those mainly for social reasons—she and her teammates almost never watched baseball of any kind, which, after all, was a close cousin of their sport of softball and was performed on a major league level—thus at the world's very top quality—barely an hour's drive from Ann Arbor. Indeed, Liz emphasized that she was a much more ardent Tigers fan and a more conscientious follower of baseball and other professional sports (mainly football and ice hockey, with the local area Lions and the Red Wings receiving special pride of place) during her high school years than as a top-level college athlete. Just like in Courtney's case, Liz's interview amplified yet again how the "doing" and the "following" of sports are truly distinct constructs in the world of female college athletics, which, after all, with few, if any, professional leagues extant for women, represent the pinnacle of women's sports in the United States.

And here is Sarah, one of our sportista interviewees, on this very topic:

Two of my best girlfriends from high school are involved in collegiate sports (both play varsity volleyball), but these two girls have the least interest out of all my girlfriends in talking about sports. These are the girls that usually tell me to stop talking about sports within minutes of me bringing the topic up, or the ones who criticize me for talking about it so much. It's interesting to me because they are two girls who are completely immersed in sports, but once they leave the realm of their respective sports, they are completely uninterested. What's even more surprising is that most of their guy friends are on the basketball and football teams at their schools, so you would think that they would want to learn/discuss these sports. But they don't.

Even in the world of top-level figure skating, this pattern pertains. In an independent study conducted under Markovits's auspices, Alex Shibutani, who with his sister Maia constitutes one of the three best ice dancing pairs in the world, having medaled only as the second team in the history of the sport in their very first World Championship in Moscow in April 2011 and being not only among the youngest medalists at such a level in the history of figure skating as a whole but also the first ice-dancing team of Asian descent to medal and part of the first-ever North American sweep of this discipline, conducted in-depth interviews with ten of his fellow world-class skaters at his rink in Canton, Michigan, which—in the past two decades—has become the mecca of global figure skating. Alex's task was to ascertain the patterns of sports consumption on the part of his fellow world-class skaters and to gauge whether there was any congruence between their "doing" and "following" of sports. Here are some of Alex's findings:

> At the rink I skate at in Canton, Michigan, the locker room chatter among the men is almost always sports related. Although we are all focused and engaged in our training, the conversation rarely approaches skating. We'll discuss topics ranging from Denard Robinson's completion percentage, to "Tebowing," to the amazing dunk we all saw on SportsCenter the previous weekend[64] . . . Through my interviews, I talked with skaters of both genders, and it is clear to me that the skating world is a microcosm of general society. The consumption of sports amongst figure skaters seems to directly mirror the commonly perceived male to female ratio in regards to interest in sports. All the males that I interviewed for this paper consider themselves sports fans, and would almost always prefer to watch a sport other than the one they are most proficient at. The females, while in some cases sports fans in their own right, had considerably less interest in watching sports and did not match the males in their consumption of sports. Much of the females' sports knowledge was absorbed through their contacts with their male skating partners and local environments such as the rink and the locker room.[65]

In a visit to the University of Washington in May 2011, Markovits conducted in-depth interviews with members of the university's women's varsity soccer team, which, just like the University of Michigan's, is a Division I participant and thus plays at the highest possible level of the sport in the United States, with the exception of the fledgling professional soccer league, sporting different names at different junctures in its existence, with "Women's Professional Soccer (WPS)" being its latest and now defunct incarnation. The patterns that we discerned in our research in Ann Arbor were fully replicated in

---

[64]Denard Robinson was the University of Michigan's electrifying quarterback from 2009 to 2012. "Tebowing" refers to an act that entails getting down on one knee and starting to pray, even if everybody around does something completely different. The term derives from a regular posture struck up by the charismatic and controversial former Denver Broncos quarterback, Tim Tebow, a Heisman Trophy winner and two-time national champion at the University of Florida, who is a devout Christian and whose popularity propelled his demeanor into a global phenomenon in which people "Tebowed" on just about every imaginable surface, in all conceivable settings, from the top of Mount Kilimanjaro to the gateway of the Taj Mahal.

[65]Alex Hideo Shibutani, "Sports Consumption among Top-Level Figure Skaters at the Rink in Canton, Michigan" (unpublished final research paper written for Sociology 395, University of Michigan, 2011), 14, 15.

Seattle. Here, too, these women were obviously superb athletes who loved play-ing soccer and took great pride in excelling at it on such a high level. They de-lighted that their team had advanced deep into that year's NCAA tournament, reaching the elite eight. They were serious athletes in terms of being in superb physical shape, preparing thoroughly for all opponents, always eager to im-prove every facet of their game. And yet, these athletes, too, just like their Uni-versity of Michigan counterparts, barely watched any soccer games, male or female, on television. They did not follow the Champions League in Europe, nor any of the top national leagues there, or anywhere else, for that matter. And to the extent that they watched a match or two here and there, they did so because their boyfriends did or for some other social reason that had nothing to do with their own interest in following the game of soccer at its top level. To be sure, all respondents informed Markovits that they would be watching the U.S. women's national team in the World Cup to be played in Germany a few weeks after these interviews. But when queried as to whether they watched this team play in venues other than the World Cup or the Olympics, the answers were solidly negative. In this case, too, there emerged a clear hiatus between being a superb and dedicated athlete while also being a rather disinterested and disengaged sports fan.

This marked disconnect among women between "doing" and "following" sports also pertains in the opposite direction, in that some who have come to follow sports, even on a professional basis, with this being their livelihood, never did any and are proud of such. To be sure, this group is much smaller than its obverse. One of our interviewees, a prominent sports writer in a major sports town, explained, "I was never an athlete. I never played any sports. I'm very un-athletic." When asked about "doing" versus "following," she re-sponded plainly, "I completely don't 'do.'" She admitted, "I almost didn't go to [my undergraduate university] because they had a PE requirement."[66]

Another of our interviewees, too, was not an athlete as a young girl. "We technically had Title IX, but it wasn't put to use in my case. I played one year of basketball very badly," she explained, "but I always loved sports."[67] The fact that "loving sports" does not mean loving to play sports for her appears to be a major marker of her being different from most women involved with sports.

Our interviewees—both the amateur and professional sportistas, as well as our college-aged and middle-aged respondents—highlighted another pat-tern that speaks to the difference between playing and following sports. In general, sports talk is not that valuable around women or young girls. Laura,

---

[66]Dana Wakiji (*Detroit News*), interview with the authors, April 25, 2011.

[67]Ann Killion, interview with the authors, May 23, 2011.

one of our interviewees, even described actively downplaying her "sports talk" when other young women are present, for it is usually not taken well by them.[68] Unlike their male peers, women do not have sports talk as a means of fitting in. It seems that *playing* sports, though, served as a social advantage for even very young girls. Many of our subjects explained how they started playing sports at a young age to fit in and become involved with their peers. Katrina, another of our interviewees, a sports reporter in a major sports city, describes how, as a 6 ft. 1 in. tall seventh-grade girl, sports provided her with a space where she could fit in.[69]

These accounts speak to a difference in terms of the social utility of sports playing versus sports following. It also highlights the important difference between these two facets of sports in terms of the way that they are accepted or resisted by men. Males do not have a problem with women being good at sports (against other women). It is a social advantage, in some situations, to be a girl who is good at sports. Thus, men in the meantime have let go of the Victorian notion that a lady is not to *play* sports. Yet men seem to hold on to the idea that women cannot watch or talk about or follow—in short, consume—sports in the same way that men can and do, and that, obviously for men, constitutes the only proper way to valorize this unique cultural good.

In only a few decades, Title IX has drastically changed the ways that young girls play sports. Christine Brennan, one of the pioneer female sports journalists in the United States, writes:

> These days, we see big, strong girls—girls like me—playing on organized teams in every neighborhood. Those girls dash from game to game and field to field wearing jerseys and uniforms and baseball caps. Count their sports: soccer, basketball, softball, field hockey, lacrosse, Little League baseball.
>
> A girl like that, today's young female athlete, plays on as many as twenty-five organized teams before she reaches her freshman year of high school.
>
> I have no trouble remembering the number of organized teams I played on before my freshman year of high school.
>
> Zero.
>
> I never wore a uniform or jersey until I entered high school.[70]

---

[68]Laura Hahn, e-mail message to the authors, January 2011.

[69]Katrina Hancock (WDIV, Channel 4 News, Detroit), interview with the authors, March 29, 2011.

[70]Christine Brennan, *Best Seat in the House: A Father, a Daughter, a Journey through Sports* (New York: Scribner, 2008), 64.

Brennan continues, describing the deficiencies in women's sports programs, even once Title IX was in place, especially compared with the programs that the boys had:

> While the boys had buses taking them to their games, either our mothers or older students drove us in cars to away games, because there were no buses for us. If there weren't enough drivers, our games were postponed.
>
> There never was talk of being good enough to win a tournament or a state championship. That's because there were none for girls until basketball my senior year. What's more, few girls thought about playing in college. There were no scholarships for women as far as we knew.[71]

Title IX's effects were not immediate, but were surely significant. Brennan writes:

> As bad as things sounded, girls' sports were emerging enough so that within a few years of my graduation, there would be all of this for the girls in Ohio: tournaments, state titles, buses, uniforms, scholarships. But back then, girls' teams were relegated to club status, no better or worse than the drama club. Girls who played sports were members of the Girls' Athletic Association (GAA), which was like any other high school club.[72]

Courtney's teammates fit into this category. They played on many teams while growing up, eventually choosing to pursue (and succeed greatly in) soccer. Their moms, however, had to play on soccer "clubs," not teams, and had much more limited opportunities in sports. Courtney and her peers on the team are not sports followers, even considering their athletic upbringings. Even Brennan avers that the effects of Title IX have not yet been able to germinate a larger degree of female fandom to date, though she also notes that we might perhaps never see women develop sports fandom comparable to men's, in both degree and kind. However, she argues that continued generations of mothers who grew up as athletes, as beneficiaries of Title IX, might start to

---

[71]Ibid., 75.

[72]Ibid.

change this. Many mothers claim to have become more interested in following a culturally popular and hegemonic sport by way of seeing their daughters—"Title IX babies"—participate in sports. Further iterations of this pattern
may possibly lead to an increase in women's following of popular sport. In Gillian Warmflash's research, this pattern appeared strengthened, as Warmflash
as well as Markovits and Albertson were surprised, by the finding that seventeen of Warmflash's thirty-three interviewees cited their *mothers* as the prime
source of their sport socialization, which contradicts the assertion on the part
of an overwhelming majority of our sportistas who mentioned their *fathers*—
just as all three of us expected—as being their most important initiator into
the world of sports consumption.[73] The degree to which such relatively recent
developments might have consequences on the enhancement of future female
sports following is impossible to predict. Nonetheless, this finding is surely a
reflection of the potential that Title IX has to reach beyond its current capacity
to include women in *doing* sports and extend to actually further women's interest in *following* popular sports.

Soccer as a Special Case:
The Women's World Cup

The 1999 U.S. women's soccer team was an amazing example of how far wom-
en's sports have come. The entire country fell in love with the U.S. women's
national team. Christine Brennan writes about how she was at a Women's
World Cup game that year at which the stands were completely full. After the
game, there was a men's MLS game, for which any member of the crowd could
stay without charge. To her surprise, as well as that of her female colleague, the
stands emptied out after the game. Brennan saw this as a tangible shift of wom-
en's soccer rising above men's at that time. As she put it, Title IX was in action
right in front of her.[74]

But was it really Title IX that was in action in front of Brennan's eyes, or
was she witnessing the immense power of nationalism that transforms every
sport's existence and augments its value beyond any other measure and imag-
ination? Were the folks who loved and cheered for our women's national team
cheering for their being women, their being soccer players, or their being

---

[73]Gillian Lee Warmflash, "In a Different Language: Female Sports Fans in America" (unpublished
honors thesis, submitted to the Committee on Degrees in Social Studies, Harvard University,
Cambridge, MA, March 2004).

[74]Christine Brennan, interview with the authors, April 25, 2011.

Americans representing the United States in a major international tournament? In other words, was this temporary enthusiasm not merely a spot-on expression of Jerry Seinfeld's famous notion of rooting for laundry in that most spectators and most television viewers did not really know these women soccer players and had few, if any, ideas about the game of soccer, but were enthusiastic about rooting for athletes that sported the letters "USA" on their jerseys, very similar to the quadrennial event called the Olympics, during which millions of viewers are captivated by sports and athletes about which they have no clue but for whom they develop emotional affinities and allegiances, solely based on the shared commonalities of their passports.

And Americans are not exceptional in having their interest and affect massively augmented for a sport and its purveyors merely by virtue of shared nationality. Just think of the Australians' near hysteria in delighting in Cadel Evans's winning the Tour de France in the summer of 2011, declaring the Monday after his triumphant Sunday on the Champs Elysees a national holiday. Or all of Germany exulting in Dirk Nowitzki's winning his first NBA championship in June 2011, making basketball, at least for a few weeks, rival the supremacy of soccer in that soccer-crazed country. Examples of this kind abound.

This is not to take away one iota from the amazing cultural feat attained by the World Cup–winning U.S. women's soccer team of 1999, which, after all, to this day, has remained the sole sports entity in American history to grace the covers of *Time*, *Newsweek*, *People*, and *Sports Illustrated* in the very same week. And if anybody came close to attaining such national prominence, it was this team's successor, the U.S. women's soccer team of 2011 that had the nation glued to its every move in distant Germany and whose final game against Japan became the second-most-watched soccer game of any kind in American history, barely missing the record set by the 1999 squad. Still, the 2011 team's telecast of its final against Japan on Sunday, July 17, attracted three times the television audience that the Open Championship at the Royal St. George's Golf Club in England, a hotly contested Major, attained. And the game broke the "Tweeting" record set by the royal wedding between Prince William and Kate Middleton in the spring of that year.[75] Indeed, the popular successes of these two World Cups are nothing short of astounding. No women's sports of any kind—not even figure skating, gymnastics, and tennis, the stalwart individual sports that have traditionally been strongly identified with female athletes and viewers—came close to having such viewership and enthusiastic following

---

[75]The Associated Press, "Women's World Cup Final Breaks Twitter Record," July 18, 2011, available at http://espn.go.com/sports/soccer/news/_/id/6779582/women-world-cup-final-breaks-twitter-record (accessed July 20, 2011).

among men and women as did these two U.S. Women's World Cup soccer teams. But there exists, perhaps, a telling reason for this.

How Did Women's Soccer Sneak In?

It is notable, though, that American soccer is not part of the hegemonic "Big Four" sports. Might it be that, perhaps, the women's sports that have a chance of garnering large, devoted audiences (of men, women, or both) in the United States are only those whose men's "versions" do not have a strong hold on sports culture, or in Markovits's *sports space*? Might that explain the gap in the WNBA audience versus that of the NBA (and the consequent salary differences),[76] compared with the event that Brennan saw at the soccer game, in which the women's version attracted a packed stadium and millions of television viewers, while the men's remained largely unnoticed in both venues?

Many men and women will cite women's alleged physical inferiority (specifically an "inability" to dunk by those in the WNBA) as the reason why they prefer men's over women's versions of sports. For example, the women who responded to Markovits's study noted that some of their reasons for preferring the men's game to the women's were that the latter is not as fast paced as the former, that the female players are not as skilled as their male counterparts, and that the overall level of intensity is less in a women's game than it is in a men's. What about soccer, though? Surely, the men are faster and stronger than the women who play that game. So why do we care more about the women's national soccer team (at least in 1999 and in 2011) than we do about the men at their World Cups? We, as a country of sport fans, do not much care about our women's Olympic basketball team that won silver in 1976, the first year that the event existed for women, bronze in 1992, and gold in every other year that the summer Olympic Games were held. It seems that if a women's sport is to get any kind of a national following, it must not overlap with a popular men's sport, meaning the Big Four in the United States. If there does not exist a men's counterpart to a sport in terms of its viability as a winner or at least as a major contender, then it seems that we grant women their place in the sun.

College softball offers a fine example of this, with the WCWS regularly drawing large audiences and television ratings. Although baseball might be

---

[76]The maximum salary for a six-plus-year WNBA player was, in 2010, $101,500 (this was also the first time in league history that players were able to receive more than $100,000). Under the WNBA's collective bargaining agreement negotiated in 2008, the 2010 team salary cap was set at $775,000 (available at http://womensbasketballonline.com/wnba/rosters/salary.html). The minimum salary for an NBA player at the same time was $473,604 for a brand-new rookie, increasing every year until, after ten years, the minimum was $1,352,181 (available at http://www.insidehoops.com/minimum-nba-salary.shtml; both URLs accessed July 25, 2011).

seen as a cousin to softball, the games are different enough that there seems to be no stepping on toes, no immediate comparisons, no head-to-head competition. Even if there is a male counterpart, a female sport can get attention as long as it is not in the culturally hegemonic space of the Big Four. In that case, the men's version is too important, and the games are too similar, easily—and perhaps compellingly—invoking immediate comparisons that point to the alleged physical inferiority of the women. Albertson (somewhat sarcastically) asked one of her male roommates why he would not keep the channel on ESPN when they stumbled on a (rare) broadcast of a women's basketball game. "I thought we liked basketball," she jokingly commented, knowing what type of response she would get. Revealing much about his perception of alleged female athletic inferiority, her roommate responded, "Yes, indeed, we do like basketball. I heard that the JV team at Pioneer [a nearby Ann Arbor high school] is having practice right now. Wanna go watch?" His comment was a clear statement as to how he viewed women's basketball as inferior compared to men's. Would he have said that with regard to soccer, though? One suspects not.

In fact, several weeks later, during the Women's World Cup in July 2011, the very same individual called the U.S. women's game against Brazil the best sports moment of the year. Does he say that when Albertson watches women's college softball or volleyball, for which there are no men's events? The answer is a solid no.

The Most Famous Sports Bra in the World

One of the 1999 team's lasting legacies, a moment that has become iconic about this team in the sports memory of the American people, much more remembered by all than the team's on-the-field feats, has been defender Brandi Chastain's throwing off her jersey after scoring the game- and world-title-winning clincher with her penalty shot. Immediately after this incident—then commonplace in men's soccer all over the world, since penalized by a yellow card—the speculations and national debate commenced as to the reasons why Chastain did this: to market a new sports bra designed by Nike, to make a point about gender equality on the field, to flaunt her sexuality, to engage in wanton exhibitionism; on and on the speculations and opinions emerged and persisted. Chastain herself claimed that her action was a result of "momentary insanity."

Whatever the reasons, this completely unimportant incident in the larger context of winning the World Cup has remained so iconic to this day that Chastain chose to entitle her excellent book on soccer and women's sport, *It's*

Not About the Bra.[77] Moreover, she claimed in conversations with Markovits over the years that, apart from the committed soccer community and the female soccer world in particular, most non-soccer people in the United States know her solely for her discarding her jersey in the moment of triumph on that hot July afternoon at the Rose Bowl in Pasadena. The point here is simple: Nothing close to anything parallel or similar exists in men's soccer or men's sports. Thousands of male soccer players all over the world ripped their shirts off after scoring any goal, let alone a World Cup–winning goal, before FIFA decided to penalize this behavior, and it still persists precisely in moments of importance like winning the World Cup, such as when the legendary FC Barcelona player Andrés Iniesta took off his jersey right after he scored Spain's only and game-winning goal to lead the country to its first World Cup title in its contest with the Netherlands in the summer of 2010. Nobody discussed Iniesta's body—his looks, his motives, the hidden sexuality of his actions—at all. His behavior, though duly garnering a yellow card by Howard Webb, the noted English referee, was readily accepted as an integral part of soccer's celebratory iconography, no more, no less.

If anything, Iniesta's disrobing attained a dignified dimension by virtue of his revealing an undershirt that had the logo, "Dani Jarque siempre con nosotros" (Dani Jarque will always be one of us), in memory and honor of Daniel Jarque, a player for Espanyol, FC Barcelona's bitter crosstown rival, who had tragically died of a heart attack earlier that season, thus demonstrating that all soccer players, even those playing for hated opponents, are brothers. The reactions to these two very similar incidents of World Cup–winning goals could not have been more telling in their difference: normalcy, even a noble gesture, for Iniesta and the men; sensationalism of some kind (sexual, commercial—both) for Chastain and the women.

To be sure, the Chastain celebration had to be placed into its proper context of various sexualized precursors. Thus, for example, late-night television talk show host David Letterman displayed a photo of the women's national team in which all twenty players appeared to be wearing nothing but Late Show t-shirts. Letterman himself transformed the wholesome term "soccer moms" into the racier and more risqué "soccer mamas," soon to be followed by the openly sexualized "soccer babes," inhabitants of Letterman's telling name for their place of residence, "Babe City." And a side-angle photograph of Chastain "crouched behind a soccer ball wearing only her cleats and her ripping muscles" drew the attention of journalists, pundits, and reporters, as well as many people with little previous knowledge of or interest in soccer. An image

---

[77]Brandi Chastain, *It's Not About the Bra: How to Play Hard, Play Fair, and Put the Fun Back into Competitive Sports* (New York: HarperCollins, 2004).

of femininity and wholesome sexual appeal was conveyed in the message that "women can be both athletic and feminine in an endeavor that, in many countries, still carries the stigma that women who play [soccer and other male-dominated team sports] are somehow unwomanly."[78]

And Brandi Chastain was not the only prominent team member to be sexualized. Julie Foudy posed for a *Sports Illustrated* swimsuit edition in which she appears with a man and is wearing a swimsuit while running along the beach, dribbling a soccer ball. Mia Hamm, one of the best soccer players ever, and arguably one of the best female athletes of all time, received attention for more than her amazing athletic feats.[79] Named to *People Magazine*'s "50 Most Beautiful People," Hamm appeared in Gatorade and Nike commercials with much makeup and her hair down. In a Pert Plus shampoo commercial, Hamm rips out her athletic ponytail and tosses her hair across her shoulder, of course looking much more beautiful and feminine than she would in her sweaty soccer attire. Hamm also became the spokeswoman for the new "Soccer Barbie." The Hamm Barbie says, "I can kick and throw like Mia Hamm." One could interpret the Chastain, Foudy, and Hamm depictions not as overt sexualization but as a celebration of the female athlete's body. This, however, was most assuredly not the case in the Women's World Cup in Germany in the summer of 2011.

Sexualization across the Globe: 2011 Women's World Cup

Even before the tournament began, five members of the junior German national team posed for the July issue of the German edition of *Playboy* with complete frontal nudity and in unambiguously sexualized depictions, using the requisite sexy lingerie and the ubiquitous stilettos.[80] The openly sexualized text accompanying these pictures was full of double entendres, such as ample usage of the word "Vorspiel," which in German means both preliminary rounds in a tournament and foreplay. Needless to say, words such as "ball," "shot," "run," and "play," among many others, appeared, describing innocuous soccer-related matters, but always, of course, hinting at their all-too-obvious

---

[78]Jeré Longman, "Pride in Their Play, and in Their Bodies," *New York Times*, July 8, 1999.

[79]When FIFA, global soccer's federation, honored the great Pelé in 2004 to name the game's all-time top 100 players in honor of FIFA's centenary, the only American soccer players who made Pelé's list of 125—the legend could not confine himself to 100—were Michelle Akers and Mia Hamm. In addition to being the only Americans on Pelé's list, they were also, of course, the only women. "Pelé names top 125," March 5, 2004, available at http://fosxsports.news.com.au/print/0,8668,8874487-2321,00.

[80]"WM-Vorspiel mit scharfen Schuessen" in *Playboy* (German edition, July 2011): 29–42.

sexual meanings. The headline "We want to refute the clichés of the butch women" graced the interview section, with the five women demonstrating that the issue of lesbians ruling German women's soccer, a widespread assumption on the part of the male-dominated soccer public, was a topic worthy of addressing (and commercializing) by *Playboy* and its models from the junior squad of the German women's national soccer team.[81] Indeed, the *Playboy* interviewer commenced one of his questions, "In the 1970s and 1980s, there was allegedly not one single heterosexual player on Germany's national soccer team. How high is the percentage of lesbian players today?" One of the players, Ivana Rudelic, responded, "I was born in 1992; thus I was not even in planning in the 1970s and 1980s. And we have not conducted any scientific surveys thus far on the topic of the players' sexual orientation. Of course, there are homosexual players. That is no secret in women's soccer." And her teammate Julia Simic added, wisely describing the massive difference between men and women insightfully, "I think that there are some homosexual players among the men, too. But that issue remains a total taboo. And with good reason: Were such a player to reveal his sexual orientation and preference, he would have a terribly difficult life in the Bundesliga [Germany's top male professional soccer league]. With and for women, the issue is a lot less complicated."

In a fine research paper analyzing femininity and sexualization in women's soccer for Markovits's sports course at the Leuphana University of Lueneburg, Henrik Frach featured an in-depth interview with Kristina Gessat, one of the young soccer players posing on the cover of *Playboy*, in assessing her conflicting position of a top-level athlete and budding national soccer star on the one hand, and a sex object on the other.[82] In addition to confirming the much-repeated official justification for the *Playboy* shoot, that Gessat and her teammates disrobed to prove that they were "totally normal, regular girls ("Maedel") who chose to play soccer but also love to shop and place a special value on their appearance," Frach points to the sad fact that millions of German male soccer fans will never know Gessat, the excellent and promising soccer player, but only the naked pin-up girl in come-hither poses.

While the article in *Playboy* was without a doubt the most egregious example of the Women's World Cup's sexualization in Germany, there were many other instances of highlighting the players' beauty and sexuality, though with clothes, often featuring them. Thus, for example, six members of the national team's senior squad, definitely more prominent soccer players and bigger stars than the five junior squad members posing for *Playboy*, appeared in suggestive

---

[81]"Wir wollen das Mannweiber-Klischee widerlegen" in *Playboy* (German edition, July 2011): 44, 45.

[82]Henrik Frach, "Fussballspielerin oder Sexobjekt? Weiblichkeit und Sexualisierung im Frauenfussball" (unpublished research paper, University of Lueneburg, Lueneburg, Germany, 2011).

poses in many commercials for the shampoo company "Schwarzkopf," whose logo in English is "Professional HairCare for you," under such headlines as "Our beauty-eleven squad storms straight to the final" and "Soccer professionals can be this beautiful." And Germany's Fatmire "Lira" Bajramaj was much more famous for being the country's "glamour girl" soccer player who, according to her widely known views, never runs onto the field without lip gloss as well as mascara and is eager to marry early, have two or three kids, and open a cosmetics salon, than for being the team's only player of Muslim and Albanian descent, having been born in Kosovo and emigrating to Germany as a young girl.[83]

In addition to these depictions of the women players, little girls could also admire and play with a Barbie doll version (i.e., busty and blonde) of a member of the German women's team. The Barbie, released in time for 2011's World Cup, wears official German Soccer Federation–licensed miniature soccer gear identical to that of the real players over her certainly Barbie-like figure. Like all Barbies, this one has visible makeup on her face, gloss on her lips, and mascara on her eyelashes, and embodies the hegemonic culture's picture-perfect femininity, even in her soccer cleats. The words "I can be . . ." appear in English and in German (*ich waere gern . . .*), followed by "Fussballspielerin" only in German (the feminine version of soccer player), clearly encouraging girls to engage in Barbie's sport, while simultaneously reinforcing all that Barbie's figure and appearance, after all these decades, have come to symbolically reinforce and represent.

The sexualization of the World Cup and of female soccer players reached well beyond the established media. Thus, an innocuous visit by Janna Bray, one of Markovits's doctoral students at the University of Michigan, engaged in her fieldwork in Berlin completely unrelated to soccer, the World Cup, or any sports, to the town hall of Treptow-Koepenick, one of the capital's important eastern districts, revealed five artful photo collages produced by students at the Merian School gracing this public building's entrance area. The first one, featuring the logo "*Fussball ist . . . SEXY*" ("Soccer is SEXY," in large letters), depicts an attractive woman dressed in a soccer uniform, sitting on a soccer ball, and sucking her fingers suggestively. The next image, with the text, "*Auf die Party! Fertig! Los! Sie ist bereit, bist du es auch?*" ("Onward to the party! Ready! Go! She is ready. Are you?"), features a mini-skirted woman's legs as they shed Nike soccer boots for stilettos. The third montage has the text "*Keine Angst Maenner, es ist nur Fussball*" ("Don't worry, men. It is only soccer.") and depicts a woman holding a gift-wrapped soccer ball across her belly, clearly

---

[83]See, for example, "Die will nicht nur spielen!" in *Freundin*, 14/2011.

emulating pregnancy. The fourth item shows a young woman kissing a glass case that holds a frog and a soccer ball adorned with a crown. The caption reads, *"Ein Maerchen wird wahr"* ("A fairy tale turns true."). And lastly, accompanying the text *"und wir haben doch Ahnung von Technik, ueberzeugt euch selbst"* ("And we do know technique. Find out for yourselves."), we see a woman's long, bare legs clad in red stilettos, kicking a soccer ball in the air with her left heel.[84] We rest our case!

Moreover, this tone and content was not at all specific to Germany. In neighboring Austria, where women's soccer plays a lesser role than in most Central and Western European countries and whose team did not even qualify for the World Cup tournament, *Sport Magazin*, Austria's most comprehensive and pedigreed sports publication, ran a huge spread on one of the country's players, a certain Mariella Rappold, the "OeFB-Beauty" (OeFB stands for Oesterreichischer Fussballbund, the Austrian Soccer Federation), whose absence in the tournament will, according to the publication, severely diminish the beauty quotient of the players in Germany and thus mar the competition's overall attractiveness and desirability à la "look what the fans in Germany will miss," decidedly referring to Rappold's attractive appearance and not her prowess as a soccer player.[85] Here, too, the sexualized double entendres appear in virtually every paragraph of the article. And though Rappold did not pose nude for the camera, a number of the published pictures—killer stilettos, miniskirts, and all—clearly accentuate her looks rather than her skills as an athlete and soccer player. And one should never forget the context wherein this has occurred: a complete marginalization of women's soccer in Germany and Austria. At least the former celebrated a World Cup in which the power of nationalism and the all-potent "we are rooting for laundry" phenomenon weighed in and created a buzz for the women's game for a four-week period. But as Julia Zeeh's fine master's thesis at the University of Vienna, written under Markovits's supervision, clearly shows, women's soccer in Austria leads a woefully marginal existence, as measured by every imaginable dimension.[86]

While such overt sexualization would be unthinkable of members of the U.S. soccer team—just recall our descriptions of Chastain, Hamm, and Foudy—or any top-level American athlete, the sexualization of women in American sport is most common not so much as a manifest flaunting of overtly sexualized images and accompanying text—pace Danica Patrick as a bikini pin-up

---

[84]We are grateful to Janna Bray for taking photographs of these five items during her visit to the Rathaus Treptow-Koepenick in Berlin on July 6, 2011, and for sharing these photographs with us.

[85]Tom Hofer, "Mara-Donna Fussball," *Sport Magazin* (July 2011), 46–53.

[86]Julia Zeeh, "Fankultur im Frauenfussball: Zugangsformen und Motivationen des Publikums beim SV Neulengbach" (master's thesis, Department of Sociology, University of Vienna, 2012).

and her GoDaddy.com commercials—as in the crucial context of beauty, health, and looks. Just think of Lindsey Vonn, the superstar downhill skier, the Williams sisters in tennis, and a number of top swimmers, basketball players, and yes, soccer stars. And then there emerged Hope Solo's post–World Cup 2011 image with the American public: a gorgeous female who progressed quite far on *Dancing with the Stars'* eleventh season and who—oh, yes—also happened to be an outstanding goalie for our national team. And when Alex Morgan scored arguably the most impressive goal of the entire tournament in, of all games, the World Cup final—a real cracker from twenty yards away from the goal—the Internet and Twitter went haywire not about this amazing shot but over her being "hot." Looks matter for female athletes in a way that they do not for their male colleagues. And women athletes know this.

Necessarily Evil?

During a panel discussion in June 2011, Lindsey Van, female American ski jumper who led the (successful) campaign to get the International Olympic Committee to include *women's* (not just men's, as was previously the case) ski jumping in the Winter Games, said plainly, "You might not want to be known as the pretty naked girl . . . but if you want to just be known for being good at your sport, you need to get attention in some other way first." She added, sounding somewhat frustrated, "Think about it: Famous female athletes are all beautiful. If you're a guy, all you need is to be the best. You don't need to do anything else. If you're a woman, to get attention, you have to be good at your sport *and* be beautiful. You can't just be good."[87] Val Ackerman, the former president of the WNBA, agrees: "Those of us who are more idealistic, particularly the people who work in women's sports, want to believe that what happens on the athletic surface is all that matters. I think the reality is sometimes it's not enough to be a great athlete. You have to have something more."[88]

This distinction between the experience of a female athlete and that of a male athlete is dramatic. Consider the reaction of male sports spectators to any kind of sexualization—from crude comments to notions of "cute butts"— of *male* athletes. While men can watch female athletes and comment all they want about appearances, focusing more on a woman's face and body than on what she is actually *doing* with said assets, for a woman to comment on the

---

[87]Lindsey Van, panel discussion at the Association of Women in Sports Media conference, June 25, 2011.

[88]Jorge Castillo, "Maya Moore's Deal with Jordan Brand Could Be Breakthrough," *New York Times*, August 7, 2011, available at http://www.nytimes.com/2011/08/08/sports/basketball/maya-moores-deal-with-jordan-brand-could-be-breakthrough.html?pagewanted=all (accessed August 8, 2011).

appearance of a male athlete equates to blasphemy among bona fide sports fans. In the case of male athletes, to comment on their appearance or sexual attractiveness is a completely irrelevant conversation to have, so much so that participation in such commentary might cause one to lose credibility among sports fans. Even the most expert, most knowledgeable sports fans, though, deem commentary regarding an athlete's attractiveness "relevant" enough in the case of female athletes. Not only is the attractiveness of a female athlete relevant, but it is also, it seems, in some cases, *more* important than her actual athletic output or success.

The "Kournikova Effect"

In what has been dubbed the "Anna Kournikova effect," it seems as though, to extend Lindsey Van's quote, "If you're a woman, to get attention," you don't even *have* to be "good at your sport"; beauty can trump athletic achievement and output. Danica Patrick became a phenomenon initially because she broke down barriers and entered Indy circuit races as a female. Naturally, much publicity surrounded her story, and much was expected in terms of her performance, which did lead to her being the only woman to win a race in the Indy car series. Years later, Patrick is still in the center of the public eye, but not completely by dint of her success. Patrick's aforementioned overtly suggestive Go-Daddy.com commercials have maintained her relevance and attention, even as she has been unable to rise to dominance and sustain attention in the position that is the very basis of her presence in the public sphere: as a NASCAR driver.

Anna Kournikova surely possesses immense athletic talent; in 1997, at age sixteen, she advanced all the way to the semifinals at Wimbledon, losing to that year's champion, Martina Hingis. Kournikova reached a No. 1 Women's Tennis Association (WTA) ranking as a doubles player. Bud Collins, Hall of Fame tennis journalist and encyclopedic tennis savant, believes that "she eventually got caught up in all the frills and notoriety surrounding her. . . . She was good and could have been very good. But her looks made her a lot of money."[89] Kournikova would eventually earn a spot on ESPN's list of the "25 Biggest Sports Flops of the Past 25 Years." It is not possible to say whether Kournikova's high profile as a celebrity necessarily resulted in her never reaching what others saw as her potential; however, we tell her story here to highlight the fact that one need not have the *most* success in a sport to become one of the most recognizable and famous participants in it. Tellingly, that is the case in women's sports, in sharp contrast to men's, where good looks could never compen-

---

[89]Michael Ventre, "'Kournikova Effect' Can Derail or Boost Athlete," NBCsports.com, February 26, 2007, available at http://nbcsports.msnbc.com/id/17203733/ns/sports// (accessed August 13, 2011).

sate for or—more starkly still—actually supersede and displace achievement in top-level competition.

Of course, Kournikova was never *the* biggest name in women's sports. Looks alone cannot attain that. One also needs to win big events with some consistency. Another Russian tennis player seems to have attained what her compatriot could not quite achieve. According to *Forbes*, Maria Sharapova was the highest paid female athlete of 2010, combining both her tournament winnings and her endorsements. To be sure, Sharapova's physical appearance is not overlooked; much of her public attention is focused on her beauty. Yet the foundation of her reputation is in her tennis prowess, manifested in four separate World No. 1 singles WTA rankings as well as five Grand Slam finals appearances, three of which concluded with championship wins (2004 Wimbledon, 2006 U.S. Open, and 2008 Australian Open). Forbes's list continues, listing Serena and Venus Williams as the No. 2 and No. 3 highest-paid female athletes, respectively.[90] In fact, in continuation of this pattern, Forbes reports that *all* of the top ten highest-paid female athletes of 2010 played *individual* sports.

This pattern may be seen as further reflecting the "sports space" argument, that consumers simply do not have "room" left to care about and closely follow women's team sports, considering the space that is taken up by the hegemonic sports. Following an entire women's team (and, most likely, the whole league) would require much more of a vacancy in one's sports space than would the following of an individual, especially one whose major relevant events only happen a couple of times annually. Notable, again, even in the cases of these highly decorated tennis champions, is the fact that their athletic careers are supplemented by photo shoots, clothing lines, and general commentary and scrutiny, all focused on their physical appearance.

The particularly strong gendering of sports pertains mainly to those that comprise what we have termed a society's hegemonic sports culture. Thus, the resistance to women's presence in these at any of their levels—the playing field, their reporting, or their analysis and interpretation—is much higher than in the myriad of sports that do *not* belong to the hegemonic sports culture. Concretely, women in the United States have a much harder time being taken seriously in football, basketball, baseball, and hockey than they do in virtually all individual sports, as well as in soccer and volleyball, both of which are team sports, but are not part of America's hegemonic sports culture.

The same pattern pertains in other liberal democracies, such as Great Britain. In a fine study of female ice hockey fans in the United Kingdom, Garry

---

[90]Castillo, "Maya Moore."

Crawford and Victoria K. Gosling show conclusively that this sport, decidedly not a participant in Britain's hegemonic sports culture, has successfully attracted a much greater percentage of female fans than has football, that country's most important representative of its hegemonic sports culture.[91] As the authors correctly note, "It would appear that 'new' and 'imported' sports such as ice hockey in the UK and soccer in the USA, which lack the masculine tradition of many more established sports, offer women more opportunity to attend as supporters."[92] We would like to supplement this by saying that such culturally non-hegemonic sports offer women a bevy of otherwise unavailable opportunities well beyond the world of supporters at the playing venues, reaching all the way to being fans at home, the office, on the Internet, and—of course—to being their reporters, interpreters, and analysts in print and the visual media. Women's legitimacy and authenticity in these sports has been much higher precisely because they have been much less dominated by men and thus have not become all-male prerogatives and remain quite marginal to men's passions, interest, and knowledge.

Female Athletes and Gender Identity

In her superb research on the University of California, Berkeley, varsity female athletes' perception of their identity as top-level competitors in a physically demanding pursuit, as are all Division I sports, Jennifer Carlson demonstrates that the women exhibit a deeply ambivalent attitude toward having muscular bodies.[93] While, on the one hand, these female athletes want to train as hard as they need to in order to excel and succeed, which means participating in grueling weight training to enhance their strength and stamina, they are openly wary of such regimes enhancing their muscles to a point where their arms might not appear sufficiently feminine. As Carlson argues persuasively, the interplay of women and sports inextricably entails not only matters of gender but also of sex. The intricate issues as well as complex and profoundly contradictory metrics that constantly pull female athletes in all directions and accompany their everyday lives is also well presented in a collection of fine articles in the anthology *Women and Sports in the United States: A Documentary Reader*. Especially the contributions comprising the sections "Negotiating Masculinity and Femininity: The Female Athlete as Oxymoron" and "Com-

---

[91]Garry Crawford and Victoria K. Gosling, "The Myth of the 'Puck Bunny': Female Fans and Men's Ice Hockey," *Sociology* 38 (2004): 477–493.

[92]Ibid, 482.

[93]Jennifer Carlson, "Sex, Gender and Female Athleticism" (unpublished paper, University of California, Berkeley, 2010).

peting Bodies: Physiological, Biological, and Psychological Issues" make the seemingly irreconcilable demands that dissect the core identities of female athletes in ways unimaginable for men emphatically clear.[94]

One of the most insightful analyses of the immensely complex problems involving sex and gender for women athletes comes from Karin Martin's work. In her unpublished manuscript entitled *From Black Pants to Bras: Gender and Appearance on Campus*, Martin devotes an entire chapter to the complexity of women athletes' appearance in their college-based environment at a large research university in the Midwest, which, with the author's permission, we can reveal as the University of Michigan, where Martin teaches in the Department of Sociology. Tellingly entitled "Tomboyish but Still Girly at the Same Time," Martin's work in this chapter seconds Carlson's findings explicitly by delineating how, for many female athletes, there exists a constant tension between having both athletic and feminine bodies. Martin depicts superbly the inevitable double bind of athletic femininity that virtually all female athletes encounter: torn between being top-level athletes, representing power, endurance, performance, and strength and being attractive young women, embodying ideals of feminine beauty, as dictated by our hegemonic culture. This deeply felt ambivalence and real tension manifests itself concretely in a very discernable "look" on the part of women athletes on the University of Michigan campus, which states to the world, "Yes, we are top-level Division I athletes, muscles and all; but we are also pretty women attractive to men." Nothing symbolizes this synthesis, this compromise, this hybridity more aptly than the ponytail: long, beautiful, flowing hair, tightly tied with purpose and a clear sense of competition.

While not quite conforming to the hegemonic femininity embodied by the sorority girls whom the female athletes in Martin's research often refer to as "sorority sluts," and whose emphatically feminine appearance and demeanor the athletes perceive as threatening and uncomfortable, yet in certain ways also desirable, the female athletes do indeed express a marked wish to appear attractive in a male-centered conventional manner, and they behave accordingly. As one of Martin's interviewees stated:

> It's funny because most of the time, if you had someone who is in a sorority and someone who is an athlete walking down the street in the middle of the day, we would look strikingly different . . . Because a lot of times, at least with my team and most athletes generally, we don't wear much makeup during the day because you're going to go

---

[94]Jean O'Reilly and Susan K. Cahn (eds.), *Women and Sports in the United States: A Documentary Reader* (Boston: Northeastern University Press, 2007).

to practice and what's the point of sweating and getting all this grime, like junk all over your face. We'd usually have our hair pulled back in a ponytail. But at night at a party you might not be able to tell the difference, because we'll have makeup on and might be wearing the same type of clothing that women who are in sororities would be wearing.[95]

Just like in other highly male-dominated and male-coded settings like the Marines or engineering, so, too, in sports, Martin argues, are women caught in the double bind of existing in a world in which it is virtually impossible for a woman to be feminine (and to be taken seriously, we might add), which, in effect, leads these women to assume almost two different, if not completely separate, identities: sort of an official de-feminized work identity by day and a highly feminine leisure identity by night. Above all, many female athletes pursue active strategies to avoid being seen as lesbians, which, they feel, is a widespread assumption about them. Thus, they actively seek to emphasize their heterosexual femininity, lest there be any suspicion about their being lesbians. Indeed, if the reader recalls, this was precisely the alleged motivation—much more than the money—as to why those five German soccer players posed nude in *Playboy*. It was meant to serve as a visual marker of their decided heterosexuality in a world that prevailing male-dominated culture sees as overwhelmingly lesbian.

The Power of the Ponytail

While most female athletes will not go to such lengths, they most decidedly introduce clear signifiers of their heterosexuality, none more so than the ponytail.

> The ponytail is an appearance strategy that attempts to signal femininity and to accommodate athletic practices. Long hair was normatively, ideally feminine at U. Sorority women at the beginning of the twenty-first century usually wore their hair long, straight, blown dry, and "down." This was hegemonic hair. Short hair, especially on an athlete, was read as masculine and lesbian. Women athletes therefore usually wore long hair. . . . A ponytail allowed [women] to have long hair and to avoid being seen as masculine and/or lesbian while accommodating their athletics.[96]

---

[95]Karin Martin, "From Black Pants to Bras: Gender and Appearance on Campus" (unpublished manuscript, 2000): 115, 116.

[96]Ibid, 124.

And the prevalence of the ponytail reaches way beyond the confines of college athletics. Indeed, it was noticeable at the Women's World Cup in 2003, shifted to the United States at the very last moment due to the SARS epidemic in China, where the tournament should have occurred, how many more ponytailed players there were on the U.S. team as opposed to the German team, for example, let alone the North Korean team, for which, as we so well know from Brigitte Weich's remarkable documentary film *Hana, Dul, Sed*..., there existed an official policy of keeping all the players' hair short. Interestingly, seven years later, in the 2010 tournament, many players on the German team also sported long hair in ponytails or buns. That the ponytail's differentiating power pertains mainly to hegemonic sports, and the often mentioned fact throughout this book that soccer in America does not constitute such, whereas by the name of football, in its many linguistic variants, it does so in Europe and elsewhere, is best confirmed by the comments of one of Martin's interviewees. Trying to distance her sport of volleyball, and thus herself, from the mere suspicion of lesbianism, when one "track and field guy told [her] that he has the statistics to prove that most volleyball players were lesbians," she responded:

> I think they maybe see us as different because ... soccer ... you don't see homosexuals or lesbians playing soccer; like you just don't hear about it. Of course, I know it happens but you usually see them more like ... it's more like the masculine sports, like I think basketball and maybe softball are more ... strong; whereas soccer in a way is more like a skill. Of course, it's good to be strong, but I think ... you see more masculine, like butchy kinds of girls playing basketball. So I think the guys they feel like, you know, they don't think a girl is a lesbian on the soccer team. They feel like, "oh, you know, she's probably straight." If they see a girl on the basketball team, they're probably like, "I wonder," just like it's a stereotype.[97]

Tellingly, in Europe and Latin America, it is the exact opposite: Soccer-playing women are seen as butch and exist under the constant suspicion and derision of being lesbians, whereas basketball-playing women are not. The minute women enter any of the male-dominated areas of the hegemonic sports culture, they are immediately seen as threatening and thus construed as the unfeminine, undesirable "other," whether on the playing fields, in newsrooms, or in living rooms.

---

[97]Ibid., 120, 121.

As a particularly egregious, even tasteless, but nonetheless extant, example of the sexualization of female athletes, let us end this segment with a brief exposé of something called the Lingerie Football League.

The Lingerie Football League

In 2004's Super Bowl XXXVII, there was a new pay-per-view halftime option for those watching the game at home. Men, lots of them, were actually choosing to watch *women* play football during halftime of arguably the biggest (men's) sporting event in the country, and one of the biggest in the world. Beyond their gender, the protagonists of this game sported one immediately noticeable difference from the men's version: clothing. Billed as "The Lingerie Bowl," the spectacle featured a full-contact game of football, with all female teams, sporting scantily clothed players. The event became so popular that its creator, Mitch Mortaza, decided to expand his idea and create an entire league by 2009, citing "overwhelming demand from fans all across the country and the desire of thousands of women that wanted the opportunity to play football."[98] In its inaugural season, the Lingerie Football League featured ten teams, mostly from cities with a big NFL presence. The games aired, usually in the form of highlight reels, on MTV2, though the season-ending Lingerie Bowl was accorded complete coverage. As reported on the Lingerie Football League's website in 2011, "the inaugural season on MTV2 drew strong ratings, significant national media coverage and created a frenzy."[99] While this apparent "frenzy" might have eluded most sports fans, the League must have attracted a sufficient number of viewers to expand to twelve teams by 2011, divided into separate Eastern and Western conferences, featuring teams with names such as "the Charm," "Crush," "Fantasy," "Passion," "Breeze," "Bliss," "Sin," and "Temptation."[100] The League's obviously successful first two seasons on television led MTV2 to commit itself to airing the entire 2011–2012 season "live and in full-length form for the first time ever." *LFL Presents: Friday Night Football* premiered on MTV2 in August of 2011.

Watching this game feels strange. The women wear shoulder pads, elbow pads, knee pads, and helmets. The shoulder pads awkwardly bulge out from

---

[98]Lindy T. Shepherd, "Balls Out: Lingerie Football League Brings Guts and Garters to Orlando," *Orlando Weekly*, August 19, 2010, available at http://www2.orlandoweekly.com/news/story. asp?id=14219 (accessed June 5, 2011).

[99]Lingerie Football League, "Lingerie Football League Returns to the Gridiron Live This Fall on MTV2," LFL360, March 22, 2011, available at http://www.lfl360.com/articles/lingerie-football-league-returns-to-the-gridiron-live-this-fall-on-mtv2 (accessed June 5, 2011).

[100]Lingerie Football League, www.lflus.com, 2011.

their bare shoulders, and the helmets most closely resemble (and probably are) hockey helmets. Every player is required to have a clear visor (no football-style facemasks allowed). As to the jerseys, the League's and the game's name says it all: the Lingerie Football League requires that all of its players wear less-than-full-coverage bras, panties, and garters on their thighs. The terms delineated by the League and agreed to by its participants specifically outline that:

> Player shall wear wardrobe[101] provided by Producer. In light of the foregoing, said wardrobe material shall be "non-see through" material. Player shall not wear any additional garments under wardrobe provided by Producer without prior written consent from Producer. Should Player violate this clause, Player shall by fined a total sum of Five Hundred Dollars ($500.00) per occurrence.[102]

Under the heading "nudity" within the League's stipulations, it states that:

> Player has been advised and hereby acknowledges that Player's participation in the Event and the related practice sessions and Player's services and performance hereunder may involve accidental nudity.

It continues:

> In light of the foregoing, Player knowingly and voluntarily agrees to provide Player's services hereunder and has no objection to providing services involving Player's accidental nudity.[103]

In a report on thesmokinggun.com, an ex-player explained that, during her time in the League, Lingerie Football League officials did not allow any players' underwear to be worn under their League-provided "wardrobes," "since that would inhibit instances where players were exposed when uniforms were ripped off or pulled down during play."[104]

The League's mission statement in late 2011 stated, "The Lingerie Football League has become the ultimate fan-driven live sports phenomenon—blending action, impact and beauty," which seems pretty accurate.[105] There is

---

[101]Notably not referred to as a "jersey."

[102]The Smoking Gun, "Lingerie League Gets Litigious," December 17, 2009, available at http://www.thesmokinggun.com/documents/crime/lingerie-league-gets-litigious (accessed June 5, 2011).

[103]Ibid.

[104]Ibid.

[105]Lingerie Football League, "LFL101," available at http://www.lflus.com/lfl101 (accessed June 5, 2011).

surely action, as the game is fast-paced and played by athletically competent, physically fit females. Plenty of impact exists as well, by the full-contact nature of the game. And beauty is in no short supply. Mortaza, the League's creator, explains that making it as a player into the LFL demands the following three requirements: "beauty, athleticism, and confidence."[106] Keith Hac, head coach of the Chicago Bliss, further details the selection process, delineating the relative importance of specific prerequisites: "The first criteria [*sic*] to play here is looks. And then we find out if they're athletic. They have to be phenomenally beautiful and can [*sic*] play football."[107]

But is it "about women taking over a man's game," as the blonde goddess in the League's commercial posted on its website would maintain, or does it have less to do with football and more to do with "selling sex with hopes of men paying to watch women in their underwear?"[108] Or might it be best described in Mortaza's own words, as "Disneyland for football fans?"[109]

The League represents significant "firsts" in a lot of ways for women and football. "For the first game, it is going to be people wanting to have a good time, wanting to see beautiful women playing football and getting down and dirty," said a member of the Miami Caliente, Taira Turley.[110] Others, such as Courtney Martin, contributor to feministing.org, saw this "first" chance at women playing football and garnering audience interest as a step backward, though. For Martin, to "give women an opportunity to participate in a sport that they haven't had the chance to do for pay and publicly previously, but only let them do it if they are stereotypically pretty and willing to do it in their underwear" represents "objectification at its most pernicious."[111]

The truth is that, however novel it may be, the Lingerie Football League is not the first league to put women on the gridiron. The Independent Women's Football League, created in 2000, now gives more than 1,600 women playing on fifty-one teams throughout North America the chance to play full-contact football in the same conventional football uniforms worn by the men in the

---

[106]Shepherd, "Balls Out."

[107]Al Hamnik, "Wiping That LFL Smirk off Smug Faces," February 2, 2010, available at http://www.nwitimes.com/sports/columnists/al-hamnik/article_ff4f8286-6ef4-5977-bdf9-2915b37c59f6.html (accessed June 5, 2011).

[108]Shepherd, "Balls Out."

[109]Ibid.

[110]Simon Evans, "New Underwear League under Debate," *Reuters*, September 4, 2009, available at http://www.reuters.com/article/2009/09/04/us-football-lingerie-idUSTRE5825Y220090904 (accessed June 5, 2011).

[111]Ibid.

NFL.[112] Additionally, the Women's Football Alliance, founded by two individuals in 2009, expanded rapidly within its first few years to now feature sixty-three teams in the United States. In both of these leagues, the goal is the same as it presumably is in men's leagues: to play football at the highest and most competitive level possible. Photos of the line of scrimmage in an Independent Women's Football League or Women's Footbal Alliance game are not exactly conventional centerfold material. The players' jerseys are worn *over* their pads, helmets are equipped with face masks, and there is no sign of any player's buttocks breaching the border of her bottoms. The disadvantage besetting these two leagues is patently obvious: Virtually nobody watches their games.

In 2011, the Lingerie Football League got a cousin: the Lingerie Basketball League. A visit to the League's main website reveals a man's voice, set to a dramatic musical background, theatrically intoning, "America loves basketball. America loves beautiful women. Now, a match made in hoops heaven." The voice continues, "Are you ready for women who are *tough* on their opponents, but *easy* on the eyes? You better be."[113] Lingerie basketball, "where beauty meets the hardwood," seeks to "bring *sexiness* to basketball," presumably by requiring, similar to its football predecessor, the players wear bras, panties, and garters strapped to laces that wrap and wind down their legs all the way to their ankles. Again taking its cues from the Lingerie Football League, the names of the four Lingerie Basketball League teams, all of which are based in Los Angeles, are "the Beauties," "the Glam," "the Divas," and "the Starlets." "It does seem as though the popularity of a particular women's sport is often unfortunately tied to how attractive its stars are," said Larry Tobin, former Vice President of Product for FOX Sports Interactive, in reference to the new basketball league.[114] Jessica Hopkins, a player in the Lingerie Football League, shares the notion that such a reality is "unfortunate": "It's not fair [for women to have to wear so little], but we all know sex sells." She continues, "I'd much prefer to have my skin covered when playing tackle football on hard Astro-Turf, but the lingerie/sexy aspect of our game is what gets people interested."[115] Even considering their distaste for such consumer preferences, some still see a completely sexualized "lingerie" version of a women's team sport as a means of

---

[112]Independent Women's Football League, available at www.iwflsports.com (accessed May 5, 2012).

[113]Lingerie Basketball League, 2011, lingeriebasketball.com (accessed August 10, 2011).

[114]Hollie McKay, "Lingerie Athletic Leagues Are Proof That Women, Men Are Hardly Equal in Sports, Experts Say," FoxNews.com, August 5, 2011, available at http://www.foxnews.com/entertainment/2011/08/05/lingerie-athletic-leagues-are-proof-that-women-have-long-way-to-go-to-equality/ (accessed August 15, 2011).

[115]Ibid.

positively advancing the world of women's sports. A *Huffington Post* article on the new basketball league wrote an intentionally sarcastic but tragically telling statement; "The only logical next step is to get rid of the WNBA and replace it with the LBL."[116]

The Future of Women's Sports

The WNBA is not, from a business standpoint, a successful venture, but a promising boost was given to its supporters and optimists when, in August of 2011, Maya Moore, the University of Connecticut superstar who led the Huskies to an NCAA championship to cap off their record-breaking undefeated season, was offered an endorsement deal with Michael Jordan's Jordan Brand. As a rookie sensation in the WNBA, Moore's joining of the Jordan Brand family, which includes such stars as Dwyane Wade, Chris Paul, Carmelo Anthony, Derek Jeter, C. C. Sabathia, Dwight Freeney, and Andre Johnson, represents what "could be a breakthrough for female athletes looking to achieve greater marketability."[117] Bob Dorfman, author of the *Sports Marketers Scouting Report*, believes that Moore's opportunity with Jordan "certainly gives her a leg up in the marketability category among female athletes." What that translates to, it seems, is being at the top of a totem pole that is completely overshadowed by the skyscraper that is men's popular sport. According to Dorfman, "It's very difficult for female athletes in team sports to rise above their sport and become marketable icons because the sports aren't as followed." Dorfman explained that these women's sports "don't bring in the casual fan . . . they bring in more of a niche fan. The attention just isn't there, which makes it harder." Even if Moore's signing with Jordan Brand *does* elevate her to Mia Hamm–like fame (especially comparable because Hamm, too, gained individual renown as a member of a team sport that catapulted her, among others, into a much-touted Gatorade commercial in which she competes with Michael Jordan in a number of sports, finally throwing him to the ground with a nifty judo move), it appears quite unlikely that the rest of the league will benefit from any ripple effects of Moore's undeniably towering stature. Ample room within the "sports space" may be available for Moore alone, but not necessarily for all of women's basketball.

The WNBA is not alone in its frailty. After the Women's World Cup in 2011, Jeré Longman published an article in *The New York Times* featuring WPS

---

[116]Dan Treadway, "Lingerie Basketball League Makes Debut in Los Angeles," *Huffington Post Sports*, August 2, 2011, available at http://www.huffingtonpost.com/2011/08/02/lingerie-basketball-league-debut_n_916213.html (accessed August 15, 2011).

[117]Castillo, "Maya Moore."

(Women's Professional Soccer), the professional league established in 2009 (after the 2003 collapse of the Women's United Soccer Association [WUSA], the former host of women's professional soccer). WPS, whose logo was a silhouette of Mia Hamm, had six teams but lost one in the fall of 2011, with a clear threat of further shrinkage and eventual disappearance in 2012. But even the presence of five teams would have proven a serious handicap since soccer's all-important sanctioning body, the U.S. Soccer Federation (USSF), "delayed approving Division I sanctioning for WPS" since the Federation requires the presence of a minimum of eight teams for it to declare a league "top flight," or "major," in the parlance of American sports. Indeed, with its former six teams, WPS had already operated under the Federation's waiver.[118] Without any doubt, this league embodied the highest level of soccer that a woman could play professionally in the United States. Longman reported that the members of the U.S. national team were greeted, on their return to the United States, with reverence, gratefulness, and pride, as though they were heroes for having positively represented the country, but that, now that the World Cup is behind them, "the far less glamorous and more uncertain existence of league soccer has abruptly returned."[119]

Although the increases in attendance at matches might foster optimism, television ratings, and social media trafficking of WPS events that followed 2011's Women's World Cup, "history suggests that operating a fully professional women's league in the United States will be difficult." Financial strains are forcing the league to pay its players even less than they are currently earning, in some cases, leaving individuals with a few hundred dollars per appearance on the pitch. Such a situation for professional players (as opposed to the semiprofessional model employed overseas, in which players simultaneously hold outside jobs) leaves Megan Rapinoe, U.S. national team member and WPS player, pessimistic. "The national team players, I think we're going to be O.K., but you can't have a league with people making nothing," she said.[120] Even on the coattails of the wildly popular and successful 1999 women's national team, the WUSA only lasted three seasons before it, too, ran out of money and had to fold. Brandi Chastain, the face of the 1999 championship team and one of the founders of the WUSA, said in August 2011—after the buzz of the Women's World Cup and during the lack of buzz surrounding the women's professional

[118]Ann Killion, "WPS still fighting for survival"; sportsillustrated.cnn.com/2011/writers/ann_killion/12/02/wps/index.html. Viewpoint at SI.com, available at http://cnnsi.printthis.clickability.com/pt/cpt?expire=&title=WPS+fight (accessed December 2, 2011).

[119]Jeré Longman, "After World Cup Thrills, Players Return to Unstable Women's League," *New York Times*, August 8, 2011.

[120]Ibid.

league playoffs in the United States—that World Cup and Olympic soccer in the women's game had virtually no connection to league soccer. And, as if on cue, only 2,057 were in attendance at the magicJack's first playoff game, despite featuring such World Cup stars as Abby Wambach and Megan Rapinoe. At the end of the season, the league terminated this franchise's turbulent existence for reasons also related to the paucity of spectators that it attracted, similar to the teams' fates in the WUSA. As expert sports journalist Ann Killion stated, "It's hard to believe we're having this conversation again. I'm encouraged that we're talking about it, but I'm discouraged that it's the same conversation."[121] And it is hard to imagine that even Abby Wambach's winning the 2011 Associated Press award for the best female athlete of the year, making her the very first individual soccer player, male or female, to receive this prestigious award since its inception in 1931, beating her teammate Hope Solo and basketball star Maya Moore in the process, would guarantee this fledgling league's solid survival. In fact, WPS folded following the 2011 season.

The 2011 World Cup team did not end its tournament in the same fashion as its 1999 predecessor, and even though the team fought its way dramatically to the final match, Longman predicts that the team, and therefore the professional version of the sport, "won't be as marketable because they didn't win." Ann Killion shares the view that the future of women's soccer, and other professional leagues, for that matter, cannot rely on the excitement that comes from a discrete event or an individual player, especially when that event or player only enters the popular spotlight once every couple of years. She maintains that the notion that the Women's World Cup in July—even though it was the most watched soccer event ever to air on ESPN[122]—should have resulted in a shift in attention to women's soccer—that "a big event should lead to sustained interest in a professional league"—is "not a fair gauge." She explains that such an expectation is

> not the tape measure we use on other events. No one thinks that the fresh face who wins freestyle aerials at a Winter Olympics can sustain a successful freestyle aerials league. Nor were MLB, the NBA or the NFL built on the backs of events that only happen every four years. A suc-

[121] Ann Killion, "After Captivating the Nation, U.S. Women Struggle to Stay in Spotlight," SportsIllustrated.com, August 19, 2011, available at http://sportsillustrated.cnn.com/2011/writers/ann_killion/08/19/wps.world.cup.boost/index.html?eref=mrss_igoogle_sports (accessed August 19, 2011).

[122] ESPN Media Zone, "2011 Women's World Cup Finals: ESPN's Most-Viewed and Highest Rated Soccer Match," July 18, 2011, available at http://www.espnmediazone3.com/us/2011/07/18/2011-women's-world-cup-finals-espn's-most-viewed-and-highest-rated-soccer-match (accessed August 22, 2011).

cessful event doesn't equal a thriving league. A team broken apart and scattered among many teams loses its appeal.[123]

Jorge Castillo, for *The New York Times*, writes:

To become marketable in the male-dominated world of sports, female athletes have needed a combination of novelty, like a Women's World Cup in the United States; off-the-field endeavors, like the Williams sisters' fashion ventures; and sex appeal. Anna Kournikova never won a WTA singles title, but she became a star largely because of her attractiveness.[124]

Unfortunately, the novelty and unprecedented success of a World Cup championship team is not always enough to keep a professional league alive in the interim before the next World Cup, and the Williams sisters are subject to commentary and scrutiny over their bodies and appearances, even when they continue their unprecedented tennis dominance. Castillo's quote mentions that the magic formula for marketability of a female athlete has included "novelty," "off-the-field endeavors," and "sex appeal." One wonders if that formula will ever be amended to include anything related to athletic supremacy.

Conclusion

One need not be a committed Marxist to realize that, while markets and private ownership are immensely potent forces for innovation and progress, they also advantage the already powerful, often at the cost of the continued powerless. Those, in turn, depend on the advocacy of public institutions apart from the market, often, though not exclusively, embodied in forces associated with the modern state, to help their cause both in a material and also in a larger existential manner. It seems that the predominance of men's sports and their concomitant cultural hegemony in modern societies have been largely the result of market forces. This is particularly the case for those very few ball-dominated team sports that have, in the course of the twentieth century, become what Markovits has come to call "hegemonic sports culture," meaning that their following and cultural presence far exceeds the world of their actual producers (i.e., the players). It was largely market forces that created and that continue to

---

[123]Killion, "After Captivating the Nation."

[124]Jorge Castillo, "The Marketing of Moore Is a Team Challenge," *New York Times*, August 7, 2011: D6.

foster the popularity of football, baseball, basketball, and hockey on the North American continent, and soccer on a global level. The prominence of the market in the creation and maintenance of this construct extended even to such anti-market entities as the Soviet Union and its orbit.

As Robert Edelman demonstrates so convincingly in his award-winning book, while the Soviet people most certainly appreciated Dynamo Moscow's producing a bevy of the Soviet Union's many Olympic medal winners, virtually none of the particular sports in which these medals were attained really mattered to the people on an emotional level.[125] That was left to the game of soccer, which was much less state controlled than the Olympic sports and in which Spartak Moscow, Dynamo's great cross-town rival, captured the hearts and love of millions of Soviet citizens, mostly men, of course. In contrast to Dynamo, which was the police's club and a symbol, representative, and beneficiary of the de-commodified state sector, Spartak was much more anchored in quasi-market structures, thus embodying something of an antinomy (if not outright opposition) to the official powers that be of party and state. In other words, it was the market and popular culture that favored the heavily, almost exclusively, male world of soccer—and thus Spartak—whereas it was the state that produced success in all the de-commodified Olympic sports, not much followed by the people on a daily basis, except in their quadrennial incarnation, when they brought a bonanza of medals to Soviet glory. Mike Dennis and Jonathan Grix confirm this pattern in the now defunct German Democratic Republic, in which soccer, just like in the former Soviet Union, represented a space of contestation, and thus popularity, partly by virtue of its relative autonomy from the state and—concomitantly—its relative proximity to quasi- if not openly market-like mechanisms.[126]

Ditto in the United States. It has been the market that continues to produce the culturally hegemonic sports comprising the Big Four followed by men, but it has been by dint of Title IX—that is, the state—that women were accorded major access to sports that the market would never allow them, and still does not, as witnessed by the more than precarious existence of women's professional leagues in basketball and soccer and their virtually total absence in football (not counting the Lingerie Football League in this tally), baseball, and ice hockey. Sports that are not popular and are basically unmarketable, in which women actually have a real chance to excel, will only flourish with the help of forces outside the market, which in the American context does not bode well

---

[125]Robert Edelman, *Spartak Moscow: A History of the People's Team in the Worker's State* (Ithaca: Cornell University Press, 2009).

[126]Mike Dennis and Jonathan Grix, "Behind the Iron Curtain: Football as a Site of Contestation in the East German Sports 'Miracle,'" *Sport in History* 30, no. 3 (September 2010): 447–474.

for the proliferation of their popularity. In contrast, the hegemonic sports cultures—all heavily male everywhere in the world—rely more or less solely on the market for their success, even in state-socialist systems, such as the former Soviet Union, and the oddity of contemporary China. Perhaps the market will never accommodate women's team sports in the same way that it has men's. Then again, the latter has had close to a century's worth of temporal advantage over the former. This pertains not only to the female producers of sport, which was our concern in this chapter, but also to the world of women sports fans, to which we now turn our attention in the remaining sections of this book.

4

Fandom and the Typical
Female Sports Fan

s the "entrance exam" for being officially recognized as a "true" sports fan
something that is unique to sports? In other areas of cultural interest, music
and film, for example, is entry free of cost, or is the required method of entry
and legitimization into those fan groups the same as it is in the case of sports?
Are there methods employed by the "gatekeepers" of sports fandom that are
not a part of a Deadhead's—or a Mozart maniac's—mode of exclusion and distinction from his or her symbolic club?

Social theory on culture features the division of culture into different hier-
archical types (usually dichotomous in their categorization) and corresponding
brands and magnitudes of capital or social benefits that come from one's accumulation or recognition of being "cultured" in certain ways. Pierre Bourdieu,
arguably one of the most influential scholars working on the social construction of culture, explains in his seminal work *Distinction* that the obtaining of
cultural capital requires "total, early, imperceptible learning, performed within
the family from the earliest days of life," and that the right kind of cultural capital, or "symbolic goods, especially those regarded as attributes of excellence,"
can serve as "the ideal weapon in strategies of distinction."[1]

It seems as though the clearest initial line to draw among the myriad
milieus of "culture" is that between what Bourdieu calls "official culture"—
virtually identical with the often-used "high (or high-brow) culture"—and that

---

[1]Pierre Bourdieu, *Distinction: A Social Critique of the Judgment of Taste* (New York: Routledge,
1984), 66.

which is commonly (and, as will be shown, tellingly, and also academically) referred to as "popular culture." Official culture attains more social legitimacy in terms of one's ability—even expectation—to display one's intellect, awareness, and distinction from the rest of the population. It receives much of its social legitimization by giving its bearers the sense and perception of being more learned, more refined, more distinguished, more "cultured," more "classy," in the vernacular uses of these concepts. It is via the cumulative benefits accrued by such "distinction" that its beneficiaries reproduce and institutionalize this social good as best they can in the hope of maintaining their guardianship over it for as long as they possibly can. Needless to say, such possession of cultural capital conveys distinction not only in terms of social standing but also— perhaps more important still—in terms of power. In notable contrast to the construct of "official culture," its popular variant has as its basis nothing more than the "informal consensus" of the masses.[2]

In her essay "Fandom as Pathology: The Consequences of Characterization," Joli Jensen outlines two major dimensions along which "official" and "popular" culture are divided.[3] The first constitutes one's "object of desire," referring to the actual subject, be it a team, musician, artist, or otherwise to which the actual "fandom" is directed. The objects of fandom included under the banner of "official culture," as explained by Jensen, are characterized as being expensive, rare, and of interest typically to upper-class populations, elements of what is colloquially referred to as "high culture."[4] These types of cultural artifacts and figures are "popular with the wealthy and well-educated," and their pursuers typically do not even use the word "fan" to describe their relationship with these objects of their desire, opting instead to use words such as "preference, interest or expertise."[5] Official culture "connoisseurs," under this simple model, collect and admire "Eliot (George or T. S.) not Elvis; paintings not posters; the *New York Review of Books* not the *National Enquirer*."[6]

The "objects of desire" within popular culture (and revered and loved by their *fans*), however, are "popular with the lower or middle class, relatively inexpensive and widely available."[7] If an object of desire fits this description, "it is [subject to] fandom," Jensen explains. "If it is popular with the wealthy

---

[2]John Fiske, "The Cultural Economy of Fandom," in *The Adoring Audience: Fan Culture and Popular Media*, ed. Lisa A. Lewis (New York: Routledge, 1992), 30–49.

[3]Joli Jensen, "Fandom as Pathology: The Consequences of Characterization," in *The Adoring Audience: Fan Culture and Popular Media*, ed. Lisa A. Lewis (New York: Routledge, 1992), 9–29.

[4]Ibid., 19.

[5]Ibid.

[6]Ibid.

[7]Ibid.

and well educated, expensive and rare, it is *preference, interest or expertise*."[8]
Jensen uses the archetypical examples of Barry Manilow as a low-brow, highly
accessible, and therefore more "popular" object of fan desire, and James Joyce
as a high-brow, exclusive example of an object of pursuers' desire within "official culture." Thus, one speaks of a Barry Manilow *fan*, but of a James Joyce
expert, aficionado, or *connoisseur.*

There is a second major difference in Jensen's categorization of high and
low culture. Beyond the specific object of desire that separates them, "the Joyce
scholar and the Barry Manilow fan, the antique collector and the beer can collector, the opera buff and the Heavy Metal fan are differentiated . . . also on
the supposed *nature of their attachment*."[9] On what basis, so this dimension
queries, does a particular fan, aficionado, follower, appreciator, or hooligan
assert her or his affection for the "object of desire?" Typically, a fan's nature of
enactment and expression, in the case of popular culture, is characterized as
being primarily emotional, with a unique element of passion. "Fans [of popular culture]," Jensen explains, "are believed to be obsessed with their objects, in
love with celebrity figures, willing to die for their team. [This type of] fandom
involves an ascription of excess, and emotional display—hysterics at rock concerts, hooliganism at soccer matches, autograph seeking at celebrity sites."[10]
The nature of attachment for fans (or appreciators or admirers) within *official*
culture is devoid of such emotional connections, and is instead understood
as being rational. One's fandom for a "highly cultured" object is the result of
a rational evaluation, and her or his affinity "is displayed in more measured
ways—applause and a few polite 'Bravos!' after concerts; crowd murmurs at
polo matches; attendance of 'big-name' sessions at academic conferences."[11]
The presumed dichotomy between "reason and emotion," Jensen explains, is
the basis on which the distinction rests between "worthy" and "unworthy"
areas of cultural interest. "The obsession of a fan [of popular culture] is deemed
emotional (low class, uneducated), and therefore dangerous, while the obsession of the aficionado [of official culture] is rational (high class, educated) and
therefore benign, even worthy."[12] Jensen continues to explain how the value
that society places on *reason* is most likely rooted in the Enlightenment notion
that "reason is associated with the objective apprehending of reality, while
emotion is associated with the subjective, the imaginative, and the irrational."

---

[8]Ibid.

[9]Ibid., 21 (emphasis ours).

[10]Ibid., 20.

[11]Ibid.

[12]Ibid., 22.

Jensen eventually, and in accordance with our conventional understanding of the world, concludes that all of these dividing lines, between "high-brow" and "low-brow" objects of desire, "official" and "popular" realms of culture, "rational" and "emotional" bases for admiration, "worthy" and "unworthy" areas of interest and devotion, between the "fan" and the "aficionado," are not necessarily distinct lines, but blurry streaks at best.[13] That is, the practical differences, in terms of fandom, between a Manilow fan and a Brahms connoisseur, even if one insists on categorizing them as adhering to low and high culture, respectively, are minimal, and are likely to begin and end with the "elitist and disrespectful beliefs about our common life," to use Jensen's words.[14]

While the presumed division between low and high culture may still have consequences for behavior (Jensen herself admits that, instead of ever professing to "love" or be [presumably irrationally] willing to die for any of her high-culture objects of affection, she might instead proclaim: "I 'admire' William James, I 'read with interest' Lewis Mumford, I 'enjoy' pre-Raphaelite design and 'am drawn to' aspects of pragmatism"), this division might not carry much weight as to the role that the assignation of a certain type of fandom assumes.[15] What consequences—positive or negative—might the recognition that one is a fan or an aficionado of low- or high-culture subjects have in a person's life? Does the fact that cultural areas of interest might be divided into high and low categories have implications for the types of social capital that they offer?

Let us suspend the judgment call in terms of whether these distinctions matter and turn to a further examination of "official culture" to apply it later to our example of sports as a representative of popular culture to show that these two modes of culture are eerily similar, if not indeed identical. We will then address the powerfully gendered nature of sports' cultural capital to explain why they represent an exceptional case that employs different entrance requirements for men and women to become its bona fide beneficiaries, interpreters, and participants.

John Fiske's discussion of culture and its associated capital contributes to the idea that the differences between *official* and *popular* culture are not, in fact, very consequential at all, for the weight of popular culture, and the modes of discrimination employed in the granting (or denying) of its possession, are virtually as strict as those employed in the case of official culture. With their basis in mere "informal consensus," to reuse Jensen's phrase, areas within popular culture quickly fall subject to the same discriminatory processes as

---

[13]Ibid.

[14]Ibid., 10.

[15]Ibid., 22.

official culture, as "fans discriminate fiercely: The boundaries between what falls within their fandom and what does not are sharply drawn."[16] As inclusion within a community defined by a certain popular culture becomes more beneficial to its entrants, economically, socially, or individually, it continues to closely replicate the mechanisms of exclusion featured in the case of official culture. Fiske avers that by way of a process in which "fans, in particular, are active producers and users of such [popular] cultural capital . . . and, at the level of fan organization," those *popular* fans "begin to reproduce equivalents of the formal institutions of official culture," further obscuring the "difference" between the two levels of culture.[17] Fiske's goal, in his own words, is to demonstrate that "fan culture is a form of popular culture that echoes many of the institutions of official culture, although in popular form and under popular control."[18]

Bourdieu characterizes "official culture" as being more discriminatory than popular culture, explaining that it "distinguishes between those who have it and those who don't."[19] Fiske employs Bourdieu's models of culture and distinction to outline a process in which "the cultural system works like the economic system to distribute its resources unequally and thus to distinguish between the privileged and the deprived."[20] Using this model, it is easy to recognize that sports are not alone in their exclusionary practices. We will now examine the socially and culturally advantageous nature of the assignation of fandom, eventually narrowing the focus on sports fandom and the ways in which it differs from other realms of both "official" and "popular" culture.

Be one a Barry Manilow fan or a Deadhead, a film buff or an opera connoisseur, each one of these assignations exacts some sort of entrance requirement as well as some kind of tangible evidence of one's continued existence as a bona fide member of this club. All membership demands tests of entry as well as maintenance of status as an insider of good standing. To a person who constitutes a part of his or her identity around being an expert follower of a certain culture, whether popular or official, there exists a significant interest and priority to maintain the exclusivity of the status of being a "true" fan of or expert in that subject. "Fans may argue about what characteristics allow someone to cross it and become a true fan, but they are clearly agreed on the existence of the line. Textual and social discrimination are part and parcel of the same cultural activity," Fiske explains.[21] "Such fan knowledge helps to distinguish

---

[16]Fiske, "Economy of Fandom," 34.

[17]Ibid., 33.

[18]Ibid.

[19]As cited by Fiske in ibid., 31.

[20]Ibid.

[21]Ibid., 35.

a particular fan community (those who possess it) from others (those who do not): Like the official culture, its work is finally one of social distinction."[22]

One seemingly universal requirement to cross this proverbial, totally elusive, invisible, intangible, and yet—for all insiders—oh-so-real "line," constitutes the main difference, the all-powerful divider, between the "bandwagon," or shallow or fair-weather, fan and his or her bona fide hard-core counterpart— the "real" fan—laying claim to being an expert or aficionado for whom affect for the object of desire absolutely necessitates a substantial amount of *knowledge*.[23] As Fiske explains, "In fandom as in the official culture, the accumulation of knowledge is fundamental to the accumulation of cultural capital."[24]

As discussed earlier in this book, one of the main gaps between men and women in terms of their sports fandom pertains to the level of knowledge that is deemed essential for becoming and remaining a bona fide member of this community. Arguably, it is the gap in the accumulation and dissemination of sports knowledge that separates men from women in the world of sports fandom. And herein, we believe, rests the biggest difference between sports and other realms of fandom. That is, while all fans have a vested interest in maintaining the exclusivity of their "club" and its associated cultural capital, the gatekeepers to sport are not only protecting their "members" for the sake of a voluntary part of their identity ("Keep it special that we're all Barry Manilow fans, all Deadheads, which is something we have decided is special to us"). Rather they are protecting a part of their identity that is essential to a much broader constituency: namely, their gender, their maleness. Just as fans or aficionados of James Joyce have "organized their life (even their 'identity' and 'community') around Joyce" to some degree, so too have sports fans and aficionados built their identity and community around this particular object of desire. What renders belonging to the club of sports so different, in gender terms, from belonging to the club of Manilow or Joyce is that sports constitute an essential part of being an ideal male, while they represent a tangential piece of culture for a woman in which she has *chosen* to include herself. It is essential to the male's "maleness" that he be a part of the symbolic community of sports fans, not only to preserve the specialness of the community but also to preserve the weight that such membership carries in terms of asserting

---

[22]Ibid., 42–43.

[23]Since we have established that the real-world practical differences between high (or "official") and low (or "popular") culture reside in their normative assignations, reflecting class and status inequalities, rather than in their empirical characteristics, we now feel comfortable in labeling the hard-core fan henceforth as an "aficionado" in our study, even though the reader will remember that Jensen, in her fine work, reserves this term solely to followers of high culture.

[24]Fiske, "Economy of Fandom," 42.

and displaying his masculinity. If one is not a Deadhead, there are no consequences for "doing gender" incorrectly; one is simply excluded from whatever social rewards might come from such an association (most likely from those within the Deadhead community, and not those outside it). Ditto for being an Elvis fan or a Beethoven aficionado.

In the case of sports, though, being a sports fan, even considering its ubiquity (something that would presumably make being a sports fan less special, less exclusive, and therefore less culturally and economically beneficial), does not just tell people that they have pursued a niche, and thus engaged in attaining distinction. Rather, by being a sports fan, one "does gender" in that membership in this collective conveys the decided meaning that is an essential ingredient of being a man in the hegemonic culture of contemporary America and that of the advanced industrial world. Deadheads want to preserve the exclusivity of their group so as to keep its cultural capital at its current value—if everyone were welcomed into the "club," then membership in it would not say anything unique or special about being a Deadhead. It is similar with sports: If all were welcome into the club (that is so essential for men to show their maleness), it would lose its exclusivity and thus its weight, especially, and specifically, if outsiders, such as women, were allowed! Thus, the presence of female sports fans—but particularly sports aficionados and experts—constitutes a direct threat to the exclusivity of this male club.

It is perhaps easier to understand, then, why men might have a particularly vested interest in keeping women out of a realm of their social and cultural world that is so important to their masculinity. What sets exclusion from sports apart from that in other cultural realms is the fact that sports do not merely represent one of the myriad of items to which one can choose to be attracted and then enter, enjoy, and leave, if one so chooses. Rather, sports constitute a core part of our culture that remains integral to the two main gender categories defining our lives. The "entrance exam," or insistence that one "prove" oneself, is not unique to sports. All fan communities look to exclude "non-experts," but the sportista's a priori virtually unsolvable predicament is that while she *does* meet the objective requirements to enter and remain in the club, this asset may well be for naught because, regardless of her achieved knowledge, her ascriptive characteristics will continue to deny her real entry and complete acceptance.

Fiske adds an interesting explanation to the discussion of (popular) sports as (official) culture: "The less a fan suffers from . . . structures of domination and subordination" (i.e., males in general), "the more likely he or she is to have developed a habitus that accords in some respects with that developed by the official culture, and which will therefore incline to use official criteria on its unofficial texts."[25] To employ Albert O. Hirschman's brilliant framework of "exit, voice and loyalty" to round out this aspect of our presentation: Women's entry into the world of sports fandom is fraught with a priori obstacles because, even if formally accepted to this world, their voice in it will still quite likely remain muted and distrusted and their loyalty forever questioned and doubted. With few incentives to belong to this world, women's exit from it bears a high probability.

ESPN, the self-proclaimed "worldwide leader in sports," garners an audience that, save the broadcasts of the National Spelling Bee and cheerleading competitions on ESPN2, is overwhelmingly male.[26] It is no secret that women, as a group, do not participate in sports fandom with the same frequency and devotion than men do. Men account for 76 percent of viewership of ESPN's programming, comprise nearly 98 percent of fantasy sports participation, and vastly dominate the phone lines at sports radio programs.[27] They "more frequently attended to the sports segment of local newscasts, more frequently watched sports newscasts on cable, and spent more time on a daily basis reading the sports section"[28] than women. Still, though seemingly impossible and most certainly contradictory and counterintuitive, the number of females who self-identify as sports fans is statistically not significantly different from that of males: 73 percent versus 83 percent, respectively.[29]

As Donald Levy illustrates, though, regardless of gender, "it is not possible to live in the United States and be unaware of, or unaffected by the constant rhythm of sport." Sports' ubiquity is undeniable and gender-blind, to the point that even a non-fan, male or female, is involved in the institution of sport. It has, as Levy states, "become part of our educational system, common language and national identity." Clearly, this ubiquity pertains much more to the realm of *following* than of playing sports; moreover, it relates almost exclusively to a very small number of team sports centered on some sort of ball-like

---

[25]Ibid., 36.

[26]Michael Hiestand, "ESPN Aims for Female Audience with espnW," October 1, 2010, available at http://www.usatoday.com/sports/columnist/hiestand-tv/2010-09-30-espnW-baseball-tv-playoffs_N.htm (accessed June 4, 2011).

[27]Donald P. Levy, "Fantasy Sports and Fanship Habitus: Understanding the Process of Sport Consumption" (paper presented at the annual meeting of the American Sociological Association, Philadelphia, PA, August 12, 2005), available at http://www.allacademic.com/meta/p21053_index.html (accessed June 20, 2011).

[28]Ibid., 4.

[29]Beth Dietz-Uhler, Elizabeth A. Harrick, Christian End, and Lindy Jacquemotte, "Sex Differences in Sport Fan Behavior and Reasons for Being a Sport Fan," *Journal of Sport Behavior* 23, no. 3 (2000): 219–231.

contraption (pace the hockey puck). It is precisely this phenomenon, the weaving of popular sports following into the general cultural milieu of society, that Markovits has come to call "hegemonic sports culture."

A given geographical and temporal hegemonic sports culture may differ based on gender, age, class, religion, and ethnicity, Markovits finds, yet each one serves as a community, with the choice to include or exclude potential members.

Considering the inescapability of sports as a part of our social fabric, an examination into women's typical sports consumption practices—or a look at the norm from which this book's main subject, namely our sportista, deviates—is a vital component of understanding the challenges that come with such a deviation.

Components of Fandom

> My girlfriends who were from the city were of course Reds fans and Bengals fans, but I don't think they had a clue why they would chant "Who dey" in the streets. None of them watched sports.[30]

In the car on the way back from conducting a very fruitful interview, we revisited the rich conversation we had just completed with a female sportscaster whom we contacted for our study by virtue of her being an obvious sports expert. While immensely impressed by our subject's erudition and her first-rate professional qualifications, we interpreted many of her responses in different ways. In no instance was this more pronounced than in her self-description as a "huge fan" of a certain basketball team of which "*everyone* in [her town] was a huge fan."

Albertson had doubts about her expertise, and even her fandom. "She's just like those girls," Albertson said, "who 'LOVE' the Celtics, but who can barely name two players on the (current) team and who don't know who Larry Bird is." "Who are you," Markovits answered, "to say that those girls are not fans? Even if they can't name a *single* player, but love the team for its famed parquet floor, or its green jersey, or whatever; how can we determine that they don't have some sort of genuine affection for the Celtics," which might thus make them totally "legitimate" Celtics fans.

This conversation began to perplex us collectively, but it frustrated Albertson especially. "Just because they have a Celtics jersey and their dad has tickets . . . doesn't make them a Celtics fan since they don't actually *know* anything about the team," she kept reiterating.

---

[30]Leah Hsieh, email to the authors, January 2011.

"Perhaps," Markovits retorted, "but we can't deny that they have affect for the team, that they have true 'love' for the Celtics which is every bit as pronounced and emphatic as is the love of those who know every current Celtics player's statistics and the life story of every Celtics great."Herein is the key to understanding one of fandom's most important components, especially in terms of our concern with identifying a pervasive and salient difference between the fandom of a typical male versus that of a typical female. It was by way of that car ride that it became clear to us that fandom cannot, and indeed should not, be abrogated by virtue of any alleged shortcoming or by a preconceived, yet elusive, body of knowledge that one needs to acquire to qualify as a bona fide fan. Put differently, even the Celtics fan who barely manages to watch an entire game, but who unwaveringly hopes that the Celts win every single one that they contest, has a place on the spectrum of fandom, if he or she claims such.

Instead of deeming our non-knowledgeable but passionate Celtics supporter a "fake" fan, or stripping him or her of proclaimed fandom altogether, perhaps this person should be filed under the category of "affective" fan, contrasted with its "knowledgeable" counterpart. In other words, fandom need not be defined solely by intellectual dimensions, such as expertise and knowledge, but can also be construed as primarily an emotional construct. A key breakdown of the components of fandom rests in the distinction between affect and knowledge, between "I love the Celtics" and "I know the Celtics," and beyond them, the entire NBA and the game of basketball. The *feeling* of fandom requires only maintaining a true preference or taking genuine enjoyment in knowing that "one's team" or "one's player" or "one's league" experiences success. After all, the NBA's slogan in defining its threshold of fandom is "I love this game," not "I know this game." While affect is clearly a broader and less sophisticated common denominator than knowledge, it need not be less legitimate.

If, on the other hand, validation as a *knowledgeable* fan defines one's entry and acceptance into the community of fandom, then such a *performance* and actual *achievement* requires many more tangible steps and specific actions. The conversation we shared in that car ride led us to a new framing of fandom in which we shed our previous, relatively crude binary categorization of fan versus non-fan, employing instead a typology of fandom on a continuum between affection and knowledge. Let the emotional fan have a place, we thought, and let the fan whose enthusiasm embodies both affect *and* knowledge become known as the *full fan* or *superfan*.

A study conducted by Beth Dietz-Uhler, Elizabeth A. Harrick, Christian End, and Lindy Jacquemotte titled "Sex Differences in Sports Fan Behavior and Reasons for Being a Sports Fan" addresses this distinction well. To be considered a "sports fan," participants in the study needed simply to "consider . . .

him/herself to be a fan of sport" (to respond affirmatively to the simple question "Do you consider yourself a 'sports fan'?").[31] Those who counted themselves as sports fans were then asked questions about their *reasons* for being a fan (e.g., "enjoys cheering," "likes sports," "enjoys watching with friends and family"); about traditional *behavior* and activities pursued by sports fans (e.g., hours per week spent watching sports on TV, frequency of discussion about sports); about how *interested* they were in sports in general; and about how *knowledgeable* they considered themselves when it comes to sports (this comment was followed with an assessment of objective sports knowledge to generate a measurable level of knowledge for use in the study). We refer to this study's results throughout our ensuing discussion. However, for now, we are only concerned with the way the researchers disaggregated important components of fandom and how they delineated that fandom's each and every component need not necessarily be present for a person to fulfill his or her own classification of being a fan—that in fact one might be accurately described as being some sort of fan, even when only possessing a bare minimum of the elements constituting fandom.

Picking up on the insightful work of these scholars, we constructed our own scheme as follows: Some balance between knowledge and affect seems to be the required path and necessary prerequisite to becoming a qualified, bona fide fan, accepted as such by both insiders and outsiders. Affect alone yields the enthusiastic dilettante; knowledge by itself furnishes the hardened technocrat. Full fandom, it seems, resides at the epitome of the intersection of each of these two ideal-typical extremes and polar opposites, which—of course—are intimately related and influence each other deeply: Affect breeds knowledge, which in turn further deepens affect. As shown in Figure 4.1, the field of fandom is wide open.

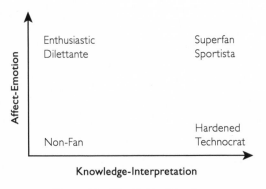

Figure 4.1   The Field of Fandom

[31]Dietz-Uhler et al., "Sex Differences," 223.

While this book's punchline, after all, depends on the fact that exceptions within gender *do* exist and deserve attention and validation, we most certainly understand the danger of typecasting women in any way, specifically concerning anything that features emotions as women's guiding cause for action, attitude, and behavior, thereby reinforcing one of the most platitudinous stereotypes about women. That being said, a review of research into the area of the "normal" woman's motivations for being a sports fan reveals a clear primacy of the emotional side of fandom as opposed to its knowledge-based component. Understanding the median woman's patterns of sports consumption will help us immensely to highlight the deviant cases that we chose to call "sportistas." It is an understanding and appreciation of their growing presence in contemporary American sports culture and society that forms the core purpose of our project.

Both the *loving* and the *knowing* of sports are necessary components of being a full-fledged fan. But their fulfillment is not binary. Rather, fandom exists along a spectrum, with any given individual's level of devotion lying anywhere from apathetic and uninterested to painfully invested. To make matters more complex, but realistic still, any given spot on this spectrum will in fact be experienced very differently. Thus, individuals finding themselves with an identical degree of devotion can express their fandom in vastly diverse ways. Some, for example, might have their bedrooms covered with photographs of their most beloved players from their beloved team, but may not follow their individual or collective stats. In contrast, others may not own any of their favorite team's memorabilia, but will never miss a game on television. Others attend their team's every home game, come rain or shine, but do not watch other teams in the sport on television and spurn any team items in their homes or on their bodies. So emotion's manifestations in fandom, perhaps even more than knowledge's, comes in a myriad of guises and many variations.

Bracketology

During the 2010 NCAA basketball season, Markovits solicited the students in his Sport and Society class to take part in a voluntary bracket competition, the winner of which would receive a small prize. The original invitation was to fill out a bracket for the men's tournament, and later the inclusion of the women's bracket was added to the contest. Very illustrative results came from these two opportunities, highlighting some key components of fandom's deeply gendered identity.

Of 182 officially enrolled students in the class, there were 101 men and 81 women. A total of 157 students filled out the men's NCAA brackets, comprising

86.2 percent of the enrolled population. In terms of the gender breakdown of the respondents, 82 were men and 75 were women, with the former representing 81.1 percent of the male portion of the class, while the female respondents made up 92.6 percent of all of the women students. The numbers for participation in the women's bracket competition, perhaps unsurprisingly, paled in comparison with those of the men's. Twenty total students (about 11 percent of the class) filled out the women's NCAA brackets, with 17 of these being men and only 3 being women. Whereas a higher percentage of the women in the class filled out the men's bracket (92.6 percent compared with 81.1 percent of men), it was, interestingly, the men who outshined the women in terms of participation in the women's bracket (about 20 percent compared with only 3.7 percent of women).

What does this disparity, the fact that women participated in the men's bracket in such high numbers, but dropped out when it came to completing the women's bracket, say about the purposes or motivations for filling out each? Both contests included a nominal but identical prize (a box of candy), so that incentive cannot be identified as the cause for this difference. As a matter of fact, the circumstances of the contests were such that the barriers to entry into the men's bracket were actually higher than those for entry into the women's. The directions for participation in the men's bracket (which was announced and set up for the class before the women's) were to follow a link sent out in an email to the entire class. The first time that the students received this email, there was some sort of technical glitch, which meant that interested participants had to start from scratch to fill out their brackets. Additionally, the host website that Markovits chose required that students create a user name, an obstacle that may have caused some students simply to pass on the contest.

These two obstacles stood in the way of participation (or at least marginally tested patience) in the men's bracket. But by the time the women's bracket competition was set up and announced, both barriers were gone. There were no problems with the link, and the required user name had already been created to permit participation in the men's bracket. Still, though, only 11 percent, as opposed to the 86.2 percent of students who completed the men's bracket, took the (very small amount of) time to enter into the competition for the women's bracket.

After seeing the lack of response to the women's bracket (particularly from female members of the class), Markovits asked women who did *not* take part in the women's bracket, but who *did* complete a bracket for the men's competition, to write to him explaining their reasons for doing so. Several responses pointed to the nature of the women's game versus the men's, for example, "I feel like the men's game is played at a much faster pace and is more 'down and dirty' with physical play." "I don't think women's b-ball is entertaining to watch. It holds no appeal," another student responded. "It has lower scoring, more emphasis on defense, and offensive plays are nowhere near the caliber of men's," a third student echoed. Is that, then, the answer to the disparity in terms of filling out the brackets, an act that does not, by any means, even require that one watch the games for which one picks the winners?

Somehow we believe that reasons pertaining to the nature of the women's as opposed to the men's game, giving clear preferences to the latter's over the former's, though clearly present, remain marginal at best in explaining the paucity of the female students' involvement with the women's brackets. Our doubt that the appreciation of different basketball skills between men and women determined the female students' participation in these brackets were well founded when viewed in the context of the widespread admission from women in the class who stated openly that they "knew nothing" about college basketball, men's or women's, but whose ignorance did not prevent them from merrily completing the men's bracket anyway, and never mind the technical glitches that seem not to have posed any "barriers to entry" to women who completed the men's bracket, but not the women's. For female students who most likely had not watched one college basketball game all year (save, perhaps, some big games played by their Michigan Wolverines), the nature of play was most likely not the determining factor in their completing a men's, but not a women's, tournament bracket. Rather, we submit, the key behind the disparity in participation is that the NCAA men's tournament, and its accompanying nationwide bracket mania, has little to do with basketball but much to do with larger American culture.

It was not because of the "high-caliber" or exciting offense exhibited by the male players, as one of the women, who refrained from filling out a woman's bracket, expertly claimed. Rather, it was "because of the hype and the interaction with others about it," meaning the men's tournament, of course, that this woman and a large number of her female classmates completed the male as opposed to the female brackets. Popular (men's) sports are much bigger than are their actual athletes or their games on the field or on the court. In stark contrast, however, the NCAA women's tournament is precisely solely about basketball. Whereas many of the women who filled out the men's bracket admitted to knowing nothing of (and, outside of the tournament, having no affinity for) basketball, they still wanted to participate in the bracket competition because of the social significance it carries as a major part of our American cultural fabric. Knowledge of the sport, its players and teams, and an affinity for sports in general or basketball specifically need not be present for an individual to reap a clear benefit and enjoyment from participating in the men's bracket competition. It is the topic of coast-to-coast water cooler conversation for the three-week duration of the tournament, and, even with no particular knowledge of the teams or players, many people want to be part of it.

The woman who *won* the entire bracket competition, in fact, admitted to knowing nothing about basketball and actually using a computer-automated automatic fill-in option for her bracket! Markovits, never having heard of such an option, was confused by her response to his query as to her winning "strategy," which, after all, bested the multitude of male bracketologists populating his class, but the rest of the class let Markovits know that this student employed a computer algorithm to complete her bracket in seconds, and it turns out, much more successfully than Markovits, who deems himself an expert in college basketball and labored over his brackets for hours, if not days. The point is that participation, and even great success, in the men's bracket competition does not require that one appear anywhere at all on our field of fandom, just as other events of great cultural diffusion and proliferation do not necessarily require expertise to be pursued, enjoyed, and shared.

The women's bracket does not possess anywhere near the cultural weight, however, that the men's does, which explains why more men than women completed it. The women who knew "nothing" about men's basketball still filled out a bracket—and even won the competition, as we just reported—but refrained from blindly filling out a women's bracket, often citing as their reason the lack of social value and meaning that participation in the women's bracket had for them. Therefore, completing the women's bracket was much more likely to involve expert knowledge of the sport of basketball, or, more probably, a true devotion to knowing and following sports in general, unrelated to and not requiring any social utility whatsoever.

And sure enough, of the seventeen men who completed the women's NCAA bracket, ten were members of Markovits's "Beanster's Group," thus named for some students who met with Markovits every Friday afternoon on a purely voluntary basis throughout the semester in the Beanster's Café on the University of Michigan campus to spend two hours engaged in "advanced sports" talk, from cricket to baseball, from basketball to hockey, from football to soccer, and all other football codes. Tellingly, all members of this group of sports omnivores were male, even though Markovits announced the group's formation loud and clear after a few of his lectures and explicitly encouraged and invited women to join, to no avail. None joined, not even Albertson, a sportista by any measure, who was a student in Markovits's class that semester and liked it so much that she continued contact with Markovits over sports, leading to her becoming his co-author of this book. When queried by Markovits as to her reasons for staying away from this group, Albertson mentioned in a matter-of-fact manner that she would not have felt comfortable in such an exclusively male

environment whose very raison d'être was to hone a predominantly male discourse. There was absolutely no animosity in Albertson's explanation, nor was
there a sense of inferiority or exclusion. Instead, she made clear that her presence could possibly have made the participants feel slightly uncomfortable and
thus she would have felt uncomfortable herself. It became clear in our conversation that Albertson's barrier to entry into the Beanster's Group was not only
the exclusive maleness of the group but also the fact that its participants were
essentially all strangers to Albertson. After all, she had absolutely no hesita-
tion when participating vigorously in comparably male settings—such as her
male-dominated housing situation—in which her interlocutors were friends
and acquaintances.

The sports omnivores of the Beanster's Group exhibited markedly similar characteristics to the male non-athlete population appearing in Markovits
and Smith's study of University of Michigan students and athletes: having accumulated an immensely detailed knowledge of and impressive expertise in
a number of globally important hegemonic sports—the Big Four of North
America, to be sure, but soccer, cricket, and rugby, among others, as well—
but not having played any of these on any meaningfully competitive level.[32] In
other words, these sports omnivores embodied the epitome of sophisticated
sports speakers and followers, but were distant from being sports producers in
any meaningful sense of that term.

Finding Our Subject: The Sportista

Since joining the faculty of the University of Michigan in the fall of 1999, Markovits has taught his sports class on seven occasions. Officially entitled "Sport
as Culture in Advanced Industrial Democracies: The United States in a Comparative and Historical Context" (renamed "Sports, Politics and Society" as
of the 2011 fall semester), the class has been featured in the offerings of the
Department of Sociology but also always cross-listed in the Department of
Germanic Languages and Literatures by dint of the emphasis accorded to Germany among the European countries analyzed in comparison with the United
States. Starting in 2013, this course will also be cross-listed with the Department of Political Science.

Designed as a reading- and writing-intensive course for upper class-
men, this offering has become a well-known staple among the University of
Michigan's undergraduates majoring in the most varied subjects but mainly

---

[32] Andrei S. Markovits and David T. Smith, "Sports Culture among Undergraduates: A Study of Student-Athletes and Students at the University of Michigan," *The Michigan Journal of Political Science* 2, no. 9 (2008): 1–58.

concentrated in the social sciences. The course's enrollment has steadily weighed in at about 180 students per semester, though with its having been upgraded from a 200-level to a 300-level course, with even more stringent writing requirements, the number of students declined to eighty in the fall semester of 2011. It is interesting and quite telling for the subject of our book that the enrollment of women increased steadily over the twelve years that the course has been offered. Starting at about 25–30 percent in the first two to three years, the presence of female students has in the meantime attained a virtual 50-50 balance with men.

In the last three iterations of the course (2009, 2010, and 2011), Markovits routinely asked in the first meeting of the class that he would like to meet women students right after the lecture who fulfilled the following "requirements": nightly watching of ESPN's SportsCenter at least five times a week; regular following of either *Pardon the Interruption* or *Around the Horn*—or both—representing popular sports commentary programs on ESPN; and a steady daily following of sports on the Internet, whether of a team, a league, many teams, or many leagues. Out of approximately eighty-five women in the lecture hall—forty-two in the fall semester of 2011—typically about six to eight proceed to meet Markovits after the conclusion of his lecture, claiming to fulfill his "requirements." Markovits then asks these women to write him email narratives covering two areas: first, the history of their sports involvement, how they came to follow sports, who was the main person, and what was the crucial event—if any—that led them to become such avid sports followers; and second, how their fandom manifests itself in their current daily lives as young adults.

The results have been nothing short of fascinating. Markovits has gathered twenty-two such detailed narratives that he then augmented with similar accounts from undergraduate women at other American universities. Indeed, it was through this venue that Markovits came to know Albertson, who, surely unsurprising to the reader, was an enthusiastic respondent to Markovits's inquiry in the winter semester of 2010. The data gathered from these detailed accounts have enriched our presentation in this book.

Markovits's inquisitiveness with regard to sports culture and the nature of fandom as they exist among undergraduates had some history; in 2007, Markovits became curious as to what—if any—differences existed in the sports cultures and their construction on the part of student athletes and students, and, even more importantly for this book, whether male and female Michigan students exhibited marked differences in their respective sports cultures. Did differing social characteristics of Michigan students and student athletes lead to variations in their experiences of sports cultures? If so, how and why? If not, what explained their commonalities?

Markovits and Smith composed and distributed a survey instrument that eventually became the quantitative basis for their article "Sports Culture among Undergraduates: A Study of Student Athletes and Students at the University of Michigan."[33] It will also serve in this discussion as a means of bolstering with enumerated data our findings and conclusions gleaned from our interviews and narratives.

In total, 845 students participated in the survey. This included 398 men and 447 women; 434 athletes and 411 non-athletes. The athlete sample included most members of twenty-four of twenty-five of Michigan's varsity teams (the only team absent was football).

The non-athlete sample derived from four sources. Three of these were classes in which the survey was distributed to students—a freshman introductory sociology class, Markovits's aforementioned sports class, and a German history class. The fourth source was a copy center in downtown Ann Arbor, where copies of the survey were deposited for undergraduate students waiting in line to purchase and photocopy their course packs. At the beginning of each semester, many students visit this copy center to obtain course packs, and frequently they encounter very long lines. To the usual distractions of reading, listening to music, and chatting, Markovits and Smith added the opportunity to participate in their survey—an opportunity taken by more than one hundred students.

This sample, then, includes only undergraduates, and is weighted heavily toward students in the College of Literature, Science, and the Arts—the University of Michigan's main undergraduate liberal arts college—especially the social sciences. All three classes surveyed were undergraduate social science classes, and the copy center caters almost exclusively to undergraduates from the College of Literature, Science, and the Arts. It must also be borne in mind that there exists a large component of students from Markovits's sociology of sport class, whom Markovits and Smith expected to be a "self-selecting" group, with greater interest in and knowledge of sports than the general student body. Still, the sizeable sample included in their study, Markovits and Smith believe, represents a valuable and telling segment of Michigan's undergraduate student population. But in no way do the authors claim that their study comprises a representative sample of the general undergraduate student population of the University of Michigan.

We will use Markovits and Smith's study, along with secondary sources and the narratives collected via solicitation in Markovits's lecture throughout the ensuing presentation of the nature of hegemonic sports culture and its different iterations in society's two primary gender categories.

---

[33]Ibid.

Attendance: Spectatorship at Live Events

One of the areas in which men and women have reached near parity in terms of sport consumption is in their attendance at live sporting events. Markovits and Smith found that women spent 2.7 hours per week, on average, and men spent 3.0 hours attending live sporting events of any kind. Even divorcing the figure from a university context, as well as removing the student athlete faction, other studies have found similar results. In 2000, the National Football League's attendance was 46 percent female, and Dietz-Uhler et al. found that the difference in the average "number of events attended" by men versus women was negligible.[34]

If one looks only at the numbers, attendance at live events does indeed appear to be similar between men and women. However, motivations for said attendance and specific behavior and attention exhibited while at the venues differ greatly, as we will argue, between the typical male and female attendee. That is, while the numbers in attendance seem to suggest that males and females grant equal attention to sports spectatorship, the differences in their *reasons* for attending and the *meaning* as to what this attendance entails and signifies reveal amply that the same sporting event is typically framed very differently for men and for women.

In general, males and females within the same stadium are there to meet different needs and ends, with women's main reasons for attending being mainly about inclusion at a social event of any kind, of which this particular sporting contest is merely a convenient and interchangeable representative, and men's reason being primarily centered on the specific event, on the game as an end in itself, often in the larger framework of the sport's other teams, its league, and beyond, with the entire experience being contextualized in a much larger comparative sports framework extending over time and space. Also important to consider is that the Markovits and Smith study included student athletes, who may be more prone to attend athletic events (including games or meets featuring sports outside of the hegemonic sports culture), and was conducted at a large university at which "football games . . . [are] a vital ceremony regardless of gender . . . a ritual of college life" and that, according to the authors, the norm of undergraduate student life expects, quite possibly compels, attendance at football games on Saturday afternoons in the fall, even for a decided (but certainly extant) minority among students who might not

---

[34]Patrick Davis, Heath McDonald, and Adam Karg, "The Role of Gender in Determining Season-Ticket Holder Satisfaction" (paper presented at ANZMAC 2010: Doing More with Less: Proceedings of the 2010 Australian and New Zealand Marketing Academy Conference, Christchurch, New Zealand, November 29–December 1, 2010): 8; and Dietz-Uhler et al., "Sex Differences."

be particularly interested in football.[35] In a senior honors thesis under Markovits's guidance, Laura Marie Biltz has researched how women in sororities at the University of Michigan construct their football lives during their four years at this university.[36] In particular, behooving her major in anthropology, Biltz conducted in-depth interviews with sorority members about their exact experiences at home games on football Saturdays in Ann Arbor. Biltz was especially interested in ascertaining these women's participation in pre- and post-game activities as well as their behavior inside the stadium during games, particularly concerning their knowledge of the timing, content, and shape of the many collective rituals that define the very being of a Michigan fan. Reading Biltz's fine work makes it very clear that on this level of identification with, love for, and knowledge of sports, women are every bit men's equals. Going to the "Big House" on fall Saturdays has much more to do with fulfilling a key ritual of undergraduate life at the University of Michigan than offering prima facie evidence for one's interest and expertise in football, college or otherwise.

TV Watching

Of the 93 million people worldwide who tuned in to the nail-biting 2007 NFL Super Bowl game between the Giants and the Patriots, 45 percent of them were women.[37] The gender distribution of subsequent Super Bowls was virtually identical. Whereas this figure might prima facie suggest virtual gender parity in terms of following the most important marquee event on the American sports firmament, it also masks important gender differences that cannot be as easily quantified and explained by numbers. To be sure, one key aspect in interpreting this figure is that if Super Bowls consistently constitute the most watched television events of any kind in the United States, regularly attracting circa one hundred million viewers, then their social importance as an inclusive annual event far exceeds their actual content. Watching the Super Bowl in contemporary America has much less to do with sports than with inclusion in a mainstay of American culture. We find Donald Levy's characterization about sports spot-on pertaining to the Super Bowl's presence in contemporary America, though as compelling for sport as a whole: "We experience sport like

---

[35]Markovits and Smith, "Sports Culture."

[36]Laura Biltz, "Sorority Women and the Body Politic: Structuring the Self Image in a World of Maize and Blue" (unpublished honors thesis, The University of Michigan, Ann Arbor, Michigan, 2012).

[37]Sarah Mahoney, "Marketers Ready to Address 45% of Super Bowl Audience," *Marketing Daily*, June 22, 2008, available at http://www.mediapost.com/publications/index.cfm?fa=Articles. showArticle&art_aid=74770 (accessed April 20, 2011).

the landscape in a painting that includes us until like the air we breathe, we absorb sport through osmosis."[38]

Thus, when it comes to watching regular, run-of-the-mill games—not mega events—and following programs featuring analysis of and commentary on sports, women's participation declines markedly when compared with men's. Markovits and Smith found that, among their undergraduate survey population, women spent an average of 3.2 hours per week watching sports competitions on television, while men spent an average of eight hours. Dietz-Uhler et al. garnered similar results, with the mean female response being 2.3 hours per week watching sports, and the male response, 8.53 hours. These numbers surely represent a gendered gap in one of fandom's most basic requirements, but still only reflect differences in the watching of actual *games* or events.

One would think that an even greater divergence between men and women would be exposed if either of the two surveys had asked respondents about additional time spent watching beyond the games proper, including pre- and post-game shows and other ancillary sports-related programming. The prototypical sports fan constituting a society's hegemonic sports culture does not turn the TV off at the final buzzer, for there are hours of post-game analyses to absorb, as well as programs completely independent of the broadcast of the actual game itself. These programs (e.g., *SportsCenter, Pardon the Interruption,* and *Around the Horn,* the very programs whose regular watching Markovits delineated as being a minimal prerequisite to describing oneself a sports fan and thus participate in writing one's story about it) are all about talking sports outside of the context of the actual event. Above all, viewing such programs on a regular basis requires that one care about sports more than the mere watching of a game itself might entail.

These types of programs are also typically less social than games. They are broadcast several times daily and are not occasions to gather with friends to watch. These programs are flipped to in the morning before work, and they are on in the background throughout the day. To wit, according to one of our respondents on this very topic, "I usually turn on *SportsCenter* as I am putting on my make-up and getting ready for the day." This fact, as well as the significant role that these types of shows play in the life of the typical male sports fan, speaks to another notable difference in contrasting male and female fans: Women rarely watch sports by themselves. Be it a game or sports talk television, the typical woman is not going to tune in to a sports program of this kind when she is alone, a pattern that reflects the notion that, for most women, sports are more of a means to a social end than an end in themselves.

---

[38]Levy, "Fantasy Sports," 1.

The fact that women spend less time than men watching sports programming that is not an actual game is augmented by the gender disparity found in the amount of time spent *discussing* sports. Dietz-Uhler found that, while men spend an average of 4.19 hours per week discussing sports, women only spend an average of 1.93 hours.[39] What this finding suggests is that those sporting events that women are watching are not candidates for continued conversation after the game ends, that perhaps the very watching of the game is serving a role other than satisfying a real drive to engage in watching sport. "I find that applies to most women," one of our subjects averred. "Again, they view watching a game as a social gathering versus something they want to actually watch."[40] On top of spending more time watching sports, men are more likely to talk about a game before it happens and to continue doing so after it ends. In this relatively basic *behavioral* component of sports fandom, we already begin to see women showing less interest in sports' following than men.

Time Deepening

> My cheerleading team would often have meets on Mondays, which meant a Sunday team dinner followed by rolling each others' hair in curlers for the next day. While doing this, we would have snacks and watch the Sunday night football games.[41]

Another component that an objective numeric value does not show is the precise meaning of spending two hours per week watching sports for the normal female sports fan. Put differently, what does her time spent "watching a game" look like, compared with, for example, her husband's? Research has found that a woman's experiences watching sports, even if they are equal in actual numbers to a man's, differ in terms of her ability or desire to become completely consumed by the game (and therefore to ignore the duties related to both the keeping of the house in which the game is being watched as well as the catering to the men who are there watching, i.e., cleaning and feeding, respectively). While watching sports, women commonly take part in what Gantz and Wenner call "time deepening," a practice "in which they participate in several activities concurrently."[42] Often having extra domestic responsibilities, Gantz and Wenner point out, women "may find it difficult to spend most of an

---

[39]Dietz-Uhler et al., "Sex Differences," 225.

[40]Stephanie Schwartz, email to the authors, March 15, 2011.

[41]Leah Hsieh, email to the authors, January 2011.

[42]Walter Gantz and Lawrence A. Wenner, "Men, Women, and Sports: Audience Experiences and Effects," *Journal of Broadcasting and Electronic Media* 35, no. 2 (1991): 241.

afternoon or evening indulging in food and libations while concentrating on an entire game,"[43] and they are "more likely to report they 'also work[ed] on household chores' while they watched sports on TV."[44] Men, more often than women, tune in to pre-game panel shows and stick around after the game for highlights and analysis, and all throughout, they snack. Perhaps a vestige of Victorian gender roles, research has found that it is no mystery how the chips and salsa get refilled.

This concept is important in terms of characterizing a typical woman's viewing experience, but it is dangerous in that it can be used to invalidate a genuine "superfan's" true devotion and desire to watch a game. That is, *time deepening* is performed often by all women, regardless of their place on the field of fandom. Men often regard a woman's multitasking during a game as prima facie evidence that she is, and women in general are, less interested in the game, a practice that can frustrate the sportista and devalue her experience. Albertson, a bona fide sportista herself, remembers the party that she and her (male) roommates hosted for Super Bowl XLV during her senior year of college. Behooving her qualifications as a sportista, she remembers the details of the game itself, but also recalls that she did not sit down once from pre-game programming to post-game celebrations. The menu for the day was extensive and, in some cases, required timely attention to the oven and stovetop. Tellingly, as soon as the game started, all of the men abandoned Albertson, leaving all kitchen duties to her. Moreover, they did so without uttering one word of explanation, comment, or excuse, simply assuming that by virtue of Albertson's gender, all would be fine and dandy. Near the end of the game, after Albertson made an editorial comment about Green Bay Packers quarterback Aaron Rodgers's performance, one guest mumbled mockingly to one of her roommates, asking if "Emily had even watched one second of the game." She had, of course, watched nearly every second of it, but was forced to do so from the adjoining room *while* attending to the sustenance of the party.

To be clear, nobody "forced" Albertson into doing anything. She could have abandoned the food, as her male roommates did, and left the party guests hungry. However, she, perhaps as a function of her gender, felt the need to provide, to be a proper hostess. Albertson's acting on her characteristically female impulse did not at all diminish her own enjoyment and understanding of the game. She loved every minute of it, followed its nuances, understood the strategies, remembered the various stats. Regardless, the assembled male viewers did not accord her any validity as a sports fan because—at least ostensibly—her

---

[43]Ibid.

[44]Walter Gantz and Lawrence A. Wenner, "Fanship and the Television Sports Viewing Experience," *Sociology of Sport Journal* 12, no. 1 (1995): 65.

physical presence was not as obvious as that of the males in the room. This fact disqualified her to speak about the game with knowledge and expertise. Even though she could "prove" her fandom or knowledge in other ways, it was obvious that her absence from the right room at the right time precluded her from being a member of the club.

The point of this anecdote is to illustrate that time deepening, a common practice by women, need not serve as "proof" that the woman who participates in it is any less interested in the game than are men. Albertson was a more knowledgeable and ardent football spectator than many of the males at her party, but she had assumed extra responsibilities to please the larger group, and therefore lost her credibility. The expectation that a woman take care of housekeeping, cooking, and other typically female tasks was at play at the beginning of televised sports culture and aided in the bolstering of the idea that sports games are for men to watch.

At the origin of widely televised sports programming, games were broadcast at times when people (i.e., men) could watch: after work. The male's workday was over, and he was now free to relax at home and tend to his hobbies, among which watching and following sports took pride of place until work the next morning. Women's work, however, did not come close to ceasing with their departure from the office and their arrival at home. In fact, this was often the busiest time for the traditional woman, as the family was home and needed to be fed and taken care of. As explained by Carol Stiff, Director of Programming and Acquisitions at ESPN, this logistical conflict may be responsible for a lot of women's lack of sports following. She noted, "Many sports events are televised during prime-time or weekend hours, precisely those times that many women are most busy with their children."[45] Even if women had discovered a love for football, the option to sit for a few hours and watch a game was not a realistic one in terms of the larger economy of their daily lives.

It seems that, even for a progressive college-aged woman—like Albertson—who is a bona fide sportista, the gendered division of labor continues to make it difficult to live and enjoy sports fandom in the same way that leisure-seeking males can. Time deepening must not be seen as precluding an individual's fandom, but rather, perhaps as a reflection of the additional barriers that women have to cross to become fully integrated and accepted sports fans.

Gillian Warmflash's research explained that, in their understanding, "women simply do not have the time to be sports fans." "Women are busy, trying to juggle being moms, working, a house, being wives. Women have a

---

[45]Gillian Lee Warmflash, "In a Different Language: Female Sports Fans in America" (unpublished honors thesis, submitted to the Committee on Degrees in Social Studies, Harvard University, Cambridge, MA, March 2004).

multitude of roles that they've always done throughout the years," says [one of Warmflash's interviewees]. "It takes time to follow a team, to watch television, to read the sports page every day. Someone has to be taking care of the kids. I just think women have a lot more responsibilities than men."[46] Kristin Johnson, another of Warmflash's interviewees, similarly argues, "Women are multi-taskers. There's so much more on their plate that it's hard to add that extra, especially later in life. You might say, 'Oh, sit down' [to a woman] and she will say, 'No, I have this to do and I have these errands to run and I don't feel like sitting down and watching a basketball game when I could be getting a lot of other stuff done.'"[47]

With Albertson representing a sportista, the exception to the typical female sports fan, the still-expected behavior of time deepening nonetheless represents a conundrum for female sports fans, from the lukewarm to the raging.

Sports Talk

As mentioned earlier, the research on sports fan behavior shows that women spend much less time discussing sports with other women or with men than do male fans. Even in a group of ten college-aged females, who were brought together under the *specific* premise that they were all bona fide sportistas (and for the sole *purpose* of discussing this aspect of their lives), on a Thursday evening before an important University of Michigan football game nary forty-eight hours later, which they all had plans to attend, the conversation at the dinner table on their first convening at the restaurant and awaiting the arrival of Markovits, who purposefully delayed his entrance so that the women would talk among themselves, unencumbered by his presence, was *not* about sports. Instead, these sportistas talked about many other dimensions of their identities along which they aligned, such as their college majors, classes they had taken, and mutual people they might know.

This finding is especially surprising when considering the fact that even men who do *not* consider themselves to be sports fans, but who simply exist as "normal" men, as regular Joes, so to speak, turn to sports more often than any other topic (even when they share a very specific commonality, say being professors of political science or account executives) in a situation in which they are seeking a source of small talk and superficial common ground. Markovits convened the aforementioned young women for the sole reason that they all were deeply interested in sports and confessed to having major passion for and

---

[46]Ibid.

[47]Ibid.

knowledge about them. And yet, they turned to other topics of conversation to make new connections. For females, it seems, discrete events seem to make up the essence of sports, something that one attends and experiences, either in the stadium or on television, and whose relevance ends at the final buzzer. The story appears to end there, with few of its extra-game facets providing relatable experiences with which to build a bridge to new people.

After the conclusion of the nearly forty University of Michigan home games that Markovits has attended since joining the University's faculty in the fall of 1999, he has witnessed first-hand how the story ends for female Michigan students with the final whistle in the Big House, whereas the very same moment opens up entirely new narratives for their male counterparts. Paying close attention to the conversations on departing from the stadium while walking up Hill Street, a major artery between the stadium and many fraternity and sorority houses, Markovits has overheard many a fascinating conversation among Michigan students. The gender divide has been overwhelming and persistent. Female students discuss a wide-ranging array of topics, ranging from a lively debate as to whether teaching hospitals offer better care than general hospitals to why feminists ought to take Sarah Palin more seriously. Women might even share a word or two about something that happened among their friends in the stadium during the game. What Markovits has yet to hear is women's passionate discussion as to why Michigan's defensive backs should have played deeper on the opposition's short yardage situations on third downs; why options should have played a greater role in Michigan's offense; why the play action was overused, especially in the second quarter; how the evening game between two Southeastern Conference teams might affect the Bowl Championship Series standings; why next year's recruiting class will be among the top five in the country; or any number of topics pertaining to technical aspects of the game that they had just attended or to college football, more generally, beyond this particular Michigan game, never mind the NFL or other sports altogether. After a game, women talk about many things, with football and sports not prominent among them. "Growing up," one of our interviewees avers, "I tried not to talk about sports in front of girls. I still try not to this day. I've toned down my sports [talk] around girls because it hasn't always been taken well."[48]

The exact opposite happens routinely with men departing Michigan Stadium, or any venue, for that matter. Sports have served men as their most universal source of bonding capital (that which can strengthen the bonds between individuals with shared characteristics) and bridging capital (that which connects individuals from different social clusters). For men, the bonding capital

---

[48]Laura Hahn, email to the authors, January 2011.

provided by sports emanates from their near essentiality for hegemonic masculinity; that is, men recognize an understanding and appreciation of sports as a quintessential characteristic of being male, as a culturally crucial marker of their gender, as it were, and therefore as an important medium in strengthening the bond among all men, sports fans or not.

In a more tangible sense, though, in instances where the similarities vested in their shared gender are not sufficient in establishing a social connection, sports provide bridging capital among men who, for lack of better words, don't have anything else to talk about. Sports constitute a safe and reliable topic with which men can build a bridge to an otherwise completely distant stranger. Above all, sports for men constitute perhaps the most potent bridging capital between different social stations, classes, ethnic groups, nationalities, and religions. Even between long-standing adversaries with such deeply held hatreds as exists between Israelis and Palestinians, sports form a crucial—and often the only—bridging capital for men as, for example, so movingly depicted in the Israeli film *Cup Final*, in which the two protagonists, who confront each other on the bloody battlefield of the 1982 Israeli incursion into Lebanon, share moments of mutual respect, even affection, merely by dint of their watching the soccer World Cup during the mayhem around them and by their both being passionate fans of the Italian national team, especially its goal-scoring superstar, Paolo Rossi, who led the *Azzurri* to their third world championship. "Having interest in and knowledge of sports are ways to assure that [a man] can communicate with other men," Warmflash concludes from her research.[49] One of her interviewees explained, "Sports are a currency for men, they're what you trade in, they're what you talk about."[50] "Most men have talked about sports most of their lives," another one of Warmflash's interviewees averred. "They know that another guy will be interested, so it is a safe place to go."[51] The idea of a "safe social currency" seems essential in understanding the male attraction to sports fandom, as Warmflash concludes that "sports are such an appealing topic of conversation for men, precisely because they are impersonal, enabling men, who do not like to 'express their feelings,' to communicate with each other without truly opening up."[52] Because of the bonding and bridging capital that sports possess, they are an invaluable social tool for men. Sports, versus politics, for example, which are more personally revealing, offer "a much easier way to open the line with another guy," explained another

---

[49]Warmflash, "In a Different Language," 75.

[50]Ibid., quote from Liz Clarke.

[51]Ibid., quote from Dana Jacobson.

[52]Ibid.

one of Warmflash's interviewees.[53] Speaking sport becomes, in essence, speaking man, as Warmflash so insightfully argues, perhaps more than any other possible subject, certainly more than personal matters, but also more than career issues, work-related subjects, financial issues, politics, or culture. "Men don't have all that many impersonal things they can talk about, and so they talk about sports a lot. Sports are a real common denominator for them."[54]

Context seems to matter as well to our typical female sports fans. Survey research has shown that often women, just like men, will use whatever sports knowledge they have to connect with men. Regardless of their eventual aim in the conversation, even casual (strictly emotional and affective) female fans make use of their fandom when trying to relate to their male peers. One of our female interviewees, a bona fide sportista with the journalistic credentials to prove it, shared that her female friends, most of whom have no interest in sports, *do* want her to share pieces of her sports expertise with them in certain situations; they ask her for help in equipping themselves with small pieces of sports knowledge to be used to impress or simply break the ice with their male peers. "What are the games tonight?" and "I'm trying to hang out with this guy. Tell me something to say about sports," are among the statements Nicole has fielded from her friends, and they reflect the motivations behind gleaning "just enough" sports knowledge to enter a male world, even most marginally and instrumentally.[55]

Simmons in Heels, a once-popular sports blog by and for women, reflects this practice. While the idea of a female sports blogger might be assumed to fall under the category of "non-typical" woman, this example reflects the motives of Nicole's friends, as well as those of many women. The short description of the blog, which appears on every page within it, reads, "sitting with my boyfriend and his friends used to be torture. . . Girlfriends! Let's impress our boyfriends, guy friends, coworkers, dads and brothers with sports knowledge!"[56]

The blog's entries are full of just the kind of tidbits that one might need to feign sports knowledge and interest, a goal that only exists because such knowledge clearly accords positive advantages in key situations. A previous post from February 2010 reads, "The San Diego Chargers released running back LaDainian Tomlinson after nine years. Wonder where he will end up next? Ask a guy, see what he says. Chances are he would love to share his

---

[53]Ibid., quote from Nicole Boden.

[54]Ibid., quote from Margaret Grossi.

[55]Nicole Auerbach, interview with the authors, April 25, 2011.

[56]Simmons in Heels, "Released," February 22, 2010, available at http://simmonsinheels.blogspot. com/search/label/LaDainian%20Tomlinson (accessed November 15, 2010).

opinion."[57] This practice of using small details and recently acquired knowledge to gain attention from males is important to our discussing and understanding of the sportista.

It seems that women are fully aware of the power of sports small talk when it comes to spending time around men. Even if it is the simple mention of how she "*loves* the Celtics," without further explanation of the reasons for her affection, or any substantiation of it by way of displaying knowledge, even a tangential connection to sports is commonly used by women as a means of connecting to men. After all, regardless of setting, fandom "provides social prestige and self-esteem, a form of cultural capital that many fans otherwise might not have."[58] John Fiske, drawing from Bourdieu, adds that "the cultural system works like the economic system to distribute its resources unequally and thus to distinguish between the privileged and the deprived."[59]

The purpose of this discussion of the "typical" female fan is to outline and describe the world in which the deviation from the norm—our sportista—has to operate, including the (mostly negative) assumptions that she has to overcome. We believe that these assumptions are by and large correct, meaning that most contemporary female sports fans fall short on the dimension of passion but, above all, that of knowledge to be accepted as bona fide fans, which renders the sportista not only an outlier but also makes her position difficult and precarious by dint of its being tested and suspected all the time. Particularly irksome to the sportista—and a further challenge to her legitimacy—is the often used instrumentalization of sports by the regular female sports fan to gain access to men. On the one hand, men are flattered by this; on the other, they see through it and denigrate such approaches as disingenuous. By having men conveniently project the superficial and instrumental practices of the typical female fan onto the rare female sports expert and aficionado also renders the sportista's legitimacy among male sports fans all the more suspect and illegitimate.

The earlier point in which the respondent admitted to "ton[ing] down [her] sports around girls because it hasn't always been taken well," illustrates this pattern as she continues to write, "I just remember in high school, girls thinking I only liked sports because I wanted to talk to the boys."[60] The benefits of being at least marginally sports literate are apparent to men and women. It seems, however, that those benefits can obstruct the objective evaluation of a "genuine" female fan's true level of expertise and devotion. According to one

---

[57]Simmons, "Released" (accessed April 1, 2011).

[58]Gantz and Wenner, "Television and the Sports Viewing Experience," 58.

[59]Fiske, "Economy of Fandom," 31.

[60]Hahn, email to the authors, 2011.

respondent, "I remember boys being suspicious whenever I talked sports with them. I never started the conversations."[61]

Merchandise

In this area of tangible display of sports fandom, females make a large statement. Markovits and Smith found that 92.5 percent of women and 94.5 percent of men reported owning some clothing displaying college logos, in the case of this study, featuring the University of Michigan.[62] For professional sports logo clothing (58.8 percent of women and 83.2 percent of men identified themselves as owners of such merchandise), the numbers revealed an important factor: The ownership of college logo clothing is most likely a function of the sample population being college students at a major public research university, where sports are accorded a particular pride of place in its overall identity. Still, though, without differentiating between college and professional logo clothing, females reported wearing sports merchandise more often than men to "watch televised events," as well as when attending live sporting events.[63]

The example of this gender equality in the ownership of clothing displaying college logos as contrasted to clothing featuring professional team logos, as well as the virtual equality of women's reported attendance at sporting events, embodies an important element of our typical female sports fans in a college setting, namely, that they "participate equally in the campus sports culture, but very differently in the broader sports culture."[64] Markovits and Smith identify a possible interpretation of females' pursuit of displaying fandom via merchandise, namely, that it might be an easy way of "*visually* identifying themselves as fans."[65] Donning a t-shirt must be the easiest way to display fandom; therefore, it exists as a popular choice for those without an abundance of additional markers—particularly the requisite knowledge—with which to demonstrate fandom. If a woman's goal is to be recognized as a fan among a team's fans, then wearing the appropriately signified merchandise is a smart way to supplement a minimal supply of alternate forms of proof of fandom and hide, as it were, any glaring lacunae in the items designating proper fandom, particularly in the areas of knowledge. This pattern conveys yet another highly gendered instance that we mentioned already: For many women, their experience

---

[61]Ibid.

[62]Markovits and Smith, "Sports Culture," 23.

[63]Ibid., 24.

[64]Ibid., 23.

[65]Ibid.

of sports fandom is mainly about connecting with their immediate community and culture more than pursuing their interest in sports per se.

Merchandise stands inside the Detroit Tigers' Comerica Park have three main types of jerseys: home, away, and pink. Women throughout the park can be seen in white-on-pink or pink-on-white Justin Verlander jerseys, with an accompanying pink cap displaying a glittery Old English "D" on the front. The introduction of the pink jersey and the welcome revenues attained from their sales are reflective of women's growing presence in sports venues as well as their participation in showing their fandom by way of logo clothing. In 2010, the NFL reported that its women's apparel business had doubled since 2004. That year, the league released a new line of clothing for women, the "Fit for You" line, which did not dye everything pink, but rather cut the apparel in a more flattering way for women.[66] Resented by some and embraced by others, pink and/or fitted versions of sports merchandise have proved to be extremely popular among women, many of whom do very little in terms of living out any other aspect of what constitutes commonly recognized sports fandom.

Knowledge

Even being known for having a working knowledge of sports does not guarantee entrance into the often male-dominated conversation.[67]

The breadth and depth of actual sports knowledge, the component along which Albertson initially dismissed our imaginary female Celtics "fan," as will be recalled, is an area in which typical females are significantly behind typical males. This aspect of fandom is often identified by most full-fledged fans, even below the superfan status, as being absolutely essential for admission to the "club" and maintaining one's membership therein in good standing. Not by chance, sports knowledge represents perhaps the single most salient component of sports fandom in which women prove to be most deficient and least invested. By and large, one can construe sports knowledge as consisting of the following two clusters: *historical* knowledge of a team, of players, of the entire sport, and of all hegemonic sports (the "Big Four" in the United States); and *current* knowledge of all of these facets.

Research shows that, even before breaking down "knowledge" into these component parts, most women fall significantly below men in terms of the entire category of sports knowledge. In their previously mentioned study, Dietz-

---

[66]Mandy Stadtmiller and Don Kaplan, "NFL Launching Women's Clothing Line," *New York Post*, September 29, 2010, for Fox Sports, available at http://msn.foxsports.com/nfl/story/NFL-launching-womens-clothing-line-092810 (accessed March 22, 2011).

[67]Sarah Moran, email to the authors, January 2011.

Uhler et al. asked their subjects first to self-report the level of sports knowledge that they believed themselves to have (on a scale of 1 = not knowledgeable to 7 = very knowledgeable). The scholars then proceeded to test the respondents' sports knowledge by using a twenty-item sports knowledge scale to determine the subjects' level of actual sports savvy.[68] While the means reported in the category of *self-evaluations* of one's knowledge were not that different between the two genders (5.44 for males, and 4.10 for females, out of a possible twenty), the impartial "tests" of levels of actual knowledge revealed a much larger gender gap (males achieving a mean of 11.42, females 4.20, out of a possible twenty).[69] This distinction reflects one of the more notable findings in these results: The men and women ranked themselves similarly when asked what level of sports knowledge they believed themselves to possess. However, an objective evaluation revealed that their actual levels of knowledge were not close at all. These results speak to the relatively lower set of knowledge required of women versus men in terms of their self-identified threshold of entry into the realm of sports fandom. It is much higher for men than it is for women in terms of self-defined expectations as well as actual knowledge and factual mastery.

An examination of the results of Dietz-Uhler et al. illustrates this point, in that they show that the entire scale of "knowledge" seems to shift based on gender. The women in the study consider themselves to be in the fiftieth percentile of being "knowledgeable" about sports when their twenty-point score is only 4.20. The male subjects, however, place themselves similarly in terms of percentile of knowledge, but their actual score is 11.42.[70] To consider oneself "knowledgeable," it seems, does not require the same objective amount of knowledge for women and men. Seemingly, a woman sees herself as relatively knowledgeable, perhaps, with a much lower objective score of factual information. According to one of our interviewees on this topic, "The standards for a 'real' female fan are much lower. If a female is aware of the team's record and whom it played last, men applaud her and think that she is really well-versed, while that is the extent of her capability."[71]

This pattern is crucial to our subject, because a woman's claiming "knowledge," that she "knows what she's talking about," will always first be understood through the lens of her gender. She may very well be a Tigers fanatic, a *huge* fan, but she is a woman, and we all know that a woman "knowing" this team, being a "huge fan," does not mean that she is on the same level as a man

---

[68]Dietz-Uhler et al., "Sex Differences," 223.

[69]Ibid., 225.

[70]Ibid.

[71]Jillian Rothman, email to the authors, March 21, 2011.

who shares the equivalent claim to being a bona fide fan. Research shows that women, in general, count themselves as knowledgeable with fewer requirements than do males, but what happens, then, to the woman—our sportista—who actually is as objectively knowledgeable as the men? The self-identification on the part of the typical affect-based but knowledge-challenged female as a fan hurts the legitimacy of the woman who is seeking inclusion into fandom on the same level and in identical ways that males seem to be given, merely by their gender; the fact that there appears to be a socially expected and accepted profile for female sports fans makes it that much harder for anyone to see why a "deviant" female should not simply be grouped there as well. There is already a place for her, as a female fan, but not as an unmarked, un-"othered," original, and unadulterated fan, notably without a gendered modifier. The presence of the "shallow" fans provides a massive barrier to entry for the few but clearly extant—and growing—"serious" and "committed" women sports fans. Making this all the more challenging and annoying for the small but growing number of such women is the fact that men—often with much inferior sports knowledge to theirs—are accorded access to the club of legitimate sports fandom, solely based on their gender. Simply put, for women, the socially deviant case is the accomplished sportista; for men, it is the sport-ignorant and disinterested male.

The females and males in the study by Dietz-Uhler et al. were equally as likely to identify themselves as "fans," even though their actual behaviors and levels of knowledge differ greatly. Markovits and Smith found that, when distinguishing between the "historic element" of knowledge and that of contemporary sports, great gaps exist between men and women. To assess respondents' level of expertise, their study asked each individual to "name members of the lineups of eight historical and contemporary teams from professional sports," the New York Yankees of the 1950s (and "today," meaning 2003–2004, the year of the survey), the Boston Celtics of the 1960s and today, the Pittsburgh Steelers of the 1970s and today, and finally, the Detroit Red Wings of the 1950s and today. Markovits and Smith chose these teams because each one of them was a dynasty in the Big Four American hegemonic sports in the era named by the survey and produced historically lasting superstars, who—like these teams' accomplishments in these respective decades—became part of the American sports vernacular and remain so to this day.

The females were able to name an average of 0.35 historical players, and the males 3.28.[72] When it came to knowledge of contemporary athletes, the females' average rose to 1.69 and the males' to 7.17. The mean number of play-

---

[72]Markovits and Smith, "Sports Culture."

ers that the males could identify was 10.93, compared with the females' 2.04.[73] These findings reinforce females' deficiency in terms of sports knowledge and further exemplify the pattern that their knowledge continues to wane as details veer into the past. Women do not know sports history. More important still, they do not care about doing so. It does not form an essential core of the very identify of their sports knowledge and their existence as sports fans.

As a relevant ingredient of their research, and highlighting the deeply gendered nature of sports knowledge, Markovits and Smith found the students' demeanor and body language, as well as the time that they took to complete their survey, extremely telling of the deeply gendered nature of sports knowledge. The survey instrument was administered to University of Michigan undergraduates—both "regular" students and student athletes—in an array of venues, ranging from large lecture halls to smaller classrooms, from practice fields (including in the natatorium right alongside the pool, in the case of the women's swim team) to locker rooms, but there was one finding that those administering the survey noticed in every single instance: The women almost always completed the survey approximately five minutes sooner than the men. This was the case in mixed-gender classroom settings, where the women departed sooner than the men, thus making the temporal difference amply visible, as well as in the gender-separated settings of the respective sports teams, where those administering the survey were asked to record the time taken for its completion.

Since the questions measuring the historic knowledge of the respondents appeared as the very last items on the survey instrument, we can assume with relative certainty that the time difference in handing in the survey had some connection to the completion—or omission—of this last section. Markovits, administering the survey himself in twenty of a possible twenty-seven instances, noticed a fascinating difference in demeanor between male and female respondents pertaining to this last segment of the instrument.[74] Invariably, the women stood up completely matter-of-factly after completing the survey and proceeded totally unencumbered to deposit their document in the box sitting at the venue's exit. In notable contrast, many of the men seemed to ponder the survey at its end, clearly conveying that they were at least attempting to answer the historical questions as best they could.

In other words, even if they could not answer any of the historical items on the survey, many men felt somehow obliged at least to try, clearly denoting

---

[73]Ibid.

[74]This happened in the case of twenty-four varsity teams, plus two sociology classes and one history class; no such observations occurred in the copy center where students filled out the survey during the first week of the semester while waiting on line to assemble their course packs.

that simply by being male one is expected to know who played point guard for the Boston Celtics of the Bill Russell era and what players furnished the batting order of the New York Yankees of the 1950s. The pained look on many a young man's face and his obvious exertion when attempting to respond to questions addressing sports-related issues that occurred well before he was born clearly revealed that at least some knowledge of sports history appears to be a necessary marker—a clear distinction—of a man's proper gender identity, as dictated by contemporary America's hegemonic culture. Some men actually handed in extra sheets of paper listing obscure bench players—in addition to the well-known stars, of course—of the teams mentioned in the survey, conveying clearly how important such knowledge and its demonstration were to them. Remember, this was *not* a test! Regardless, for many men, not knowing these historical facts must have appeared as a definite lacuna, perhaps even a stigma, that made them, at least to some extent, self-conscious, maybe even slightly ashamed. In contrast, to the female respondents, not knowing these details did not matter at all.

Markovits believes that historical awareness and knowledge constitute key signifiers of sports following and immersion. It is for that reason that he included the questions about naming players of prominent teams that attained their fame well before any of the study's respondents were born. The massive gender difference that emerged in his University of Michigan study conducted with Smith had its exact counterpart and precursor in Germany and Austria, where Markovits first employed this device. While teaching summer school at Schloss Salem to a group of thirty superb German students (equivalent to our National Merit Scholars) in the summer of 1995, after the very first lecture, he asked the students in his class to write down as many names as they could of players from the West German national soccer team that won the World Cup in 1954 and created the legendary "miracle of Bern" that has assumed mythical proportions in the history of the Federal Republic. Of the fourteen female students, only one wrote down one player's name; of the sixteen male students, *all* listed a minimum of three players, with some listing as many as seven players and three listing the entire starting eleven. Markovits replicated the same experiment at the University of Innsbruck in Austria in 1996, where he was a Fulbright Professor. In this case, the iconic instance was the so-called miracle of Cordoba, when at the World Cup in Argentina, in the summer of 1978, the Austrian national soccer team defeated its arch-rival Germans, the longtime tormentor of the Austrians in soccer and often experienced as the Austrians' almighty and arrogant Big Brother in areas way beyond soccer and sports. This, too, became an event of mythical proportions in Austria, with convincing data demonstrating that this victory sealed the final consolidation of the legitimacy of an Austrian nationhood, thus cementing Austria's final and complete separation from Germany. Again, Markovits asked thirty-six students to list as many members of the victorious Austrian national team as they could. Of the fourteen women, all listed one player's name, with three respondents mentioning two. Among the twenty-two male students, three enumerated the entire starting eleven, and all mentioned at least four players.

In early June of 2011, Markovits was at Leuphana University of Lueneburg in Germany, teaching a class of twenty-five students who were twenty years old. When he entered the room on the first day and introduced himself as their teacher of a class on comparative sports culture for which they signed up voluntarily, he handed out a sheet of paper to every student and asked the students to write down the names of as many of the players of the victorious German men's world champion soccer teams of 1954, 1974, and 1990 as they could. Additionally, Markovits asked the students to list as many names of the German women's world champion soccer teams of 2007 and 2010 as they could. These players were the reigning champions, with the impending Women's World Cup tournament in Germany barely two weeks away and already in the daily headlines. The immensely telling results emerged as follows: Of the twenty-five students registered in the class, Markovits received twenty-four responses, seventeen from male students and seven from female students. Of the seven women, three knew absolutely no member of the women's team and four knew only one player's name: Birgit Prinz, three-time FIFA player of the year and the Women's World Cup all-time scoring leader (at the time). That was it! They did not know any other player from either the 2003 or the 2007 women's teams. In terms of knowing any of the male soccer players, one woman knew ten men from the combined 1954, 1974, and 1990 teams. Three women knew seven men from these three teams. One woman listed five names, another woman listed four, and one woman mentioned two players in total. Most decidedly, the women knew many more players from the 1990 team than from its two predecessors. But three women did mention Fritz Walter of the 1954 team, though they did not know anyone else, not even Helmut Rahn. Four women got their players mixed up between the 1990 and 1974 teams, though all players listed did in fact play for one of these two teams. One respondent listed Bastian Schweinsteiger, Jens Lehmann, and Lukas Podolski as members of the 2007 team, which, of course, is wrong since they were all members of the 2006 men's team that did not win a championship. However, that individual most definitely listed these names under 2007, thus not making it quite clear to us whether this denoted an error in gender (Did she think that these were female players?) or whether she thought that the men's team of 2006 did indeed win a championship, which it did not. Whatever the case, this was an odd error.

And here in contrast are the markedly different results for the male respondents: Of the seventeen men, all knew at least two female players, with literally all seventeen listing Birgit Prinz, who, by having been listed by all seventeen men and the four women whom I already mentioned, was the most mentioned soccer player—male or female—among these students. None of the men listed Prinz all by herself. Ten listed her with another player in tandem, just the two of them. Three male students listed Prinz and two additional players. One male student knew four female players, another listed six, one student mentioned eight, and one even listed nine. The man who listed nine members of the German national women's team also knew five members of the 1954 men's team, nine members of the 1974 team, and a whopping fourteen—yes, fourteen—members of the 1990 team, meaning the starting eleven plus three reserve players. None of the men listed fewer than seven male players of the three combined men's world championship teams, with ten men listing more than ten players. Tellingly, not one of the male students assigned any of their listed players erroneously to a team for which the player did not play, with only one exception: For some reason, this respondent mentioned Horst Hrubesch as a member of the 1954 team, which is doubly wrong since Hrubesch played for the 1982 German World Cup team, in Spain, which made it to the final game but lost to Italy, thus not meeting any of the criteria that Markovits had delineated at the outset of his brief study.

Once again, the point is crystal clear: Men know women's sports a lot better than women do, and they obviously know men's sports a lot better as well. These small studies conducted in Germany and Austria offer confirmation from two different cultural settings involving a different sport, yet with identical structural positions to that of the Big Four in the United States: Men's knowledge of sports, historical and current, male and female, far surpasses women's.

The gendered knowledge divide in Markovits's class at Leuphana University of Lueneburg constituted a proper microcosm of a similarly gendered divide in terms of the German population's normative orientation to the impending Women's World Cup. According to a comprehensive survey, 43 percent of German women were happy with their country's hosting the tournament, while 45 percent declared their complete disinterest in it. Conversely, 63 percent of German men were happy about this championship occurring in their country and declared that they would follow its matches. Germany's female population does not much care for women's soccer.[75] It is rather doubtful whether the men do, but their love for this game that so much represents the country's male-dominated hegemonic sports culture is so vast that their at-

---

[75]Darya Brjantzewa, "Replika: Hotjat li Zhenshiny Futbol," Deutsche-Welle-World, November 10, 2011, available at http://www.dw.de/dw/article/0,,15517386.html (accessed November 12, 2011).

traction to it is most catholic and includes women, but only when it pertains to the national team in a large tournament, such as the quadrennial World Cup.

There is an incentive, an attraction, a quality of real fandom to certain men that bears some kinship to the world of "nerds," whose hyper-masculinity is defined solely by their stellar intellect, as manifested especially by their facility with numbers, statistics, and computers, and decidedly not at all by their physical ability and prowess. In other words, these nerd-type fans embody the ultimate in following, in that they know and love sports as an intellectual good, the details of which they love to collect and display, often in competition with others of similar predilections, while at the same time totally neglecting sports as an activity. Nerds, like these sports fans, collect objects associated with knowledge like atlases, maps, mathematical and scientific equipment, computer-related paraphernalia, and also, of course, sports statistics and trivia of all kinds. Above all, sports that are, by definition, physical pursuits and thus involve the human body in some manner, mutate to an intellectual artifact for these male superfans in which the game becomes an amassment, display, and competition of knowledge, to the total exclusion of the body. While there are apparently female nerds, or "nerdettes," as expressed by the NrrdGrrls! site on the World Wide Web, which sees itself as a space for the woman who rejects "the prevailing, confusing, impossible societal [presumably also physical and beauty-related] yardstick and found herself coming up short,"[76] male nerds do not need such a virtual refuge. They are perfectly content with—perhaps even proud of—their nerdy existence.

It is particularly one aspect of knowledge that receives special pride of place in gauging sports expertise: that of history, of detail. One can also call it trivia. To know any field of interest's history arguably constitutes one of the most

---

[76]As quoted in Lori Kendall, "Nerd Nation: Images of Nerds in US Popular Culture," *International Journal of Cultural Studies* 2, no. 2 (1999): 276–277. We also learned a lot from Mary Kirk, "Nerds, Geeks & Barbies: A Social Systems Perspective on the Impact of Stereotypes in Computer Science Education," available at http://www.marykirk.net/articles/nerds-geeks-barbies-a-social-system-perspective-in-the-impact-of-stereotypes-in-computer-science-education. Although in a different setting, Kirk uses—just as we have—the concept of "stereotype threat" extensively to analyze women's subpar performances in a male-dominated field, in this case, computer science education. Lastly, we found the work of Belinda Parmar, the founder of Lady Geek and Lady Geek TV, of much interest and value. In an article entitled "Why Don't Girls Want Careers in Technology?" Parmar argues that while "these days just as many women as men count themselves as tech users, and teenage girls and teenage boys have almost identical Internet usage statistics, yet when it comes to careers, boys are five times more likely to go into technology." Parmar believes that the major reason for massive gender discrepancy lies in girls' wanting to go into "creative" endeavors, such as advertising, public relations, and publishing, and their being bored and put off by the "nerdy, dull and—dare I say—male" worlds of spreadsheets, databases, PowerPoint slides, and "games consoles (made by boys, played by boys)." See http://www.huffingtonpost.com/belinda-parmar/women-technology-jobs_b_1120068.html.

vital markers of having expertise in that field. After all, how can one speak authoritatively about a topic if one is ignorant about its most basic foundations, meaning its past? It is on this very essential dimension that many women lose their confidence in the subject of sports. They love their teams, wear their colors and jerseys, display their banners, and know their players. But they will most likely not be well versed—or interested—in much factual and historical knowledge beyond the immediate boundaries of the object of their affect and passion. This pertains even to sportistas like our interviewee Alisa, a rabid Cleveland Indians fan, who

> by the age of 2 was able not only to replicate the Chief Wahoo war chant perfectly, but also to name the majority of the lineup of the team. Before I could correctly pronounce his name, Albert Belle was my favorite player (later to be replaced by Robbie Alomar). The one picture that I would carry with me at sleepovers and summer camp, to prevent me from getting homesick, was a picture of my parents, my two sisters, and me decked out in Indians paraphernalia.

And yet, this Cleveland Indians fanatic did not know much about baseball beyond the purview of her beloved team, meaning the American League. "Although I pride myself on my love of sports," Alisa confessed to us,

> I am nowhere near as well-versed in sports as the average guy. I follow my teams and watch sports with a good degree of enthusiasm, but I couldn't list the all-star players in the National League. When tested about my knowledge of sports, which happens pretty often, I don't normally do that well.

It is safe to assume that were Alisa a young man who exhibited the same degree of love for and involvement with the Cleveland Indians as she has, he would in fact not only know all the National League's all-star players but also their individual stats and then some. Women speak team and players. Men speak sports. The latter, in many ways, is not much different from speaking another foreign language, particularly in terms of the importance that they both be mastered early in life if one wishes ever to speak them fluently, without an "accent."

People who are traveling to Italy may choose to do so with a few important phrases or words in their vocabulary, so as to fit in on the most basic and superficial levels while visiting that gorgeous country. A traveler might pick up some basic vocabulary to impress the locals and show them that he or she is respectful of their culture and therefore took the trouble to learn a few words. In the same way, a woman entering the foreign nation of a Monday Night Football viewing party may take a look at, or even bother to learn, the basic elements of the game so as to provide herself with some sort of connection to the community and to display a basic understanding of the cultural world in which she immerses herself. However much native Italians might appreciate the gesture of our visitor's effort (and courtesy) to memorize a handful of Italian phrases, they will never see him or her anywhere close to being one of them. Indeed, the American transplant to Italy, even if speaking Italian perfectly, might never be accepted by those born in Italy as being truly one of their own. To be sure, such acceptance of incorporation and acculturation varies widely, with societies adhering to a völkisch, jus sanguinis-based construction of belonging—like Germany, Italy, and many countries in Central and Eastern Europe—having a much higher and exclusive acceptance threshold than societies following a jus soli-guided notion of citizenship and inclusion, like the United States, Canada, Great Britain, and France, for example. Still, this language analogy extends to sports talk as well, with any "outsider," or late arriver to the culture, having difficulty and facing obstacles in being able to find acceptance as a genuine member of the native community, free of any suspicion or discomfort coming from the native fan. If one wishes to speak Italian or football fluently and without any accent, and to be accepted as native and genuine, the process of learning must begin, linguistics and social science research finds, extremely early in life. Studies of language acquisition show that, if one tries to learn a new language beyond the age of twelve to fourteen, one will almost never speak that language without an accent; to be truly fluent and accent-free, a speaker must learn the language at a young age.[77] We find analogous patterns in sport.

Peter Mewett and Kim Toffoletti's delineation of four categories of female sports fans illustrates how late entry may result in different practices once a person joins the ranks of the fans.[78] The authors' first category, the "in the blood" fans, are those women who were born into a family of sports fans, who learned the "language" at birth, and for whom fandom was part of their overall cultural development. Those in their second category, the "learners," acquire their interest in sports later in life by way of friends, family, or other exposure, most notably by playing sports themselves. Then there are the "converts" and the "sexually transmitted fans," the latest to join sports fandom, who were uninterested in sports until a specific relationship or individual eventually inspired their interest.

---

[77]Wilder Penfield and Lamar Roberts, *Speech and Brain Mechanisms* (Princeton: Princeton University Press, 1959); and Eric Lennenberg, *Biological Foundations of Language* (New York: Wiley, 1967).

[78]Peter Mewett and Kim Toffoletti, "Rogue Men and Predatory Women: Female Fans' Perceptions of Australian Footballers' Sexual Conduct," *International Review for the Sociology of Sport* 43, no. 2 (2008): 165–180.

Most likely because of the widespread societal assumption that women are somehow a priori not interested in sports, many females are not included in conversations about them as young girls in the same way that, for example, their brothers most likely are. In our interviews, almost every one of our thirty-three respondents wrote of an experience in which she was—willfully or not—excluded from some event involving sports talk, with this experience effectively leaving her behind in terms of being able to speak about sports history, for example, making her road to becoming a bona fide sportista in her current young adult life certainly much harder, if not virtually impossible. Many women are forced into the second category, forever branded as a "learner," who will most likely have a very hard time catching up in terms of accumulating the requisite historical and detailed knowledge of sport that constitutes such a key component of the granting of legitimacy and acceptance as a bona fide sports fan.

Much of America's typical female population, though, falls under the third and forth categories, if not having been influenced by a specific person, then at least by a group or even a cultural focus on a sports team. This pattern helps to explain the origin of another characteristically female act of fandom: focusing on a specific team or player as opposed to an entire sport or multiple sports.

Jeffrey D. James and Lynn L. Ridinger found that once women became fans, "they exhibited strong support towards a specific team; however their level of motivation toward the general sport was not as strong as men's."[79] This characteristic emerges in much of the research that shows women identifying themselves as "fans" as often as men. That is, the way that these women live and understand their fandom (being a *diehard* follower of, for example, the Detroit Red Wings, without knowing players on another NHL team or watching other hockey games) differs markedly from the way that the typical male who identifies as a fan acts.

Citing perhaps differences in aggression and types of play experienced and fostered in childhood, research contends that male spectators focus more closely on the competitive outcome of a game, of the moments of victory and defeat.[80] The most important detail of the game for these male spectators is the designation of a winner and a loser. In notable contrast, it seems as though the women, even while watching the same game, are doing so from a background of "a deeper interest in the athlete and the sport."[81] Whether the root of this

---

[79]Jeffrey D. James and Lynn L. Ridinger, "Female and Male Sport Fans: A Comparison of Sport Consumption Motives," *Journal of Sport Behavior* 25, no. 3 (2002): 260–278; quote from Davis, McDonald, and Karg, "Ticket Holder Satisfaction," 2.

[80]Stephanie Lee Sargent, Dolf Zillmann, and James B. Weaver, III, "The Gender Gap in the Enjoyment of Televised Sports," *Journal of Sport and Social Issues* 22 (1998): 46–64.

d., 47.

difference lay in the gender-typed toys and activities that the different groups were led to as children, innate drives toward aggression and competition, or an unbalanced nurturing pattern that combines both the former and latter components is clearly well beyond the purview of our study as well as our competence and expertise. The consequences of the difference, however, as it plays out on game day, is that females are more often attracted to less violent sports, as well as to the less competitive aspects of sports in general.

Motivations

In the sociology of sport, several different attempts have been made to develop a motivation scale to determine *why* people choose to watch sports. In 1987, a groundbreaking attempt at developing a workable spectator motivation scale was developed and named the Sports Need for Achievement and Power Scale.[82] The scale employed five different motivation theories: salubrious effects, stress and stimulation seeking, catharsis and aggression, entertainment, and achievement seeking. In 1995, Daniel Wann developed the Sport Fan Motivation Scale, a twenty-three-item assessment of eight different motivational categories: stress relief, self-esteem benefits, escape from everyday life, entertainment, economic factors, aesthetics, group affiliation, and family needs.[83] Four years later, in 1999, Robert Madrigal and Dennis Howard created a measurement tool composed of four different categories of motivation: suspense, technical aspects, vicarious achievement, and physical attraction.[84] None of these scales of motivation have been sufficiently used to be considered generally accepted, but they contain elements that are relevant to our discussion of typologies of fans.

The question of *motivation* for engaging in sports consumption is an illustrative component of fandom's picture. To glean the purpose or reason—or in pursuit of what goal—an individual participates in sport consumption is helpful for an understanding of fundamental differences in the typical fandom of women versus that of men. Whereas men are more prone to identify the excitement of the game or the chance to "get psyched" and "let off steam" or escape as a motivation for tuning in to a sports broadcast, women, in contrast, "are more likely to watch because their friends and families are watching," and, similarly, "because it gives them something to do with friends and family."[85]

---

[82]Daniel C. Funk, Daniel F. Mahony, Makoto Nakazawa, and Sumiko Hirakawa, "Development of the Sport Interest Inventory (SII): Implications for Measuring Unique Consumer Motives at Team Sporting Events," *International Journal of Sports Marketing & Sponsorship* 3, no. 3 (2001): 291–316.

[83]Ibid., 293.

[84]Ibid.

[85]Gantz and Wenner, "Men, Women, and Sports," 237.

With this as women's underlying motivation, it is easy to understand why their priorities to take care of household chores and to continue to feed the fans, for example, remain important, even in the case of a strong accompanying desire to watch every second of the game. Ultimately, for most women, it appears that the Super Bowl party is not so much about the Super Bowl, but about the party.

Participation in the consumption of sports, as fundamental a part of contemporary American culture as it can be, is important to most women because of the opportunities that such participation offers for social inclusion. Women often play the role of fostering the environment in which the ardent—mostly male—fans can comfortably indulge in their brand of consumption, characterized by close attention to and emotional investment in the game.

Once one is compelled, by whatever sets of motivations, to pursue sports consumption, many choices still lie ahead. These choices can result in differently perceived levels of fandom. Interestingly, research has demonstrated an existing pattern between a fan's level of intensity concerning an event and the motivations that typically have brought him or her to such a level. The *Miller Lite Report on American Attitudes toward Sports*, published in 1983, outlined clearly seven different activities that encompass the array of participatory options we have as sports fans: watching or listening to sports news, reading the sports page, talking sports with friends, watching sporting events on TV, listening to them on the radio, reading magazines on sports and athletes, and reading books on these subjects. (We submit that the Internet has added a whole new level in terms of both the quantity and quality of sports fandom that a current study of this kind would most definitely include.) The researchers asked respondents about the frequency with which they participated in each of these activities, and from there divided the subjects into four "fan" groups: non-fans, low moderate fans, moderate fans, and "ardent" fans.[86]

Even in a comparison of males and females who are identified as "non-fans," motivational differences in the participation of fandom exist. Male non-fans, in a study by Walter Gantz and Lawrence A. Wenner, scored higher than their female counterparts with regard to the identification of items such as "it gives me something to talk about," "it gets me psyched up," "it is a good way to let off steam," "it lets me relax and unwind," "I like the drama and tension involved," and "to see how my favorite team does" as motivations to watch.[87] That is, it seems that a person's gender is often a stronger indicator of his or her motivations for participation in sports consumption than is his or her actual level of "fandom." Even in a population of non-fans, or people who do not

---

[86]Miller Brewing Company, *Miller Lite Report on American Attitudes toward Sports* (Milwaukee, WI: Miller Brewing Company, 1983).

[87]Gantz and Wenner, "Television and the Sports Viewing Experience," 65.

identify with sports culture, sports still play different roles in the social worlds of men and women.

Celebrity

During the 2010 winter semester, Markovits invited the University of Michigan's punter Zoltan Mesko to address the students in Markovits's large sports class. Markovits befriended Mesko at the latter's arrival as a freshman at the University of Michigan since the two shared a common background, having both been born and raised until the age of nine in the West Romanian city of Timişoara, albeit thirty-eight years apart. They shared, among many things, the languages of Romanian, Hungarian, and German that were commonly used by this city's middle classes since the nineteenth century. And they also shared their love for football, both of the Association and the American kind. Mesko became quite the cult figure during his four-year playing time for the Wolverines, attaining a star-like status often bestowed on a quarterback, a running back, or a wide receiver, way beyond that of a usual punter. Markovits asked Mesko to use his autobiography to describe to the students the cultures that he transcended in his twenty-odd years, from Romania to Ann Arbor, in which sports played a crucial role. After Mesko's erudite lecture, which was rewarded with thunderous applause by the students, Mesko answered an array of questions. Their gendered nature was striking: While every male's question pertained to some aspect of Zoltan Mesko's football playing—the technique used in his punting, the exact round in which he expected to find himself in the forthcoming NFL draft, the ways in which various strategies used by the Wolverines affected his performance as a punter, to mention but a few—every female's question focused on Zoltan Mesko, the person, such as how he coped with immigrating to a Cleveland suburb from Timişoara; how he adjusted to attending an American junior high school; how he managed to learn English; how his grandmother, whom Mesko presented to the class in a picture taken in Michigan Stadium during a football game, which was both the very first game she had attended in her life and her very first visit to the United States, felt among all these crazy fans.

It seems as though, for many women, athletes are celebrities first, people second, and only then athletes, on a much less important level. A female sportswriter attending the 2011 annual meeting of the Association of Women in Sports Media convention in Charlotte, North Carolina, said to Albertson, "I write about people, people who are in the public eye but who have other stories to tell. Those people *happen* to be athletes." Women are interested in the players' personal lives and histories as much as, or perhaps even more than, they are interested in their athletic performances. Women tend to follow athletes in the same way that they follow movie stars and famous musicians. One reads supermarket tabloids about movie stars, not to glean more information about their professional pursuit and the perfecting of their craft, and talent, but rather to gauge the story of a celebrity's life that one cannot obtain at all by seeing the celebrity deploy the very qualities that rendered him or her a celebrity in the first place. This pertains to athletes, just as it does to musicians and actors. Most men are interested in Kevin Durant because of his athletic skill and success as a basketball player earning his living in the NBA: his scoring, rebounding and assist statistics, his ability to run the floor, his leadership qualities on a young and immensely promising team. It is by dint of his sensational numbers and his success on the court that an athlete (a man) like Kevin Durant becomes a celebrity in the first place, but once he is in the public eye to the point where a woman might come to know his name (or at least recognize his picture), she is most interested in his background story and personal life, neither of which is of particular concern to the typical male sports fan.

Unique Female Preferences

Research into actual levels of enjoyment of different sporting events has revealed gendered differences in terms of the aesthetic and competitive values that men and women appreciate in different sports. As spectators, men and women have different "tastes" in sports and recognize as well as value different components of the athletic competition or performance.[88] If participation in viewing appears as an indication of devotion to following sports, it seems that women find less value and enjoyment in the following of the "Big Four" North American hegemonic team sports of football, baseball, basketball, and ice hockey than do men. There are sports programs, though, that women actually report finding more enjoyable to watch than do men. That is, while men are undoubtedly the bigger fans of the sports that have matured to constitute our hegemonic sports culture, female spectators seem to have cornered more niched areas of sports following, in terms of both the *ways* they watch the Big Four as well as the time they spend and the manner in which they watch totally different, usually less popular sports.

Ageliki Nicolopoulou's research, outlined in the first chapter of our book, looked into the differences in storytelling styles of young boys and girls and, in several studies, found that the boys' stories (a word that hardly seems appropriate, given their insanely chaotic nature) were most often centered on the themes of violence and competition, almost always featuring chase scenes, bat-

---

[88]Sargent, Zillmann, and Weaver, "The Gender Gap," 46–64.

tles, and the threat of doom or death.[89] The girls' stories, in contrast, contained characters whose nurturing relationships formed the basis of a far more cohesive plotline that, unlike the boys' stories, did not end with the Lizard King blowing everything to pieces. The stories appear to have parallels in the realm of play, with boys gravitating more toward games involving violence, physical competition, and winners and losers, and girls more often preferring and participating in role-playing activities devoid of competition. The gendered difference in the overall valuation of violence and chaos might be a possible foundation for the different levels of enjoyment that men and women eventually find in sports as a whole.

It does not seem implausible, then, to suggest that these gendered preferences may carry over and manifest themselves in the types of sporting events that men and women eventually find enjoyable to watch. With the very broad generalization of men finding more value and pleasure in violent, competitive, relatively chaotic events, and women being more attracted to and entertained by artistic, aesthetically graceful, relatively gentle pursuits, a closer look into the two groups' evaluations of American football games will further illustrate the different components of the game—and of sports in general—that the two gender groups value and enjoy.

In a 1981 study, Jennings Bryant, Paul Comisky, and Dolf Zillmann compiled an aggregate of different football plays and classified them in terms of their level of aggressiveness.[90] The researchers removed the plays from their contexts within games in an attempt to get a more accurate evaluation of each play as an isolated event. They found that the amount of aggression displayed in each play had a direct positive relationship with the enjoyment that the male subjects reported when watching it. The female subjects' evaluations did not depend as heavily as the males' did on the level of manifest aggression in each play. Most notably, though, the study ascertained that the higher the level of aggression in a particular play, the greater the discrepancy became between the amount of enjoyment reported by the male versus the female groups.

Somewhat similar to the observed gendered preference for aggression is one that emerged for the element of suspense as a relatively common feature of popular sports competitions. In a 1997 study, Gan Su-lin, Charles A. Tuggle, Michael A. Mitrook, Sylvere H. Coussement, and Dolf Zillmann recorded 105 college students' ratings of enjoyment of the second half of eight games from the 1995 NCAA Division I men's basketball tournament better known

---

[89] Ageliki Nicolopoulou, "The Elementary Forms of Narrative Coherence in Young Children's Storytelling," *Narrative Inquiry* 18, no. 2 (2008): 299–325.

[90] Jennings Bryant, Paul Comisky, and Dolf Zillmann, "The Appeal of Rough-and-Tumble Play in Televised Professional Football," *Communication Quarterly* 29 (1981): 246–253.

as March Madness.[91] The games used in the study featured varying levels of suspense in terms of how close they were, with each response being placed into one of four levels of enjoyment. The responses by the women closely resembled those by the men, except, notably, in the case of the most suspenseful "nail-biter" games. In this case, the females' overall enjoyment level dropped to that close to the levels reported for the least close "blowout" games (which got the lowest enjoyment ratings from both the male and female groups). The ratings for both gender groups featured a direct relationship with the suspense levels, until the suspense reached its highest level, at which point the women's enjoyment diminished significantly. This research suggests that one of competitive sports' most highly valued features for men may actually be a deterrent to enjoyment for the typical female viewer.

To return to the study conducted by Sargent, Zillmann, and Weaver, let us now look at a discussion of specific types of sports that men and women have been found to prefer. This particular study employed questionnaires covering such topics as enjoyment, ratings of excitement and boredom, evaluations of violence, activeness, and elegance, and danger, as well as the frequency with which the sport is usually viewed by each study subject.[92] Nine different "clusters" were arranged to include twenty-five different sports, each cluster serving as an attempt to group similar sports; the clusters were then grouped into three categories: combative (football, hockey, basketball, soccer, baseball, boxing, and karate); stylistic (gymnastics, skiing, diving, figure skating, swimming, tennis, and aerobics); and mechanized (fishing, golf, polo, archery, hang gliding, mountain biking, rock climbing, scuba diving, whitewater rafting, hunting, and auto racing).[93]

The combative sports were construed to feature and emphasize "physical strength, stamina, power and domination."[94] One of their most important characteristics is the fact that one party's victory necessarily implies the opposing party's defeat. Within this group, the sporting activities were divided according to the classifications of "violent team," "aggressive team," and "violent individual." Stylistic sports were characterized by "perfection of form" and featured qualities such as grace, mastery of body movements, and elegance. This group included the subheadings "risky," "elegant," and "nonrisky." The main shared feature of the mechanized sports was that they require use of a

[91]Gan Su-lin, Charles A. Tuggle, Michael A. Mitrook, Sylvere H. Coussement, and Dolf Zillmann, "The Thrill of a Close Game: Who Enjoys It and Who Doesn't?," *Journal of Sport and Social Issues* 21, no. 1 (1997): 53–64.

[92]Sargent, Zillmann, and Weaver, "The Gender Gap," 52.

[93]Ibid.

[94]Ibid.

tool, and the group was divided into the subcategories "nonrisky," "active," and "violent."[95]

The study results revealed significant gender difference in the enjoyment of the different sports groups. As a whole, the male respondents recorded the most enjoyment in watching the "violent combative" sports. Their lowest levels of enjoyment were reported in the case of watching "nonrisky mechanized" sports. The females did express enjoyment when watching the combative team sports, but reported the highest level of enjoyment when watching the "risky" and the "elegant stylistic" sports. Just like for men, the women's least favorite sports belonged to the "nonrisky mechanized" category.

It is notable that the evaluations for each sport, in terms of assessing it on the dimensions of violence, activeness, elegance, and danger, did not garner significantly different responses from the male and female groups. That is, the understanding and interpretation of the characteristics of the sports were wholly agreed on and consensual. It was rather in the reporting of how much each of these sports was *enjoyed* that gender differences became apparent. For example, men and women evaluated the different sports similarly in terms of each sport's level of violence, but the males' enjoyment levels were highly correlated (positively) with higher levels of violence, while the women featured negligible to negative correlations between perceived violence and reported enjoyment.[96]

In a follow-up to her study, Sargent undertook a closer examination of specific sports and their featured characteristics. She studied different clips of basketball, boxing, ice hockey, figure skating, golf, and auto racing "so that the varying degree of activity that exists in each predominant sport type" (again, those being combative, stylistic, and mechanized) "was adequately represented."[97] In this study, Sargent sought to isolate the intrinsic characteristics and values within each sport so as to eliminate the potential bias that respondents' personal experiences with *playing* sports could have played in their evaluations of specific sports as *spectators*.

Sargent's results very much replicated those reached by previous research; that is, the male respondents reported the highest levels of enjoyment for the sports that they had rated as being the most "violent, dangerous, raw and ugly," while the women showed the strongest preference for the sports that they evaluated as "refined, elegant, and involving a modest level of activity."[98] Again, a

---

[95]Ibid.

[96]Ibid., 59.

[97]Stephanie Lee Sargent, "Enjoyment of Televised Sporting Events: Evidence of a Gender Gap," *Communication Research Reports* 20, no. 2 (2009): 182–188 (quote from p. 185).

[98]Ibid., 187.

higher level of violence and danger, as perceived by the female subjects, seemed actually to detract from women's enjoyment of a specific sport. As a reflection of this difference, one of the study's findings was that the single most violent, raw, and ugly sport—boxing—was most enjoyed by males and least by females, while the unanimously most elegant sport—figure skating—was least enjoyed by males and most enjoyed by females.[99]

Conclusion

Most women do not consume sports in the same way that most men do. This is not a comparison that we are refuting or challenging in any way. Indeed, the very purpose of this chapter was to confirm the existence of these differences on many levels associated with the following—as opposed to the doing—of sports. We spent time delineating the differences between men's and women's consumption of sports to analyze the norm that informs the latter in the United States and all advanced industrial democracies. We wanted to do so precisely to highlight a small segment of female sports consumers who massively deviate from the world depicted in this chapter. It is this minority of sports-savvy women whom we have labeled our "sportistas." It is to their world that we now turn in our next two chapters. In Chapter 5, we concentrate on the professional sportista, the one who has opted to make the reporting of sports her livelihood. We then follow in Chapter 6 with a presentation of the amateur sportista, for whom sports have become an integral part of quotidian life but remain very much a hobby.

---

[99]Ibid., 186.

5

Sportista I:
Professional Women in the
Contested Space of Sports Media

Issues of Entry and Acceptance

ven if the production of sports has become close to gender equal in the wake of the phenomenal reforms wrought by Title IX and the larger context of increasing women's presence in virtually every public aspect of American culture and society, nearly every other component of the large institution of "sports" belongs to men, including the media, the reporting of sporting events, and their dissemination as well as interpretation. Regardless of the disconnect between being good at sports and being good at pontificating about them (e.g., the group of couch potato sports encyclopedias sitting at the bar, or the nerd on TV who was cut from his Little League team but who is now updating his world on the Texas Rangers' spring training developments in comparison to those of the Chicago White Sox and how each differs in their respective approaches to the teaching of base stealing), sports journalism remains an area in which women's experiences do not mirror those of their male colleagues. Like female IT firm workers, ROTC participants, and engineers, female sports journalists face challenges and barriers to entry, promotion, and, most detrimentally, credibility in this massively male word. Tune in to *SportsCenter* tonight and you may very well find two female anchors running the show, a clear representation of the advancement that women have experienced in the field. A closer look, though, at the systematic and cultural obstacles that these women have overcome historically, and are confronting daily, will reveal the great distances that have yet to be covered before parity in this field is reached, if ever.

Let us concede that a 50-50 male-female representation in all venues of sports media is currently unrealistic and might not even be what women want in terms of altering the continued gender discrimination of our male-dominated public life. After all, as we discussed in previous chapters, women's involvement with and knowledge of sports—other than their production—lags severely behind men's and perhaps offers a correct reflection of women's equanimity toward sports consumption. Maybe women do not want to attain equality with men in terms of the quantity and quality of their sports consumption. Perhaps sports—in stark opposition to politics, business, law, medicine, and other domains—do not represent an area in which equality matters to the hitherto disadvantaged gender. We doubt this to be the case but remain agnostic on the normative aspects of this matter as to why women *should* attain such equality and how, if it were to be reached, it would enhance the inclusive and democratic aspects of our lives and—at a minimum—reduce one of the many obstacles in communication that impede, or most certainly complicate, current relations between men and women. However, given the current reality of the pool of available female sports experts—of sportistas—being woefully smaller than the pool of male experts, it is not surprising that fewer women will rise to become sports journalists in any medium—television, radio, newspaper, or Internet—than men. But it is not in the quantity of the absence of gender equality that we perceive the real issue of gender discrimination in sports journalism. Rather, it is in the quality of the extant structures and discourse where we detect the real problem.

Thus, the crux, in our view, lies in the immensely difficult—perhaps well-nigh impossible—process of attaining full legitimacy for the voice of *any* woman operating as a reporter and interpreter of the hegemonic sports, which remain so heavily male coded. The obstacles are many and multifaceted. First, female journalists had to gain access to the athletes, an absolute sine qua non for doing their job properly since these journalists needed quotes from the athletes for the stories that they had to write and file immediately after games. After years and years of proving themselves as consummate professionals, female journalists have come to be accepted as such by a vast majority of players. Thus, a small group of female sports journalists seems to have attained at least a workable level of legitimacy in the eyes of the players; ditto with their male colleagues in the newsroom and television studio. This, too, did not happen overnight. Just like in the athletes' locker room, so, too, did women sports journalists face a phalanx of male domination in the newsroom, where—to put it mildly—their welcome was anything but hearty. But in this environment, too, the professionalism of these female pioneers eventually won the battle, and as a result, women's presence in the country's sports rooms have come to be accepted. Alas, this does not pertain to perhaps the most important constituents of the journalists' work: the sports consumers in the form of readers, viewers, and listeners. Predominantly male, many of them remain deeply resentful of having women talk sports to them, of having a female voice not only tell them a game's facts but also interpret its many complexities. Somehow women are simply not to know such matters, and if they do, the validity of their voice remains suspect at best, and ignorant and illegitimate at worst. In short, female sports reporters as a collective—of course, there are individual exceptions that merely confirm the rule—have a serious problem in terms of having the authenticity, authority, and legitimacy of their work fully accepted by a vastly male audience.

Making matters more complex still is the clear division between women sports reporters working primarily as print and radio journalists compared with their colleagues in television. Needless to say, the socially charged issues of beauty, sex, and sexuality assume a much less prominent role for the former than they do for the latter. Clearly, virtually all women working on television—sports journalists included—have to conform to the hegemonic male notions of beauty just to be considered for a job. Though immensely powerful, beauty constitutes a highly ambivalent currency for women in many professions, none more so than television-based sports journalism: While beauty represents the absolutely necessary entrance ticket to this profession, it also delegitimizes the woman possessing it by having her views, her opinions—her very work—degraded as being unworthy and not really serious since she clearly got her position by dint of her beauty (partly true!) and ipso facto does not know her stuff (definitively untrue!). Men revere and extol female beauty; however, once it is coupled with professional accomplishment and intelligence, the issue becomes much more complicated, with the very beauty that provided the initial access and attraction mutating into a burdensome force that constantly calls into question the woman's professional legitimacy. While beauty still remains major currency for women, it often comes with the serious cost of diminished legitimacy in the perception of a woman's intelligence and intellectual output and standing.[1] With sports expertise lacking any of the crucial credentialing mechanisms that we discussed in Chapter 2, an attractive television reporter quickly becomes a "babe" or a "pretty face," regardless of how well she knows

---

[1] It would be way beyond the purview of this book to discuss in any manner worthy of the topic the creation of female beauty's often impeding and most certainly tension-producing dimensions in men's acceptance of female intelligence and mental prowess. Just think how the U.S. Navy refused to take seriously Hedy Lamarr's invention that undoubtedly would have benefited its efforts during World War II in good part because of Lamarr's great beauty. See Richard Rhodes's wonderful book *Hedy's Folly: The Life and Breakthrough Inventions of Hedy Lamarr, the Most Beautiful Woman in the World* (New York: Doubleday, 2011). For many men, women are either beautiful or intelligent, but never both. When Markovits asked his late father (1911–1990) once what the profession of one of his acquaintances in Vienna was, the old man answered earnestly and without any sense of irony, "beautiful woman!" In no way did the elder Markovits mean anything untoward by this, as in this woman's prostituting or somehow commodifying her body in the style of Julia Roberts in *Pretty Woman*: Far from it. To that generation of men—and most certainly in Central Europe—female beauty was tantamount to a bona fide full-time profession of the finest order.

her material. With no Cal Techs and MITs legitimating sports knowledge and expertise, sports consumers (mostly men) remain completely free as to what credentialing criteria they accept as offering full legitimacy to a female sports reporter's work. While "looks" and physical appearance clearly matter to the job prospects of male television reporters, this consideration does not come close to the potency that it has for their female colleagues. If anything, in the world of sports, "schlumpy"-looking men might indeed enjoy greater legitimacy than their handsome counterparts in terms of the perception of their acumen and the authority of their knowledge in the eyes of sports consumers. Without mentioning the names of an array of male sports mavens, we leave it up to the reader to confirm our statement by picking his or her very own favorite male television sports gurus who fit the bill quite nicely.

The State of the Art

Data on journalism school students make a patently clear point: For the past two decades, their female graduates exceed or are, at a minimum, on par with men in journalism jobs, as well as many other positions of all types, but not in sports. A 2006 article produced by the Sports Journalism Association reports that "While it was common 30 or 40 years ago to see disparity between the genders, this is no longer the case in areas such as medicine and law, nor, judging by the number of women in senior positions elsewhere in the newsroom, in journalism."[2] This pattern also pertains to other advanced industrial democracies that report similar statistics coming from their news desks. In Britain, in 2006, it was reported that "the editors of *The Sun*, *The Sunday Mirror*, *The Sunday Telegraph* and London's *Evening Standard* are all women," and many of the region's other major newspapers have had female editors at some point in their past. "Yet there has yet to be a woman sports editor of a national newspaper in Britain."[3] Ever! At the 2006 World Cup, arguably one of Britain's (and most of Europe's) largest and most important sports events—and one that only happens every four years—there was literally only one female journalist in Germany representing a British newspaper among surely close to one hundred men from all the British sports media.

In the United States, the majority of journalism students at universities are female, and in some cases, overwhelmingly so. Thus, for example, at the University of California, Berkeley, for the incoming journalism program in the

---

[2] Sports Journalists' Association, "Sports Journalism—Women's Final Frontier?" posted in Journalism News, Sports Digest, September 6, 2006, available at www.sportsjournalists.co.uk/sports-digest/sports-journalism-womens-final-frontier/ (accessed July 17, 2011).

[3] Ibid.

fall of 2009, 34 percent of the students were male and 66 percent were female.[4] Women have been attaining graduate degrees in journalism in significantly greater numbers than men have. However, reports suggest that women only account for around 12 percent of sports news teams at American newspapers, radio stations, and television channels.[5] This disparity is not really surprising; it does not seem strange that many more men than women might choose to put their journalism degree to use behind a sports desk as opposed to in other departments. Most men love sports, and most women don't, so, presumably, many more men would choose to work in an area so dear to their hearts and so congruent with their intellectual interests. While this may account for part of the massive gender gap still extant in sports journalism, reports on hiring practices, as well as women's experiences when attempting to enter this particular profession, point to additional impediments featuring more insidious procedures and practices that might be keeping women out.

In the 2008 Racial and Gender Report Card of the Associated Press Sports Editors, the Associated Press Sports Editors received, on an A–F scale, straight "F's" in every category related to "gender hiring in key positions," including "Total Staffs," "Sports Editors," "Assistant Sports Editors," "Columnists," "Reporters," and "Copy Editors/Designers."[6] The study found that, in the United States and Canada, 94 percent of the APSE sports editors, 90 percent of assistant sports editors, 93 percent of columnists, 91 percent of reporters, and 84 percent of copy editors/designers were men. The numbers also represented a *decrease* in female representation, with the 2006 numbers showing that women made up 12.6 percent of staffs at APSE newspapers and websites, and the 2008 report indicating a drop to 11.5 percent.[7] The numbers tell part of the story, but more significant is that these important media institutions received "F's" for their gendered hiring practices. This sheds light on the fact that the vast numerical disparities in sports writing's gender composition should not be merely construed as reflecting a difference in the career preferences of male and female journalists; instead, they are reflective of concerted efforts to maintain sports as a male domain.

---

[4]Berkeley Graduate School of Journalism, "Admissions," available at http://journalism.berkeley.edu/admissions/admissionsinfo/ (accessed May 31, 2011).

[5]Sports Journalists' Association, "Women's Final Frontier?"

[6]2008 Racial and Gender Report Card of the Associated Press Sports Editors, available at www.tidesport.org/RGRC/2008/2008_APSE_RGRC_Press_Release.pdf (accessed June 11, 2011).

[7]Comparing these numbers with those in other areas of journalism further highlights the uniqueness of sports' disparities. In 2007, for example, a study found that men reported 48 percent of stories on all news programming on ABC, CBS, and NBC during a sample one-week period, women 40 percent, and the remaining was reported on by a joint male-female team (Media Report to Women, Sheila Gibbons, updated August 2010). At this time, full-time positions held by women at daily newspapers was reported to be 37 percent.

Research finds that, in terms of "hard" credentials, women are not fall-ing behind men. In a study by Marie Hardin, Jason Genovese, and Nan Yu, a survey was administered to 216 individuals who were identified as "sports reporters," "sports anchors," or "sports directors" on television sports news teams in large (Top 50) markets.[8] The study found that 62.5 percent of all of the subjects graduated from college with degrees in journalism, notably with *no* reported difference between men and women in terms of this statistic.[9] Men and women did not report differences in their histories of working with cam-pus media, but significant differences were found in terms of internship expe-rience, revealing women to have actually had more experience in this area than men. The findings showed that 94.1 percent of female sports broadcasters sur-veyed in this study reported having completed journalism-related internships while in college, while only 69.2 percent of males confirmed the same.[10] Given the specificity of the survey population, which focused on directors, anchors, and reporters in Top 50 markets, the finding that women possessed stron-ger "hard" credentials than the men—at least in terms of tangible facts listed on a resume—may perhaps reflect credentialing's democratizing and access-enhancing dimensions found in other male-dominated realms. This inter-pretation becomes especially salient when assessing the fact that, of the entire survey population in this study, 41 percent of the males were "sports direc-tors," while only 11.8 percent of women carried this title.[11] Even in the case of the female subgroup being more qualified "on paper" than the male subgroup, women did not appear to be enjoying any better placement within their profes-sional organizations and, in fact, they confronted skepticism about their being qualified to garner any type of sports broadcasting job in any position.

Encouraging Figures?

Tuning into any of the four major of the nine cable networks in 2005 would have allowed one to see 127 female sportscasters, an undeniable leap forward from decades past in terms of female representation.[12] These women, though,

---

[8]Marie Hardin, Jason Genovese, and Nan Yu, "Privileged to Be on Camera: Sports Broadcasters Assess the Role of Social Identity in the Profession," available at http://citation.allacademic.com//meta/p_mla_apa_research_citation/2/7/1/5/5/pages271552/p271552-14.php (accessed June 20, 2011).

[9]Ibid., 14.

[10]Ibid.

[11]Ibid., 13.

[12]Heather Michelle Toro, "Public Perceptions of Credibility of Male and Female Sportscast-ers" (doctoral dissertation, Virginia Polytechnic Institute and State University, Blacksburg, VA, 2005), 4.

combined to report on fewer than 29 percent of all sports stories (a result of the fact that many of them do not cover men's sports, i.e., the topic that provides the vast majority of popular sports news).[13] When looking at more than three hundred daily newspapers in the country in 2006, Mary Lou Sheffer and Brad Schultz found women to comprise 12.6 percent of sports staffs, again a sign of a move forward from the situation of the past. Research conducted in 2007 hinted at gender parity in the hiring of sports reporters, with 51 percent of male and 50 percent of female news directors interviewed reporting having hired a female for an on-air sports position. Another encouraging finding was that, among news directors with fewer than ten years' experience, men were even *more* likely than women to hire a woman for on-air positions (compared with the subgroup of presumably older individuals who had been involved in the industry for eleven or more years).[14]

Still, Jane McManus's research with the Curley Center for Sports Journalism at Penn State University reports that "the numbers of women in sports journalism haven't increased in a decade."[15] She continues, answering her own question, "Why don't women stick around? Here's a guess: With just a few female sports reporters in any given market, the gender remains a novelty. A segment of each new class of young women is constantly fighting to gain the same ground a generation before thought it had already established."[16]

Help: Wisdom from Veterans

Perhaps unsurprisingly, there is evidence that female news directors hire significantly more women sportscasters than do their male counterparts.[17] This means that a paucity of women at the top only compounds the problem of having a larger number of women entering the profession. In a pattern that plays out in other male-dominated realms and that has been delineated in previous chapters, there is no chicken because there is no egg, and vice versa. Christine Brennan recalls thinking of her career prospects: "A sports writer? Did women do such things? It sounds ridiculous now. But that is the power of role models,

---

[13]Ibid.

[14]Mary Lou Sheffer and Brad Schultz, "Double Standards: Why Women Have Trouble Getting Jobs in Local Television Sports" (paper presented at the International Communication Association in San Francisco, May 2007), 16.

[15]Jane McManus, "It Gets Better. 'Til Then, Wear a Wedding Band," January 14, 2011, available at http://espn.go.com/espnw/news-opinion/6015645/it-gets-better-til-wear-wedding-band (accessed February 21, 2011).

[16]Ibid.

[17]Sheffer and Schultz, "Double Standards," 17.

or in this case, a lack thereof."[18] At the 2011 Association for Women in Sports Media (AWSM) conference, one of the veteran female journalists echoed the importance of supportive people being in positions of authority to help women enter the field and give them a chance to rise to the top one day. "The young women today are dealing with the same stuff I was," the speaker explained. "If they're lucky though, they have a good editor that they can go to."

During a panel discussion at the same conference, one of the presenters offered three pieces of advice, after first explaining that her initial idealistic approach as a new journalist ("I'm just going to be the best at everything and I'll surely make it to a management position!") was not realistic.[19] The first was to "live with your reality," a common notion that was echoed by many women throughout the conference. It is, on the one hand, fascinating, and, on the other, quite telling that all of these women seem to share a common belief that a keen awareness of "their reality" (i.e., minority, token, novelty, oddity, outlier, second string, clearly some status within their organizations that is not a priori positive, even if it is not outright negative and hostile) is necessary to have a chance at succeeding in their chosen profession. Concretely, all of these women live with a keen sense that this "reality" is not something to combat, but rather something to be worked around somehow, diplomatically and with humor, and that, hopefully, with time, the male environment will accept and even appreciate them and their work, even if it will rarely fully incorporate them as one of its own. "Be yourself, but be prepared to adjust to the situation you're in," an industry veteran reiterated.[20] "Stay away from stereotypical woman's behavior!" one presenter urged, "and you better learn to communicate with the men the way they want to be communicated with," she continued. One of her colleagues added further specificity to this advice: "Don't bob your head up and down while people are talking! The men don't ever do it, so you shouldn't either."[21] In a visit to Markovits's sports class on December 8, 2011, Joanne Gerstner described to the students in riveting detail her decision to become a sports journalist and the travails she encountered, particularly in the early days of her career. She made it clear that she was determined from day one not to tolerate any kind of sexist denigration of herself or her work and that she would fight such in all venues available to her. But she also informed

---

[18]Christine Brennan, *Best Seat in the House: A Father, a Daughter, a Journey Through Sports* (New York: Scribner, 2008), 95.

[19]Ann Caulkins, panel discussion "Q & A with the Veterans," Association of Women in Sports Media Conference, Charlotte, NC, June 24, 2011.

[20]Judy Rose, panel discussion "Q & A with the Veterans," Association of Women in Sports Media conference, Charlotte, NC, June 24, 2011.

[21]Caulkins, panel discussion "Q & A with the Veterans."

the students that she would not have survived the first ten minutes of the first day in the newsroom—let alone become a successful sports journalist who has flourished in her job and loves it—had she objected to the tenor of regular guy talk banter, with all of its innuendos, put-downs, and off-color humor.

The second piece of advice was to "get a great mentor," either female (if one is lucky) or a supportive male (as is often the case, given that there are only a handful of females in top positions as sports writers). The presenter explained that her promotions would not have happened had her mentors not been actively advocating for her. This, of course, is not unique to the world of sports media, and this situation was detailed in earlier chapters as a barrier that women in many male-dominated professions face.

The last piece of advice was to "be tough, and don't downplay your achievements," which is a lot easier said than done, and is a complex conundrum that takes us all the way back to Chapter 1, as well as our discussion on stereotype threat in Chapter 2, in which we delineated that self-doubt and deprecation can have real consequences in terms of performance.

Challenges with Discrimination and Resentment

Jacquelin Magnay, the woman who brought the case to the Human Rights and Equal Opportunities Commission in 1994, which accorded all reporters (including women) full and equal access to locker rooms at sports venues, wrote, as recently as 2002, about the continued antagonistic culture of sports media toward women, describing "the desperation of men to keep the game a male-only domain," and a "culture of harassment of women journalists who cover Rugby League," notably *the* most significant component of hegemonic sports culture in Sydney, the city in which she lives and writes for the *Sydney Morning Herald*.[22] Marie Hardin and Stacie Shain found the following in their research on female sports journalists:

---

[22]Sports Journalists' Association, "Women's Final Frontier?" We mention that Rugby League is Sydney's hegemonic sport to highlight that the resistance that these women journalists face is less pronounced when they cover sports or events that are less popular with the hegemonic sports audience—men. Many of the women in AWSM, for example, explained that they loved to cover soccer (in the United States) or the Olympics for the room that those events give them to write about the "story behind the story," or the human interest angle, as well as the fact that there was not such fierce competition to get those beats or assignments. "I always loved Olympic sports . . . soccer and tennis . . . they're really untapped because everyone wanted to cover the Big Four—you can really move up fast in other areas," one of our interviewees shared. In response to why she prefers to cover the Olympics, another woman explained, "You really get to stretch as a writer; it's the best! You get to write about the dad who raised the money for his kid to compete, and see the parents crying in the stands . . . that's the beauty of the Olympics." Once again, we have confirmation of one of our book's main arguments that when women attempt to "intrude" on what is sacred space to males (i.e., hegemonic sports culture), the women confront serious male resistance, resentment, and hostility.

Most respondents believed that opportunities for women are better than ever but that female sports journalists have a tougher job than do men and that women in sports media are not taken as seriously by fans as are men doing the same jobs. More than half of their respondents reported that they had experienced on-the-job discrimination, and 72 percent indicated that they had considered leaving their careers.[23]

In a subsequent article, the authors showed convincingly that, at least in 2005, women were nowhere close to being where men were in the world of sports journalism.[24] Things have undoubtedly improved in the past seven years, but the gap remains deep and wide.

In 2005, Joanne Gerstner, then president of the AWSM, described the experience of being a female sports writer with the following words: "You look different, you are different, and you might not fit into the paradigm of how that editor feels his paper should look. I've had [AWSM] members tell me stories of applying for [jobs as] editors or columnists, only to be told that the paper wasn't 'ready' to have a woman in that position."[25]

Pressures

According to Ted Kian's research, "Once they enter the profession, female and male sportswriters have many different gender-specific experiences, which lead to different attitudes and views toward women in the profession. In general, men are treated as the 'standard' in sports writing, while women are considered 'the other' in the profession."[26]

Female sports journalists report a "lack of respect directly related to their gender from male colleagues and fans as a regular part of their work experience."[27] Our interviewees informed us that they faced animosity for their mere presence, with many of their male colleagues assuming, without knowing any-

---

[23]Marie Hardin and Stacie Shain, "How Women in Sports Media Assimilate into Their Careers: A Survey of Practitioners" (paper presented at the Association for Education in Journalism and Mass Communication, San Antonio, TX, 2005), 15.

[24]Marie Hardin and Stacie Shain, "Female Sports Journalists: Are We There Yet? 'No,'" *Newspaper Research Journal* 6, no. 4 (2005): 22–35.

[25]Joanne Gerstner, "Women Aren't Getting a Fair Shake in Sports, Either," *Newspaper Research Journal* 26, no. 4 (2005): 20, March 8, 2005, available at http://www.editorandpublisher.com/eandp/search/search_results_taxo.jsp?id=1128527100344 (accessed June 17, 2011).

[26]Edward (Ted) M. Kian, "Gender in Sports Writing by the Print Media: An Explanatory Examination of Writers' Experience and Attitudes," *The SMART Journal* 4, no. 1 (2007): 5–26 (quote from p. 11).

[27]Ibid., 7.

thing about these women's professional backgrounds, that they received the job as a "diversity hire" (or, notably, as a "pretty face") who will not contribute anything to the coverage or interpretation of sports by virtue of lacking the requisite knowledge.

Research shows that females entering sports broadcasting in search of being taken seriously as expert sports reporters—being viewed and treated in identical ways to their male colleagues—feel that they must, from day one, outperform their male counterparts to stand a chance at eventually being accepted as legitimate. "Because women are perceived to be less qualified than men, they feel they are held to a higher standard. Andrea Kremer, a veteran female sports broadcaster and journalist, says that, as she sees it, if ESPN anchor Chris Berman makes a mistake, it's just a slip; If *SportsCenter* anchor [Linda] Cohn gets something wrong, she doesn't know what she's talking about."[28] John Shannon, the NHL's senior vice president of broadcasting, seconds this notion by confirming that women broadcasters need to be "20 percent better" than their male counterparts to be accepted as credible journalists by a largely male audience. "If they make one mistake, they're going to get hammered [by sports fans and the media]," Shannon said.[29]

Linda Cohn, one of the most prominent and respected women in sports media, cites an example of how men and women are judged differently. "Let's just say I'm hosting *SportsCenter* on ESPN and a baseball score comes in and it's 14–7," she said. "And I'm kidding around and I say the Red Sox beat the Yankees by a touchdown, just for a joke, which is done all the time. You can bet there would be phone calls and e-mail. 'Doesn't she know sports? What is she talking about?' I've been at ESPN for 16 years and been in the business for over 20. But even at this stage in my career, I can't say that."[30]

To be sure (and fair), plenty of men in the industry are aware of this challenge for women, as is exemplified by one veteran male sports reporter's admission that "when a boss has a male come in and say, 'I know a lot about sports and this is what I want to do,' unfortunately, that's different than if a woman walked in and said, 'I know a lot about sports.'"[31] Even to be considered for hiring, it seems, women are already called on to "prove" their expertise in ways that are not required of men, most likely because of the assumption that any man seeking entry into the world of sports already comes with the requisite

---

[28]William Houston, "Looks First, Knowledge Later," December 20, 2008, available at http://www.theglobeandmail.com/sports/looks-first-knowledge-later/article729251 (accessed June 10, 2011).

[29]Ibid.

[30]Ibid.

[31]Kian, "Gender in Sports Writing," 13.

background and, most importantly, possesses a vast array of sports knowledge. While this assumption is, in many cases, a safe and accurate one, the perpetuation of the cycle that reinforces it is only bolstered by an exclusion of truly knowledgeable, talented women sports broadcasters, simply because of their gender. Thus, it is surely the case that more men than women can "speak sports" with fluency, but it is a blatantly unfair practice (not to mention one that feeds the aforementioned cycle) to assume, even in the case of equal credentials, a woman's seemingly innate inferiority for a job in sports, merely based on her gender.

Our culture essentializes in both directions: As a baseline, we assume that all men know sports and all women do not. But there is a notable difference in the quality and consequence of these two essentializations. Men, as a rule are not punished for being exceptions, for opting out of the norm, for not knowing sports, with the possible exception of bearing the cost of not being one of the guys. However, there are no tangible, job-related consequences for men breaking this norm.

This, alas, is not the case for women. Here, the norm breakers are punished by the very group whom they are trying to join via the very act of norm breaking. The costs here are not only potential informal sanctions by one's own gender, as is the case for men—though, to most women, it is completely immaterial whether a woman knows or does not know sports—but also very real losses and tangible disadvantages experienced daily in the labor market and at work.

The aforementioned study by Sheffer and Schultz looked into the issues of demographic identification and managerial decisions for sportscasters in which news directors were given questionnaires and phone interviews meant to illuminate any differences in the expectations for men versus women in the industry. One of this study's questions addressed the issue of differing expectations, illustrated by the tested hypothesis that "managers hold female sports broadcasters to a different standard than male broadcasters in terms of abilities, work roles and job performance."[32]

With regard to this question, Sheffer and Schultz found that the respondent group, as a whole (made up of news directors from different national markets, who were 79 percent male), did *not* believe that the standards to which their sportscasters are held differ based on gender. This majority male group's understanding of this process, however, did not match that of the subgroup of female news directors (the remaining 21 percent of the whole sample); after the results were segregated based on gender, the *female* news directors *confirmed*

---

[32]Sheffer and Schultz, "Double Standards," 12.

the hypothesis that women sportscasters are held to a higher standard than their male colleagues.[33]

This finding, based on quantitative research, was echoed by our own interviews with female sports journalists. As seems to be the experience of women in most male-dominated domains, heightened expectations apply to them as women compared with their male coworkers. "Like many women in fairly non-traditional positions," Sheffer and Schultz write, "women sportscasters are still held to a higher standard because there is greater attention to their true abilities."[34]

This quote confirms that the intensified scrutiny that women face in their work can be seen as a reaction to an underlying assumption that their abilities *are*, in fact, inferior. That is, if a person tunes in to a sports broadcast with the understanding or expectation that it is a place for men (a reasonable understanding, given the reality of women's lack of visibility in significant sports broadcasting roles), it is reasonable to assume that this person will watch the broadcast in hopes or in search of an affirmation of his underlying assumptions; he will most likely identify the same subtle missteps, if taken by a man and a woman, as more damaging when perpetrated by the female. We wrote earlier about how a playground supervisor may identify and react to "aggressiveness" in boys more often than in girls, presumably because of an *expectation* that the boys are more likely to be aggressive and not necessarily because of a real difference in behavior. In a similar process, a viewer of a female-delivered broadcast of a male-performed team sport will likely be primed and scouring for a slip-up on the part of the broadcaster because that is what the viewer expects, based on the notion that the female broadcaster is out of place and possesses inferior knowledge. Our discussion of stereotype threat in Chapter 2 pertains to this point. In an interview, a female news director averred, "I think it is such a stereotypically male profession that women must outperform."[35]

"Diversity Hires"

Another complicating issue for women in sports media is their minority status, as well as the discrediting that they often face as others (mainly men) in the industry maintain that the women who are there are the beneficiaries of affirmative action–type hiring practices. The concept of a "diversity hire," or

---

[33]Ibid., 12.

[34]Ibid., 22.

[35]Ibid.

a person who was hired solely to satisfy (often legal, sometimes self-imposed) demographic quotas, and not necessarily because of the possession of credentials and the mastery of skills, is a common impediment to women's pursuit of credibility and respect in sports media, even though (as quoted in Kian, "Gender in Sports Writing") Marie Hardin found that "only 59 percent of surveyed sport editors felt they had any obligation to have female representation on their staffs."[36] In his compilation of the "different gender-specific experiences" that men and women face in sports journalism, Ted Kian found that the issue of perceived preferential hiring was substantial in terms of differentiating women's experiences from men's. "Male reporters believe that female sportswriters receive preferential hiring and treatment from management due to their sex. This, in turn, leads to some animosity toward female journalists amongst the mostly male sports staff members," Kian summarizes.[37]

Women do not necessarily, as a whole, refute the notion that their minority status may help them enter into sports media. In Hardin, Genovese, and Yu's research, there was interesting disagreement among the study respondents, particularly pertaining to the following statement: "My gender was part of the reason I was hired into sports broadcasting."[38] When responses were categorized based on the gender of respondents, a significant difference appeared: Female sportscasters were *less likely to disagree* with this statement, or were more likely to assert that their gender *did* have something to do with their being hired than did their male colleagues.[39]

It seems that, for women, the benefits of being a "minority hire" may end on entry. That is, while many women understand that, in the words of veteran male reporter Bill Jones,[40] even though a position may not have been "advertised for a woman . . . the position was created with a woman in mind," most women do not believe that they are advantaged in terms of being *promoted* or

---

[36]Marie Hardin, "Stopped at the Gate: Women's Sports, 'Reader Interest,' and Decision-Making by Editors," *Journalism & Mass Communication Quarterly* 82, no. 1 (2005): 62–77.

[37]Kian, "Gender in Sports Writing," 11.

[38]Hardin, Genovese, and Yu, "Privileged," 15–16.

[39]One interpretation of this finding can take cues from research that has found that those individuals who (believe that they) are in subordinate positions or even who "have internalized a second-class status in their organizations," as research has shown many women in sports broadcasting to have done within their institution, are often "inculcated to adopt attitudes that justify their disadvantage" (Hardin, Genovese, and Yu, 82). This work points to the possibility that those women who reported the belief that their gender influenced their being hired may be simply buying into the dominant view that their presence must be explained by some means besides their credentials, experience, and talent; even as victims of such male chauvinist perceptions and attitudes, these women may, to some extent, buy into them and understand their experience in terms dictated by them. See the discussion of stereotype threat in Chapter 2.

[40]Kian, "Gender in Sports Writing," 12.

otherwise advancing their careers within the industry. Shelley Smith, a seasoned reporter herself, voices this opinion:

> A lot of people I remember would say, "Oh, you're a woman in sports. That's considered a minority and that's really cool, because you're going to end up getting whatever you want." Well, actually for the most part at least in the last five or six years from what I've seen it hasn't worked that way at all. In fact, I feel that it has worked against women.[41]

As part of a focus group at the AWSM convention in 2004, a twenty-year veteran copy editor echoed Smith's impression that once "quotas" are met, a woman is often at a disadvantaged position compared with her male colleagues, whose entry may have initially been more contested. "There are no women in management, but I can't imagine a man, you know, applying [for] a sports editor opening and [management] saying, 'Oh, they already have a man.' They aren't going to do that," this woman explained. Referring to the fact that their minority status often transforms from a means of advantage to one of tokenization, she continued, "When they get their woman, they got their woman."[42]

It seems as though there are few "safe" places for women in sports media, where their presence is neither resented nor actively resisted. We will now examine the avenues to inclusion and legitimation in the eyes of colleagues as well as audiences that are most commonly available to women.

Avenues to Credibility (Not Just Entry)

One way for a woman to enhance—though far from guarantee—her credibility in the world of sports media is to have arrived at her position by way of having been an elite athlete. Clearly, having played a sport at a top competitive level bestows at least some credibility to speak about that sport with authority. While it is not the only route to expertise and authority as a sports commentator, having been an elite sports producer gives one the aura of being able to interpret at least that very sport to its consumers. What is most notable about this route to legitimacy and acceptance, though, is that it effectively excludes women from being authoritative interpreters of at least three of the Big Four sports. That is, no woman, in North American sports culture, can make a

---

[41]Ibid.

[42]Focus group participant, Association for Women in Sports Media Annual Convention (Milwaukee, WI, June 4–6, 2004), taken from Hardin and Shain, "Are We There Yet?," 29.

name for herself in baseball, football, or hockey. Thus, no woman will, then, be able to find her way to the booth at an MLB, NFL, or NHL game by way of this career path and attain prominence as a broadcaster, much less an interpreter, of games in these three sports. Interestingly, and tellingly, basketball furnishes an important exception in that a number of women who were former star players in the game—Doris Burke, Cheryl Miller, Nancy Lieberman being perhaps the most prominent—have indeed parlayed their excellence on the court, even if "only" in the women's game, into prominent positions in the broadcasting of top-level men's NBA and Division I college games.[43] Doris Burke has also become a much-respected analyst of NBA games. As such, one should perceive her career as a rare, perhaps singular, success by having reached the pinnacle in sports journalism and broadcasting in that she has been accorded the authority not only to call a game but also to evaluate, analyze, and criticize it and its male players. We would be remiss not to mention Pam Ward and Beth Mowins as well-established play-by-play announcers for televised Division I college football games. This is all the more remarkable—and exceptional—because, clearly, neither of these women attained their nationally prominent positions by having been former stars on the gridiron. Lastly, we need to acknowledge Suzyn Waldman, the longtime play-by-play radio voice of none other than the venerable New York Yankees, and Renel Brooks-Moon, the public address announcer at AT&T Park, home of the San Francisco Giants.

Sports Illustrated reported in 1991 that women held "less [*sic*] than 20% of the on-camera sports jobs at ABC, CBS, NBC and ESPN," but that this percentage did not accurately represent women's presence in the field, because many of the women included in this number were only invited on air every four years to report on the Olympic sport in which they competed.[44] It seems as though people were ready to accept that, for example, a former Olympic swimmer might be capable of reporting credibly on Olympic swimming or, as has been the case, in soccer's World Cup (both men and women), a former female soccer star clearly possesses the authority to give her views on the game and its players. Note, of course, that the Olympics as well as soccer World Cups are quadrennial events that do not constitute integral parts of the quotidian North American hegemonic sports culture featuring the Big Four. Underlining soccer's continued marginality to the core of American sports culture is the fact that former women stars like Julie Foudy have regularly served as color commentators of the men's game, thus, in essence, having the liberty, indeed the task, to interpret and criticize it to the television viewers. Julie Foudy and Brandi Chastain

---

[43]Carolyn Peck and Kara Lawson have been ESPN's long-time studio analysts of—thus voices of authority on—WNBA as well as women's Division I college basketball games.

[44]Sally Jenkins, "Who Let Them in?" *Sports Illustrated*, June 17, 1991: 80.

have been the only women who—with Doris Burke in basketball—have parlayed their excellence on the playing field in the women's game into becoming
authoritative analysts and thus inevitable critics of the men's game. A parallel phenomenon in Europe or Latin America is unthinkable where soccer, of
course, is *the* most crucial ingredient of hegemonic sports culture and thus remains the solid purview of exclusively male voices, views, and interpretations.[45]

It is notable, though, that a woman's specific athletic success affords her
credibility to report only on "her sport," but does not extend further by bestow-
ing her authority to report or interpret other sports. This constitutes a telling
contrast to the situation for men, for whom a background as an athlete is far
from a necessary requirement to be viewed as a credible commentator on and a
respectable interpreter of a bevy of sports. It might be the basis for one's inclusion as a color commentator, but former athletic prowess need not—and most
often does not—serve as a basis for a man's credibility as a sports maven. A
man can be a couch potato and a sports expert. Such a combination is impossible in a woman's case.

Dana Wakiji, in an interview, spoke to this clearly, saying, "I've never
played in the NFL, but neither has Bob Costas, but he's a perfectly legitimate,
credible sportscaster . . . so I always thought that [having to be an athlete in
order to be a credible reporter] was a silly argument."[46] Wakiji could have
added the NBA and MLB to the NFL, in neither of which Costas had ever
played, although this did not prevent him from becoming one of the country's most respected interpreters of all three (and then some), bordering on
being a veritable baseball sage and savant. Costas, of course, is not the exception, but the rule. Such iconic figures of American sports journalism and television mainstays as Chris Berman, Al Michaels, Bob Ley, and, of more recent
vintage, Mike Tirico, just to name a few, have attained unparalleled gravitas in

---

[45]Even though soccer's image in the United States, both domestically and most decidedly by the rest
of the world, is that of a "feminized" team sport, Messner's research of his children's American
Youth Soccer Organization league in Southern California reveals just how dominant men remain
in this purportedly "feminized" sport, even at its most youthful level, let alone at its higher echelons: "Among the league's head coaches, 133 were men and 23 were women. The division among
the league's assistant coaches was similarly skewed. Each team also had a team manager who was
responsible for organizing snacks, making reminder calls about games and practices, organizing
team parties and the end-of-the-year present for the coach. The vast majority of team managers
were women." These women were regularly referred to as "team mom." Still, when compared with
Little League baseball, Messner cites a study that reveals an even greater paucity of women in that
sport on a comparable level, thus revealing soccer's relatively greater integration of women, but
not, we would argue, by dint of Title IX, as Messner submits, but purely by virtue of its being apart
from the country's Big Four hegemonic sports cultures. Michael A. Messner, "Barbie Girls Versus
Sea Monsters: Children Constructing Gender" in *The Sport and Society Reader*, ed. David Karen
and Robert E. Washington (New York: Routledge, 2010), 186, 192.

[46]Dana Wakiji, interview with the authors, April 25, 2011.

their stature as sports journalists without—at least to our knowledge—having distinguished themselves as athletes on any playing fields.

The second route to a less contested career in sports media is to choose to cover non-hegemonic sports, meaning none of the Big Four in the United States. As Ann Killion explained, "It was easy to get into soccer because it was clearly important in the rest of the world . . . but not in the US." She shared that "in '94, no one at my newspaper wanted to cover the soccer World Cup. The general columnists had zero interest in it, and so I said *of course* I want to cover it!"[47]

The prevalence and prominence of women soccer commentators, analysts, and experts on American television furnishes a perfect example of how such authority figures have become more or less accepted in sports that clearly do not comprise a society's hegemonic sports culture. Thus, for example, it was clear that during the Women's World Cup held in Germany in the summer of 2011, which became a huge ratings success in the United States, women were the major analysts and color commentators of all of the games. Other than the studio anchor Bob Ley, the fine play-by-play announcer Ian Darke, and Tony DiCicco who, of course, was the solidly victorious and multiple top-level tournament-winning coach of the United States national women's team between 1994 and 1999, garnering, among others, the gold medal at the Atlanta Olympics in 1996, the very first time that women's soccer had become an Olympic sport, and the world championship in 1999, culminating in that infamous Brandi Chastain jersey-shedding penalty-shootout-clinching victory at the Rose Bowl, all of ESPN's major commentators on the tournament in Germany were women, such as the aforementioned Brandi Chastain and her former teammate Julie Foudy, with their former teammate Mia Hamm also making the occasional appearance.

There is a third promising method of entry, but not necessarily an avenue to credibility, that women have employed since their first appearances in the visual domain of sports media: fulfilling the role of the "pretty puppet." It is to a brief discussion of the complex issue of sports, beauty, women, and intelligence that we now turn.

History: Beauty Queens from the Start

Women had their first experiences as sports anchors during the 1970s, most likely, many believe, because of pressure felt by stations to comply with the FCC's post–Civil Rights Act regulations regarding minority representation in

---

[47]Ann Killion, interview with the authors, May 23, 2011.

hiring (recall our "diversity hire" discussion). While the number of women on sports programs increased noticeably, it was clear that these women were not accorded the same role as their male co-anchors. As one veteran male news director explained, "Most men are sports fans . . . and are largely ignorant knuckle draggers easily threatened by women; hence women anchors are not accepted by fans."[48]

Heather Michelle Toro writes that, during this time, "rarely were women with actual knowledge of different sports *and* broadcast experience hired to fill network positions."[49] Even when women were discovered and hired by virtue of having possessed both of these skills, such "women . . . were either greeted with remarks concerning their appearance, not their credibility, or were so disenchanted with the field of sport media they left for positions in broadcast news or other venues."[50]

It is a fact that female representation in television sports broadcasting has experienced massive increases in the past fifty years. In Atlanta, in the 1960s, Jane Chastain got a spot on her local news broadcast predicting (with exceptional success) the outcomes of college football games. That role garnered her enough of a reputation to earn her a job at a local Miami station in 1967, where she became America's first female sportscaster, not yet engaged in any announcing—let alone commentary and analysis—but filming canned segments about current sports stories that were available for cable television outlets across the country. Chastain was hired by CBS in 1974, and on October 13 of that year, 18 years after the station's first airing of a professional football game, she became the National Football League's first female announcer. Chastain also appeared on some of CBS's NBA broadcasts during her time with the network. It seemed as though the stage was set for women to enter the world of sports broadcasting in meaningful numbers, if not en masse. Unfortunately for some (but, of course, fortunately for others), this world would soon mutate into a stage for beauty pageants.

Just as women's participation in sports exploded in the wake of Title IX, so too did the emblematic barricade that had previously excluded them from sports media. As soon as women began to enter this domain, they immediately came to be judged by different criteria than their male colleagues. Phyllis George joined Chastain at CBS in 1974, bringing with her a relatively unremarkable background in journalism but a dazzling one from the world of beauty, which included the 1971 Miss America title. It matters little to our

---

[48]Sheffer and Schultz, "Double Standards," 19.

[49]Toro, "Public Perceptions," 4.

[50]Ibid.

argument that Phyllis George became a first-rate journalist whose work became well respected by her peers and who has rightly become an iconic trailblazer for the still-difficult road for women in sports journalism. The fact that she succeeded to parlay her position attained by virtue of her beauty into one of genuine expertise speaks to George's personal talents and professional integrity, but in no way negates our argument about women's different access to and function in the world of sports journalism. In a continuation of a pattern that would eventually come to have significant effects on women in sports broadcasting, soon Jayne Kennedy, another beautiful woman with little actual sports background, was added to the roster of women in sports television. Women had arrived, and their presence was met with relative acceptance, an undeniable step forward for the gender equality of the industry. What muddles the "success" of women's advancements in this case, though, is that they had not entered by way of the same criteria that their male colleagues had. The requirements that these pioneering women possessed were based neither on their prowess as former athletes nor on their profound knowledge of sports. Thus, while these women's mere presence could be gauged as a proper sign of genuine female advancement toward gender parity in sports journalism, it in no way embodied any kind of equality, be it of the cognitive or the symbolic kind. The notion of women reporting sports had become less foreign to the American public, but this in no way meant that the substance of their reporting had attained legitimacy and credibility on the part of American sports fans, most of whom were men. Beauty provided a welcome entry for women into this virtually all-male world, but it could not buy respect.

Christine Brennan writes about her memories as a young journalism student, and lifelong devoted sports fanatic, as she was contemplating career choices:

> In 1976, I never knew women wrote about football, baseball, basketball—any sport, really. I saw no hint of this in the Toledo or Detroit sports sections.[51] I saw no women reporting sports regularly on TV except for Phyllis George, Miss America 1971. She was one of the stars on CBS's *The NFL Today*. It was an awe-inspiring role for a woman, but I never looked at George as a role model for me. Her career path was not going to be my career path. If you had to be Miss America to land on sports television, I knew I wasn't going to be on sports television. And if she was the only woman in all of sports media, as far as I knew,

---

[51]This is likely because there were none! An Associated Press estimate held that during the 1970s, about twenty-five women (a nationwide total) were employed as full-time sportswriters on staff at U.S. daily newspapers.

except for Olympic coverage every four years, then I wasn't going to be in the sports media.[52]

Brennan's reflections at the time illustrate the complicated nature of women's entry into sports media. Was there a "good" way to do it, a way that would have employed equal, fair credentials and requirements, but that also would have been met with acceptance from the predominantly male audience? In the larger scheme of women's places in sports, were they better off continuing to be absent, or was it better to be finally brought in, but under different selection criteria and to serve different roles than men?

Report Versus Commentary

There is a marked difference between sports *news* and sports *analysis* or commentary. Simply put, the latter exacts a much higher degree of credibility on the part of the speaker than does the former, which in turn raises issues of trust and legitimacy in the eyes of the all-important audience. Informing the viewers (or listeners) of a game's final result and the steps that led to it requires little more than the reading of a cut-and-dried text. Interpreting the results and commenting on the players' mistakes and achievements demands expertise, which is an absolute sine qua non for the communicator's most minimal credibility in the consumers' perception. To return to the concept of *credentialing*, it is when the truth is more objective that the dismissal of the speaker becomes less viable; when "right" and "wrong" are more subjective, the speaker is at much higher risk for criticism and invalidation, based on his or her opinion (or demeanor, or voice, or appearance, or pretty much any part of the performance that a recipient chooses to like or dislike).

It was this fundamental dichotomy between the topics of reporting and "commentating" that put many a male station manager into a quandary: He could put women on the air in positions that required virtually no sports knowledge (in which, for example, they simply read a story written by another person from a teleprompter or repeat to the cameras a quote from a player or coach), effectively meeting female "quotas," while not jarring the (almost all-male) viewership too significantly. Eventually, though, the well-informed female sports analyst entered the scene, and the real challenges of being a woman in a man's world (and, more specifically, in a man's particular role *within* that world) became more pronounced.

Ironically, it is when a woman in sports broadcasting does not contest the notion that she is actually not an expert, and admits to her status as an outsider

---

[52]Brennan, *Best Seat*, 95.

who is perfectly able to read the factual news from a teleprompter, but does not deign to have a voice of her own as an analyst or commentator, that sets her free of the incessant "testing" that a woman seeking to prove that she is an expert and an insider must face. Feminist theory accurately points to this facet of patriarchal culture, in which men desire to project the image of the silent woman who is "still tied to her place as bearer of meaning, not maker of meaning."[53] Applied to the question of men's acceptance of females on television sports broadcasts, this concept addresses precisely the division between being accepted as a female reporter devoid of commentary, as opposed to one who offers it. This argument then suggests that, in narratives that are deemed male, women are to operate as objects of male attention but not as propagators of the narrative itself. Andrea Kremer recognizes the following distinction between groups of women in sports broadcasting. "There are women who grew up loving sports, and, by the way, they do television, or they write about it or talk about it on radio," said Kremer, who started in print journalism in 1982. "And then there are women who think they want to be on TV, and sport is a cool thing. And I do think the audience knows the difference between the two. So I just hope people are getting into it for the right reason."[54]

Studies that cover *all* television programming have shown that this medium often highlights women's appearance over their intelligence and often presents women as helpless, incompetent, and dependent.[55] In a Sports Journalists' Association report, we learn that

> the idea that women are used for "window dressing," particularly in broadcasting, is widespread. The bottom line that cannot be ignored in this discussion is that any television station's primary goal is to attract and retain a viewing audience. This means giving people what they want to see; [even] in newspapers, picture bylines might be used, with a glamorous photo "more akin to being a WAG ['wife and girlfriend' of a prominent English soccer player representing the national team] than a journalist," according to one woman sportswriter.[56]

Additional research has confirmed that women are presented as sex objects more often and more blatantly than men.[57] These practices can be under-

---

[53]Toro, "Public Perceptions," 6.

[54]Houston, "Looks First, Knowledge Later."

[55]Peter J. Boyer, "TV Turns to the Hard Boiled Male," *New York Times*, February 26, 1986: C4.

[56]Sports Journalists' Association, "Women's Final Frontier?"

[57]S. A. Seidman, "Revisiting Sex Role Stereotyping in MTV Videos," *International Journal of Instructional Media*, 26 (1999): 11.

stood as reflections of the male hegemonic society to which the television industry is "selling" its product. They come as no surprise to any of us who have watched television, be it sitcoms, CNN, or *SportsCenter*. The reproduction of this practice makes perfect sense in a context in which, as is the case with national media, ownership is extremely lopsided in favor of males, with women comprising only 14 percent of top executive positions and accounting for only 13 percent of board members at ten of our major entertainment companies. Women make up a total of 16 percent of top positions at 120 broadcast and cable channels.[58] Elissa Perry, Alison Davis-Blake, and Carol T. Kulik, in their research on gender bias in selection, found that "When job applicant gender systematically affects organizational selection decisions, women tend to occupy primarily female-dominated jobs and men are concentrated in male-dominated jobs," meaning that, in cases when gender matters most, gender norms are concomitantly most strongly reinforced.[59]

What Does Looking Good Have to Do with Being a Respected Sportscaster? The Ambivalence of the "Babe" Factor

> You have to be pretty to be on sports TV—but it can also be a detriment in terms of being taken seriously. There's a thin line to toe between looking good enough to get put on TV and being good enough to be a respected sportscaster.
>
> —*Joanne Gerstner*

The role of the on-screen "babe" has been a route to incorporate an increasing number of women into the sports crew of a news station, often with very little, if any, sports knowledge as a prerequisite for entry. There is one important case that serves as an exception to the requirement that a woman constantly "prove herself" as being a worthy voice in sports, holding a job on par with men: her physical appearance. Once she passes on that count and is admitted to the inner sanctum of sports reporting, and if she makes certain to maintain her attractive appearance, her place is safe, barring, of course, violations of her professional conduct and the on-air repetition of egregious errors that would render her an embarrassment to the station that her beauty could not overcome. Paradoxically, women who are hired to serve as "pretty faces" might,

---

[58]Sheffer and Schultz, "Double Standards," 9.

[59]Elissa Perry, Alison Davis-Blake, and Carol T. Kulik, "Explaining Gender-Based Selection Decisions: A Synthesis of Contextual and Cognitive Approaches," *Academy of Management Review* 19, no. 4 (1994): 786–820 (quote from p. 787).

perhaps, have an easier job than many of their (male and female) colleagues, by dint of the (mostly unmentioned) lower expectations placed on them by their co-workers and, of course, their mostly male viewers. After all, in this case, the woman's real function is that of looking attractive, not of shining with brilliant insights. Beauty most decidedly trumps knowledge in this situation.

To be sure, data provide evidence that physical attractiveness offers a decided advantage for both females and males on television, as in virtually all walks of American life. This is not surprising. However, in the case of sports broadcasting, for women, beauty seems to embody far and away the single most important ticket to entry, even at the cost of knowledge that most male fans would regard as rudimentary. In Hardin, Genovese, and Yu's study of sports broadcasters in top markets, not a single female survey subject was older than forty-five, pointing to an industry pattern of letting women go when their youthful beauty can no longer grace the screen.[60] When applying, at the age of forty, for a sports broadcasting job in Vancouver, Norma Wick, a woman with nearly sixteen years of broadcasting experience, recalls being turned down for the job because "she was told she lacked experience."[61] In the 2008 article presenting her story, Wick, who now teaches broadcast journalism in Toronto, replied to this assertion of her alleged lack of experience by saying, "It's interesting that experience is high on your list, because you're hiring people who have none." She recalls the response she received: "That's because they have magic and you don't."

What are the requirements for "magic," then? Within the framework of credentialing, the criteria for "magic" seem to be an ideally ambiguous way to put aside solid qualifications (such as Wick's years of experience and accumulated expertise, which could have presumably made her an excellent hire for a sports broadcasting job) and instead hire based on requirements not prima facie relevant to the job. As William Houston points out in his article "Looks First, Knowledge Later," "the 'magic' cited in Wick's job interview is code for women in their 20s or early 30s. They're attractive. The guys call them sports babes . . . sideline hotties."[62]

As a woman seeking entry into the industry of sports broadcasting, it seems as though any level of actual sports knowledge may not even be necessary. In what a major sports writer from a large Midwestern city described as a "fast track to a short career," a woman can rely on attractiveness alone to propel her into the sports industry to serve in positions in which she can simply

---

[60]Hardin, Genovese, and Yu, "Privileged," 19.

[61]Houston, "Looks First, Knowledge Later."

[62]Ibid.

be, according to legendary veteran ESPN anchor Linda Cohn, "instructed by a producer or director through the audio device in the ear."[63] In other words, she becomes a pretty puppet.

While the numbers of women in sports media are growing, it is not necessarily a sign of forward progress in terms of them catching up to the men in credibility and expertise in sports. In fact, many women in the industry see a pattern that, as women's numbers increase in sports journalism, so too does the focus on their physical appearance (and the concomitant displacement of the valuation of their real sports expertise). *Playboy* publishes an annual docket of the "sexiest sportscasters." Google "female sportscasters," and the search will yield, in its top five hits, a Top 25, Top 15, and Top 10 list of "hottest" or "sexiest" female sportscasters, lists that may be flattering to those included, but that are representative of the value that female sportscasters seem to have in society.[64] While women in the industry recognize that an increase in female presence is positive in that it at least creates opportunities for more women to prove themselves (however hard that may be), Linda Cohn recognizes the negative consequences of the current trend, which, she explains as, "to go for looks first and then knowledge." "When people who just have looks going for them and are told what to say, that sets women in the industry back decades," Cohn says.[65]

Social psychologists inform us that, as a general rule, a person's physical attractiveness correlates positively with his or her perceived credibility. This would suggest that the more physically attractive a male or female sportscaster is, the greater his or her credibility will be with the viewing audience. Empirical data confirm the relevance of this pattern to sports broadcasting as well, but reveal an interesting—and telling—exception: The positive correlation of the reporter's physical attractiveness with his or her credibility with the audience ceases to hold in the case of sportscasters who are deemed "highly

---

[63]As quoted in ibid.

[64]The results are virtually identical in the multitude of their sexualized presence when the search focuses on "female sports reporters" instead of "female sportscasters." In 2000, *Playboy* magazine ran a contest called "Choose America's Sexiest Sportscaster." There was also a contest hosted by *Playboy*'s website in which "voters" were to choose their favorite (i.e., the "hottest") of ten female sports personalities. A Google search for "female business reporters" and "female weather reporters" will feature the prominence of an almost identically sexualized representation, as does the search for "female sportscasters." Interestingly, this is not the case for searches of "female science reporters" or "female politics reporters," although a search for "female reporters of politics" does yield a link to the "15 hottest female anchors" among the top five. We are not sure what conclusions to draw from such spontaneous and unsystematic searches and comparisons other than perhaps that the more "popular" the domain, and hence the more it is privy to the public's access, its interest, and thus its alleged expertise, the more it will attract the voice of men as well to whom the physical appearance of women matters a great deal—perhaps as much as and maybe even more than sports.

[65]Quoted in Houston, "Looks First, Knowledge Later."

attractive."[66] At that peak level, as it were, "attractiveness has been found to be a persuasive liability," according to Michael J. Baker and Gilbert A. Churchill, Jr., "when the advertised product was obviously unrelated to attractiveness."[67] A highly attractive woman on a television sports broadcast, research shows, will actually be perceived as less credible than anyone else on the sports news broadcast team, partly because of the well-worn pattern of hiring women simply for their good looks, regardless of their actual sports knowledge. Television stations summoned beauty queens into sports studios as early as the 1970s, and while these women did, in fact, gain entry into this male world, their doing so did not necessarily help women sports reporters as a whole in their gaining credibility with an almost exclusively male audience. As Toro points out, a "pretty female face . . . could actually lead audience members to believe she is less of an expert because she was only hired for her looks."[68]

Alas, this stereotype has some validity, as research shows that, in fact, most women in sports broadcasting, throughout its history, have been "beauty queens or cover girls," with little to no sports knowledge.[69] In an industry with such a heavily male-dominated audience, it might not be too surprising that news directors would employ attractive females to do sports, as it is what many male viewers want to see. The "sideline hottie" is a nice image for the typical (heterosexual male) football fan to behold between exciting catches and runs, and, so long as she refrains from any serious commentary on the game itself, her presence may very well be appreciated as an innocuous visual diversion or, perhaps even a welcome aesthetic enrichment of the serious issue at hand, which, of course, is the game. Male sports fans will appreciate attractive women as visual props. But they will not ipso facto accept them as credible interpreters of their beloved sports.

A conventionally unattractive woman will not have a chance of making it onto a television sports broadcast (or any other type of broadcast, for that matter). Thus, at the most basic level, attractiveness is required for entry. "Female sports broadcasters might have to be perceived as attractive to grab the interest of a predominantly male audience," Sheffer and Schultz explain.[70]

---

[66]Daniel Cochece Davis and Janielle Krawczyk, "Female Sportscaster Credibility: Has Appearance Taken Precedence?" *Journal of Sports Media* 5, no. 2 (2010): 1–34.

[67]Michael J. Baker and Gilbert A Churchill, Jr., "The Impact of Physically Attractive Models on Advertising Evaluations," *Journal of Marketing Research* 14 (1997): 538–555.

[68]Toro, "Public Perceptions," 27.

[69]Pamela J. Creedon, "From Whalebone to Spandex: Women and Sports Journalism in American Magazine, Photography and Broadcasting," in *Media and Sport: Challenging Gender Values*, ed. Pamela J. Creedon (Thousand Oaks, CA: Sage Publications, 1994), 108–158.

[70]Sheffer and Schultz, "Double Standards," 6.

What is notable is that sports knowledge is *not* required; in addition, those roles in a sports broadcast that do not involve original analysis or commentary are essentially reserved for good-looking women. "In a world where women's sport grows in importance daily . . . we have to expect that the media will focus [their] attention on beauty instead of achievement from time to time. The public wants it," Jeff Hollobaugh submitted.[71] Beauty provides access, but once attained, it seems to become a burden for a woman seeking validation as a credible sports expert. In short, the presence of the pretty face who does not know sports makes the job of the pretty women who *do* know sports significantly harder, for the former reinforces the stereotype and the assumption that the latter are only there because of their looks. The irony here is that the very asset that made access possible mutates into a liability on the job.

Women in the industry reported getting the most negative feedback whenever they voiced their opinions and spoke their minds. That is, men can accept these women's presence so long as it is limited to their looking nice and to their reporting the news, the event, the action, the production. But as soon as this mutates into analysis, commentary, criticism, challenge—in other words, once it features the female journalist's opinions and views—male tolerance decreases rapidly and mutates into anger, hostility, contempt, and derision. A female reporter in a major Midwestern city had this to say to the authors: "I'll get more negative emails when I give my *opinion* on the air than anything else." On first entering the industry, this reporter was issued two warnings, one by a veteran reporter, letting her know that she would have to work ten times harder than any male in the industry, and also by her own station manager, who told her, "You have three strikes against you: You're tall, you're pretty, and you know what you're talking about."

Outside of sports, these three credentials would most likely not be considered "strikes against" a person, but rather advantages, especially in combination, though, as we mentioned earlier, invoking the U.S. Navy's inability to accept Hedy Lamarr as a serious inventor, merely by dint of her exceptional beauty, demonstrates that this sports-related phenomenon exists in other realms of male domination as well.

The increasingly marginalized nature of sports pertaining to the salience of the mutual incompatibility of beauty and professional credibility is best illustrated by the fact that this pattern, though still present in many male-dominated realms, has noticeably decreased in other areas of broadcast journalism. It speaks to the distinctive nature of the male exclusivity in sports that

---

[71]Jeff Hollobaugh, "1,500 Runner Not Just Another Pretty Face," ESPN, August 30, 2000, available at http://www.espn.go.com/moresports/hollobaugh/archive.html (accessed August 3, 2011).

a woman who is both attractive and knowledgeable would be resented instead of celebrated. The intersection of these two bastions of maleness—sports and attractive women—causes problems for men—be they fellow journalists or viewers—and therefore also for an attractive female who is trying to succeed as a credible and bona fide sports journalist on television. Our interviewee pointed out that, whereas her combination of attractiveness and expertise in sports was repeatedly met with male resentment, in "news or weather . . . that combination is fine. Sports are a whole different animal." This distinction speaks to sports' near-sacred centrality for masculinity to which an attractive female expert appears, almost by necessity, as an unwelcome and threatening intruder. While women in all areas of broadcasting are, for the most part, conventionally attractive (it is television, after all), the important difference is that being *too* attractive as a news or weather reporter does not lead to a doubting and diminishing of the woman's professional *credibility*. There seems to be increasing room in men's consciousness for an expert meteorologist, a profession that at one point was completely male dominated, just like sports, to be an attractive female and to be taken seriously as an accomplished and knowledgeable professional. While the female pioneers who first broke into television undoubtedly continue to overcome barriers in their professional lives on a daily basis solely because of their gender, society has arrived at an acceptance of attractive female experts in most areas of the news but sports. This is not to say that, except in sports, men will desist from sexualizing professional women, as we mentioned briefly in footnote 64. Alas, we are nowhere close to that state of enlightenment.

What does a shift toward beauty necessarily have to do with the credibility that the public perceives in female sportscasters? Obviously, sports in our culture constitute an essential part of hegemonic masculinity. Attention to attractive women, too, is a crucial component of the very same hegemonic (heterosexual) masculinity, and, as such, attractive women and sports television broadcasting do in fact comprise complementary entities. "Hot" women and sports *can* indeed be safely symbiotic, so long as both bolster masculinity. But intelligence and knowledge exhibited by these attractive women somehow disturbs masculinity in sports more than in other realms; thus men seem to experience the combination of beauty and knowledge in sports negatively and as threatening.

Every woman whom we interviewed expressed an unmistakable frustration with, bordering on contempt for, female sportscasters whom our interviewees perceived not to have the requisite sports knowledge for their job. Our interviewees were all aware of the widespread practice in television of hiring an attractive woman with little to no sports background. All of our interviewees had a definitive disdain for this practice, often asserting that they did not think that such a "pretty face" accomplished positive things for women in the industry. Especially our interlocutors employed on the print side of sports journalism seemed to be dismissive of those of their colleagues in television, whom they deemed to have garnered their position more based on physical appearance than on factual knowledge. In a sense, they viewed female sports journalists working in print media and even on radio to possess superior professional qualifications to those making their living in front of television cameras. "In television," one female sports writer reflected, "it's all about how you look . . . you *have* to be pretty to be on sports television. Looks do not matter when your medium to the world is your voice or your words on paper."[72] While it can be argued, with considerable weight, that good looks are the absolute sine qua non for any appearance on *all* of television, far beyond sports, our interviews (as well as our own tuning in to sports television) revealed that this "requirement" in the country's sports television is much less stringently applied to male as opposed to female journalists.

The process of credentialing, then, holds that the vaguer the requirements, the easier it is to exclude potential entrants based on seemingly secondary or even tertiary factors. The entry requirements for sports journalism's print side appear to have attained a relatively concrete and tangible form: the successful completion of some kind of journalism program, the holding of a degree awarded by such a program, and some concrete experience in journalism. Given that these criteria have emerged as norms for hiring a sports journalist, it is harder for male colleagues, for example, to presume, assume, or convince themselves and others that a given woman was hired just for her looks. This, of course, does not obviate the suspicion—and the ensuing stigma—that any woman constitutes a "quota" or "diversity hire." Still, the possible cloud of being a "quota" does represent less of an a priori disqualification and delegitimation than being a "babe" or a "pretty face." Because of the cover girl's prevalence in television, "serious" women in all of sports journalism—print and electronic—constantly have to prove their mettle and professionalism to men, other women, their audience, and also themselves. Reflecting the complexity of this issue, Jeanne Zelasko, a reporter for Fox Sports, said in response to *Playboy*'s "Choose America's Sexiest Sportscaster" contest, "When I talk to young women about careers in this field, do I advise them to get a solid background in sports and reporting, or do I tell them to enter a beauty contest?"[73]

---

[72]Joanne Gerstner, interview with the authors, April 15, 2011.

[73]John Walters, "Hottie Topic," available at sportsillustrated.cnn.com/vault/article/magazine/ MAG1021425/index.htm (accessed July 20, 2011).

"Brains are an asset, if you hide them."
—Mae West

It seems as though, on some level, men—well beyond sports—are generally uneasy, perhaps even threatened, by the combination of physical beauty and intelligence in women. It is threatening to them to mix an attractive, feminine woman with expertise and intelligence, both of which our male-dominated culture fully claims to be in the purview of male judgment, expertise, and power. On the one hand, male-dominated hegemonic culture accords beauty to women. It indeed demands that beauty be arguably women's most prized currency. Beauty is an asset that women are not only demanded but also awarded to have *over* men. Beauty is the realm in which men grant women (relative) power.

Once, however, a beautiful woman also possesses brains (i.e., intelligence, expertise, knowledge), a realm that men most decidedly have never granted women, and continue to claim as their very own sphere in which to excel and make their mark, men run into serious trouble because they perceive such a combination in a woman as a genuine threat to their privilege of power. Hence, men must maintain supremacy in at least one part of this interactive relationship. And since they would be hard put to do so in the realm of female beauty, it has to be in the brains department where contestation occurs. Thus, it makes prima facie sense that males be averse to the idea of a beautiful woman possessing commensurate power in brainy matters that still continue to be culturally coded as decidedly male.

Lest the tension between physical and mental prowess and, thus, power, be solely construed in gendered terms, let us recall that intragendered competition between "brain" and "brawn" exists as well. Handsome men are not supposed to be brilliant intellectuals; that is the bailiwick of nerds and geeks. We grant jocks the good looks that define their very being in our culture, but we do not expect them to be intelligent and learned, and we act suspiciously, perhaps even hostilely, if they are that, too. Ditto on the women's side; the dumb blond stereotype is also alive and well in the female world. Somehow our culture does not like to accord too much power to any individual by having her or him excel at "brain" and "brawn" as well. We like winners, but not overwhelming ones. Being beautiful and intelligent at the same time is like running up the score in an already lopsidedly decided victory.

We return now to a previously discussed space of male dominance, namely, science, to explore further the threat of beauty in consort with brains, and, to analogize the situation of sports media to that of another male-dominated realm as a means of outlining possible implications of the "brain-less" beauty, the "pretty puppet," the "babe," for women in the male world of sports journalism. Imagine a physics lab: A woman's place there might be somewhat contested; in fact, it most likely will be, simply by such a place (still) being heavily male in the gender composition of its members, as well as, of course, the dominant cultural construction of the field's identity. To be sure, a woman's presence in such a lab might likely be perceived as some kind of threat on some level; it might likely invoke awkwardness and a sense of tension among the lab's denizens. But it is less likely that this woman's professional credibility would be doubted and questioned because it is highly improbable that she would have gained entrance to the lab without her being a bona fide and credentialed physicist. Importantly, the credentialing practices in this setting completely preclude the entry of any non-expert. We thus come back to our "pet peeve" about the difference between physics and sports for women: The former is rigidly credentialed, and an example of hiring someone merely on his or her looks is preposterous, whereas the latter is loosely credentialed and thus makes the barrier of entry very low and thus arbitrary. Clearly, a woman hired to join a physics lab just because she is beautiful would delegitimize not only her place in the lab, but also the entire lab itself. It would be absurd for a woman to be hired at a physics lab without her being a credentialed expert; physics labs have no positions for a "pretty puppet," a "beauty queen," or a "babe," devoid of expertise in physics.

But what if there *were* such a position? What if it was known that many female physicists were hired to their specific positions mainly because they were "hot"? Might that make life harder for the bona fide expert female physicist in terms of having to prove (especially to outsiders) that she has her position in the lab for the same reasons that her male colleagues do and that she should therefore be accorded the same level of legitimacy for her work, in her position, for her knowledge and her expertise to disseminate information and analysis? We submit that the bona fide, qualified, highly credentialed, while still feminine and attractive, female physicist's position might be undermined, if not in formal structures then in the equally powerful informal ones. Thus, we do not think it coincidental that women in highly male-oriented and male-dominated professions that feature the brain instead of the body as the most essential "means of production" consciously and consistently de-emphasize their femininity, precisely to be taken seriously on an intellectual level.

If this position for a "hottie" were to be introduced in physics, it would constitute a precise temporal reversal of women's arduous access to a position in sports broadcasting. That is, in sports broadcasting, women *first* entered as pretty faces with little to no sports knowledge. The sports world's very loose to nonexistent credentialing allowed access to specially designated positions for attractive women who were devoid of sports knowledge. The male creators of these positions, as well as the male viewership of the programs where these positions became newly integrated, completely condoned—actually welcomed—this new arrangement since the newcomers' legitimacy and added value were never meant to be their actual knowledge of the subject matter (i.e., sports), but simply their fine physical appearance. This construct makes it well-nigh impossible for an attractive female sports journalist who has indeed attained a level of knowledge that is on par in every possible way with that of her male colleagues to have the largely male audience accord her the legitimacy and respect that she fully deserves, and that her male colleagues receive as a matter of course. In an absurd way, she would have to make herself less attractive to be fully accepted as a bona fide expert. Physical attractiveness is a sine qua non for entry into television, well beyond sports departments, and for men as well, though manifestly less so than for women. Yet, at the same time, this requirement undermines the entrant's legitimacy, more so in the male-dominated world of sports than in those of culture or news or political analysis or weather.

Might, then, the relegation of "hotties" to decidedly female positions in sports broadcasting, with few, if any, opportunities to offer commentary or analysis, make the task of overcoming the widespread notion that 'women don't know sports' even harder? Just like in our hypothetical example of the physics lab, the existence of female positions reserved for intellectually challenged and professionally ill-prepared "hotties" could make it easier to undermine the legitimacy of those women *with* brains (especially for "threatened" men who are scouring for an opportunity to discredit the expertise of these women), so, too, might the "cover girl" role within sportscasts aid in the ease with which male viewers can diminish the perceived credibility of women in sports journalism.

The fact that *some* women are hired based on their appearance provides men with a helpful and prima facie plausible excuse that *no* woman has attained her position in the sports world based on sports expertise, knowledge, credibility, or credentials that are identical to men's. Men may want to promote this perception so as to allow them to quell the threat that they feel when they encounter a combination of beauty and brains in a professional woman. For women in sports media, beauty has thus far proven to be a double-edged sword: a necessary condition for entry and a potentially delegitimizing asset on the job.

Conclusion

Lest we be misunderstood, we are fully aware of ample research, substantiated by our real-life experiences, that our culture—indeed, probably all cultures—favors beauty and bestows all kinds of advantages and privileges on those deemed to possess it, be they male or female. Indeed, research by two Israeli scholars shows that members of the U.S. Congress receive substantially more television coverage purely by dint of their perceived good looks.[74] In an earlier work, the authors demonstrated that identical mechanisms favor the public lives of Israeli legislators in the same way.[75] We all know that John F. Kennedy's good looks—in marked contrast to Richard Nixon's crumpled appearance cum sweaty upper lip—helped him to win the presidency in 1960. While the "attractiveness effect"—"what-is-beautiful-is-good"—has a few drawbacks, such as pretty women being viewed as more snobbish and materialistic (note, once again, the drawback of beauty for women, with no parallel for handsome men), there can be no doubt that beauty offers its holder—male or female—immense benefits, such as better grades in school, more friends, lighter court sentences, and greater success in the labor market, let alone the marriage market.[76] We do not mean to argue against the benefits of beauty. Nor do we see its social rewards as illegitimate. But when the primary, if not sole, qualification for a job centered on the construction of words in speech and writing, the awareness of history, the mustering of statistics—in short, the mastery of a body of knowledge—becomes physical attractiveness, and mainly, if not exclusively, for women, then clearly beauty attains a discriminatory dimension that borders on the sexist.

Pamela J. Creedon found that sport is both "an expression of the sociocultural system in which it occurs" and a "mirror [of] the rituals and values of the society in which they are developed."[77] Toro adds, "As metaphors for gender values, both sport and media work to describe what is considered to be male and female in our culture."[78] Women in the field of sports media are immersed in a world that is not only male dominated in terms of their colleagues within the industry, but also in terms of the larger population that "consumes" their products. Sports' ubiquity, or the connection that so many millions, indeed billions, of people maintain with it, as opposed to the relative obscurity of physics, for example, on a popular level, results paradoxically

---

[74]Israel Waismel-Manor and Yariv Tsfati, "Why Do Better-Looking Members of Congress Receive More Television Coverage?" *Political Communication* 28, no. 4 (2011): 440–463.

[75]Yariv Tsfati, Dana Markovitch-Elfassi, and Israel Waismel-Manor, "Exploring the Association between Israeli Legislators' Physical Attractiveness and Their Television News Coverage," *International Journal of Press/Politics*, 14 (2010): 67–90.

[76]Waismel-Manor and Tsfati, "More Television Coverage," 441–442.

[77]Creedon, "From Whalebone to Spandex," 111–112.

[78]Toro, "Public Perceptions," 4; citing Pamela Creedon, "Women, Media, and Sport: Creating and Reflecting Gender Values," in *Women, Media, and Sport: Challenging Gender Values*, ed. Pamela Creedon (Thousand Oaks, CA: Sage, 1994): 3–27.

in a democratically generated and broadly legitimated—though highly male-coded—possessiveness that is determined to keep women if not *out*, then at least in specifically designated positions. "Privilege, a tool which represented dominance exerted by virtue of social identity, favors men in this arena, as they embody the standard and therefore are in a place to rise through the industry free of the barriers that the less powerful must face."[79] A privileged individual within an organization or community, such as a male in the milieu of sports media, is able to operate under an uncontested "sense of belonging" as well as, in many cases, an attitude characterized by "unearned entitlement," both advantages, of course, that are not available to women in the field.[80] Women's challenges in sports media start on entry and become even more complicated when (or if) they seek to earn positions equivalent in consequence to those of their male colleagues. The widespread practice of employing "babes" in specifically designed roles in sports media also has consequences for those women *not* in the industry, but who are devoted sports followers in their own right. It is to an examination of these women's, our amateur *sportistas'* experiences, that we now turn in our final chapter.

---

[79]Hardin, Genovese, and Yu, "Privileged," 187.
[80]Ibid., 82.

6

Sportista II:
Following as a Hobby,
the A-Typical Female Sports Fan

Superfans in Their Own Right,
with Their Own Voice,
and Speaking Their Own Language

We devoted the previous chapter to a detailed discussion of female sports journalists in the print and visual media. Some of them are most definitely devoted sportistas, though we also know that many are not. Clearly, to be an accomplished sports journalist, one must score very high on the possession of sports knowledge. To use the language of our graphic from Chapter 4, sports journalists need most definitely be "hardened technocrats," at a minimum, in that they must know their facts and figures, if only to fulfill their professional duty. But it is entirely possible to be a superb sports journalist and not to have the requisite affect for sports, to love sports, to be a sports fanatic in the conventional sense of that term, a genuine sportista in our book's parlance. To use the distinctions discussed in Chapter 2, one can indeed be a fine sports savant or connoisseur without being a fan.

Albertson attended the annual convention of the Association for Women in Sports Media (AWSM) in Charlotte, North Carolina, in June 2011, where she noticed the virtual absence of any sports talk, sports chatter, sports schmooze, among the attendees gathered in the informal settings of the convention hotel's hallways, coffee shops, and bars. While, clearly, all attendees were well versed in sports and extremely knowledgeable about them, their centrality remained confined to the convention's formal venues, namely, the various panels and workshops. And even Joanne Gerstner, sports journalist extraordinaire, former AWSM president, and one of its leading and most active members, who, by anybody's criteria and definition, most importantly, her very own, qualifies as a sportista, informed us repeatedly that when she gets together with women who are as well versed in all of the arcana of sports as she is, they rarely, if ever, speak about sports of any kind, and if so, only briefly. Thus, even sports-savvy women speak sports differently than men do. But this in no way implies that sportistas—women who *love* to follow sports with a passion and know them extremely well—do not exist. Quite the contrary!

We argue that they most decidedly do, though not as a large and visible and discernible collective, but rather as individuals and small groups who love and know and understand and follow their sports at a level every bit as high and as sophisticated as any male superfan does, though most definitely employing a different language, in their own right, as it were. Such sportistas are ubiquitously strewn all over society. They are among doctors, lawyers, professors, accountants, managers, workers, students, and—yes—even sports journalists.

For our study, we gathered thirty-three young women, who in no way constitute a statistically representative sample. They are all between twenty and thirty-five in age; they are all white; they are all college educated and then some; most hail from middle-, even upper-middle-class families; virtually all of them grew up in the Northeast and Midwest; and only two of them are married and have children. And yet we are convinced that their collective voices bespeak certain discernible patterns that identify the common denominator constituting a bona fide sportista. It is to these voices that we now turn in the first part of our last chapter. We then discuss the introduction of espnW as a fascinating, controversial, and unique entrant to the complex arena of gender in American sports. We analyze this phenomenon briefly and shed some light as to how the sportista relates to this still new, tentative, evolving, and highly important experiment in the possible re-gendering of the sports discourse in America's public space. We then end with some brief thoughts as to how sportistas' sports language continues to remain distinct from that of male sports fans and is likely to remain such for the foreseeable future. We now turn to the presentation of a few crucial clusters that emerged from the rich responses that our interviewees offered in their accounting of how, why, and when they became sportistas.

Hooray to Dads: The Central Role of Male Figures from Birth to Adulthood

Just as, for boys, the space of watching sports with their dads has become, over the span of more than a century, one of the key entry gates to their becoming fluent and passionate sports speakers for life, just as, for boys, the sanctity of sitting next to dad on a couch following football on Sunday afternoon, so, too, has an identical ritual been crucial in the formation of our sportistas.[1] Needless to say, this strengthens the nurture-culture argument in that it provides evidence for the decidedly acquired quality of such tastes and preferences. Yet, it also confirms that our sportistas remain outliers from the norm of both genders, somehow betwixt and between: They are like men in their love and knowledge of sports, yet are not quite accepted by them, and at the same time, their engagement with this culture and its languages remains alien to most of their sisters.

Dads were given pride of place in the story of virtually every one of our typical sportistas. Fathers were reported as being the decisive initiators of our subjects' love for sports and devoted following of them, from girlhood to their contemporary existence as young, educated, accomplished women. "Dad was critical," Gillian immediately explained in her narrative. "He took to laying out the sports page for me every morning at breakfast . . . I became a fan because my dad always had [games] on." Caitlin echoed this, explaining that her "father was always glued to the television watching sports," and when she got old enough, she began watching with him.

Beyond just having been introduced to sports, the sharing of loving to watch and learn them provided these women with a means of bonding with their fathers; many of our interviewees informed us how their shared experiences of *sport following* became their sole but all-the-more cherished medium to bond with their fathers when they were young girls. As Sarah described:

> The first memory that I have concerning my sports history dates back to when I was about 7 or 8 and my parents (both from Cleveland) took me and my brother to a Browns game. I remember my dad explaining to me first downs and touchdowns and other very basic aspects of the game. After this, my dad and I started watching all sorts of things together when he would come [home] from work. We had a really great father-daughter relationship, and his favorite thing to do was watch sports, so that's what we spent most of our time doing. We would watch hockey together, drink water and try to fake burp . . . as strange as that sounds, it was something we developed and just always did, but only when we watched hockey.

As Katrina recalls, when she would go to visit her dad, who lived in a different state, "nine times out of ten we were going to sporting events. It was what

---

[1] Douglas Hartmann, "The Sanctity of Sunday Football: Why Men Love Sports," in *The Sport and Society Reader*, ed. David Karen and Robert E. Washington (New York: Routledge, 2010), 151–156.

we bonded over, even when we didn't get to see each other all the time." These girls recognized that a knowledge of and love for sports was often the best way to foster a strong and special relationship with their fathers.

"Through sports, my dad and I could share a common interest," Kate writes. "So therefore I wanted to learn as much as I could in order to keep that as a way to bond with him." Emma informs us that, as the daughter of a man who had no "son to watch sports with," she believes she "started watching sports to get closer to [her] dad."

It seems that being invited by dad to participate in his sacred sports space constituted a source of great confidence and specialness to these daughters. It is also clear from many responses that these women realized already, as young girls, what a special, indeed unique, place sports held for dad. Somehow it was different from everything else in his life: from his work, to be sure, but also from his other activities, interests, and passions. The girls picked up on their fathers' emotional involvement with this construct as well as the seriousness that they accorded this pursuit. "There is no one I love to get attention from more than my Daddy-Dearest," Jillian admits, "I knew there had to be a way for me to be a part of his Sunday ritual. I started watching football just to spend time with my dad." Kate shares this experience, citing that she "always felt really special that he picked me to join him in watching the team that he loves." According to Alisa,

> My life ever since my birth has been rooted in sports. Since I can re-
> member, my parents joked that the night of my birth was distracting
> for my dad not because I was born 10 weeks prematurely, but because
> it was both the Cleveland Indians' home opener and the final game in
> the NCAA basketball championship in which my dad's beloved [Uni-
> versity of Michigan] Wolverines faced the [Duke] Blue Devils [April 6,
> 1992] . . . While I was still in the hospital after being born prematurely,
> my dad (not one for reading) would read me the baseball box scores
> from the [Cleveland] *Plain Dealer* so that I could hear his voice through
> the incubator. Every year, it became a ritual that my dad and I would
> watch *Field of Dreams* before the start of the baseball season and *Rudy*
> before the Michigan-Notre Dame game. I had undertaken some sort of
> apprenticeship with my dad, in which I learned how to throw a curve-
> ball and a spiral, what "not even batting his weight" meant, and why
> overtime in college football was infinitely better than that in the NFL.

The connections forged via sport following continued to help many of these women maintain strong relationships with their fathers as they grew up. "My dad was a *huge, huge* sports fan . . . *huge*! And that was kind of our main way of having something to relate to, especially when I was a teenager," Ann explains. "[Sports] gave my dad and me, who otherwise would not have been getting along great, something to bond over." For the future sportista, loving and knowing sports became inextricably linked to attaining and securing her father's respect and affection. "I became interested in sports so that I had some common ground with my father," Kathleen said. "I simply was trying to win Daddy's love."[2] Alisa informs us that "I state to this day that I became the sports fan that I am because my dad had all girls and needed someone with whom he could share his love for sports."

Sports fandom, for these sportistas, began in many ways as a means of connecting with their fathers. Virtually identical to the much more conventional father-son relationships, the special nature of these father-daughter relationships first emerged and then solidified through a shared love for following rather than doing sports. These bonds were forged in the family den, in front of a large television screen, or at the kitchen table, while going over the box scores at breakfast every morning, rather than on the playing fields. Our research reveals that, even more important than getting a young girl involved in *playing* sports, the first and crucial step in the raising of a sportista seems to lie in the hands of "Daddy-Dearest." As will be clear in a number of quotes that follow, quite a few of our respondents specifically mention their fathers as being the sole male figures throughout their lives who not only acknowledge their daughters' prowess in sports history and detail but also revel in this as an accomplishment. Dads are really proud of their daughters' having become sportistas. Few, if any, men in the sportistas' lives express approval, let alone pride, in their sports knowledge, interest, and enthusiasm. But their dads do. Reading Christine Brennan's impressive autobiography makes it crystal clear that she would never have become the first-rate sports journalist that she is without her late father's full-fledged support of and pride in Christine's making sport the center of her professional vocation as well as her private interest and passion.

Sports give fathers—virtually all men, really—a good source of bridging capital with which to reach out to others (even their children) and thus create shared space in terms of affect and knowledge. Often these relationships had been created when the future sportista's dad had no sons and so availed himself of his daughter's presence instead. But we also received reports in which it was precisely the presence of brothers or other male figures, such as uncles, cousins, and grandfathers—in addition to the influence of dads—that spawned

---

[2]Kathleen Nelson, as quoted in Gillian Lee Warmflash, "In a Different Language: Female Sports Fans in America" (unpublished honors thesis, submitted to the Committee on Degrees in Social Studies, Harvard University, Cambridge, MA, March 2004).

sportistas. This is not to say that mothers or female figures have no role in transmitting a love of sports to girls. Recall how we mentioned earlier Gillian Warmflash's interesting—and surprising (to us and to her)—finding in her research on thirty-three leading female sports journalists, among whom almost half reported that it was their mothers' interest in and involvement with sports that led them to their own engagement with this world. Warmflash, of course, was more interested in ascertaining these women's success as professional sports journalists and thus in their knowledge of, rather than passion for, sports, but still her study offers evidence of women's role in the socialization of sportistas. But even when women are the transmitters of this culture, young girls realize that, in its very essence and deep core, this culture is heavily male. Moreover, it is also quite clear that most of our respondents perceived themselves as interlopers, perhaps even intruders, into a world that was not theirs and whose main representatives and purveyors did not welcome them with open arms. We found the phenomenon of constantly having to prove herself to ever-suspicious men as both a knowledgeable and a passionate sports fan mentioned by virtually every one of our respondents. Here are some examples grouped under this rubric.

The Need for Constant Proof,
Which Still Does Not Allay Suspicion

Jillian informs us that "in 8th grade, this boy Alex said he was going to the Mets game that night—I was too. I said I was a huge Mets fan and was so excited. He said (and I quote), 'I hate when girls say they are fans of a team. They don't know anything about it.' I said, 'Of course, I know about the Mets.' He told me to prove it and asked me to name three players on the team—I named the entire 40-man roster." Apparently things have not changed in Jillian's life now that she is a college graduate and a law student because she insists that "with new guys, I still do have to 'prove' myself without fail and every time."

And Joanne Gerstner confirms that boys' suspicion of women as equal interlocutors of sports does not abate when they become grown men, perhaps ever. She had the following to say about women's position in sports journalism: "You walk into the newsroom and people assume you were a 'minority hire'; that you didn't earn your position in the same way they [men] did."[3] One of Gerstner's professors at Northwestern University's Medill School of Journalism, arguably one of the country's finest, and alma mater to Gerstner's sports journalist colleague Christine Brennan as well, had these parting

---

[3]Joanne Gerstner, interview with the authors, April 15, 2011.

words to young Joanne on learning that she had chosen sports journalism as her livelihood: "You are entering the one male-dominated field that may not be integrated by the time you leave it . . . it's like you're walking into the Vatican. It's not going to happen and you're setting yourself up for challenges that you could avoid if you wrote features, news, pretty much anything but sports." Did the professor's assessments ever prove prescient! Here is one of Gerstner's experiences from the *Detroit News*: "People call the sports desk and I answer, [and] then they ask for someone from sports. I tell them that I can help them, and they say, 'No, no, I want someone from sports.' One guy called in asking how many championships Michael Jordan has won . . . I gave him the answer, and he wanted to be put on the phone with a guy to 'verify' my answer. Sometimes I just said that I was the secretary and passed the phone to someone else."

Here are just a few comments in which the verb "to prove" plays a central role. We italicized the word for easier detection: "Innocent until *proven* guilty! For guys . . . women are not sports fans until they have *proven* themselves to be," says Sarah. Samantha seconds this by saying, "When I watch a game with guys, I feel as though I'm ignored a lot of the time until I *prove* that I know just as much about the sport as they do." And Caitlin tells us, "I have always had to *prove* to other people, males and females, that I am knowledgeable about sports. Most just assume that since I am a female, I have no interest and no knowledge." Nicole informs us that "when they hear, 'oh, she knows more about sports than you,' guys are looking to *prove* you wrong . . . that you don't know what you claim you do." And Michelle asserts that "it is assumed that you're less knowledgeable, and you've got something to *prove* in a conversation with men about sports." And Laura states, "I definitely feel like I have to *prove* myself as a female sports fan. I feel the pressure to *prove* that I know stuff about every sport because boys know about almost all sports and I feel like they don't take girls who only know things about a specific sport seriously." This is what Alisa had to say on this issue:

> In relation to guys, my interest in sports is the way that I have to *prove* myself. Off the bat, they seem to respect the fact that I truly care about sports, that I know what a cornerback is, and that I know the difference between AC Milan and Inter; with my guy friends, and even more so for guys that I'm interested in, I use sporting events as a way to spend time with them. It's a way for me to be approachable and to interact with them on their 'territory' . . . I use sports as a way to get in with the guys and to *prove* myself to them, but that doesn't always hold up.

Seasoned journalist Dana Wakiji says, "I remember one time I was at some bar or whatever and there was this football game, and the guys were so condescending and were like, 'Ohhh, well . . . really, you know about sports? Well, can you tell me what a nickel defense is?' and I'm like, 'Yes, it's an extra defensive back. You wanna know what a dime defense is? Would you like me to break down the left wing lock?'"

It is, of course, not surprising that women find themselves on a constant and perpetual probation with men regarding sports, that they always have to prove themselves, since virtually all women—by definition, so to speak, and as an indelible marker of their gender—operate on this almost exclusively male territory with a severe credibility deficit and with virtually no legitimacy. Let us turn to a brief illustration of this cluster.

Lack of Legitimacy and Credibility

Here is Samantha: "One thing that is frustrating is that males and people in general just assume that I don't know anything about sports because I am a girl . . . males just automatically either ignore you or don't pay attention to what you are saying in a dismissive manner. They will immediately dismiss you in a way that they would never do with other males." And Nicole's anger was obvious in the following comment: "Covering the Cape Cod League . . . I had good relationships with the coaches, but this one coach . . . I asked him about one of his players and whether he was going to leave the team . . . the coach told me, 'That's not for the paper.' Then at the end of the interview, he said, condescendingly, 'Did you understand all of that?' He clearly thought that I didn't understand baseball, the way that he talked to me, and I was *so mad.*" (The emphasis in the original, meaning Nicole's voice, is unmistakable.) And she continued, "I remember well that 'Right, sure, you know your sports . . . ha ha.' I did not get invited to watch the games with these guys when we first met," referring to her male friends and colleagues with whom she socialized over the summers while covering the Cape Cod League. When asked about how her male friends related to her being a sportista, Samantha replied, "Male friends, well, they would just assume that I didn't know what I was talking about when it came to sports since I am a woman, so they would ignore me completely or talk over me." She then continued, "I actually know a tremendous amount, yet they do not listen to what I have to say unless my dad is standing there agreeing with me. This is extremely frustrating." Kate seconded this frustration while also lauding her dad, saying, "Rarely will anyone besides my dad take what I have to say seriously. It is very annoying that men don't take me seriously a lot of the time when any discussion about sports begins." And Laura detected this credibility gap and lack of legitimacy in her childhood, saying, "I remember boys being very suspicious whenever I talked sports with them. I never started the conversations . . . When I formed friendships with boys based solely on the fact that we both liked sports, I had a hard time shaking the 'legit girl who likes sports' label. . . . The worst feeling is when people don't think you are being genuine or don't take you seriously . . . and dismiss your knowledge out of hand."

Thus, even when men take women's sports knowledge seriously, it is not in a matter-of-fact manner, but with a good dosage of incredulity, followed by a kind of patronizing approval that exhibits admiration reserved for some kind of exotic being. Here is Sarah on this issue: "The only problem that I usually face due to my 'manly' interest in sports is that for most guys I am immediately put in 'bro' zone and never seen as anything more than that (or at least never told that I am)." It seems, then, that men cannot handle knowledgeable female sports fans as women. Thus, women either need to be dismissed as irrelevant and ignorant, or they have to be de-feminized and inducted into the "bro" zone as that exotic "legit girl who likes sports." Somehow, the sexual tension between the genders makes it very difficult for men to accept women as their unencumbered equals, with no baggage of any kind, when it comes to sports.

Maybe Jillian's resigning tone is not that misplaced when she says, "It's just very hard to gain credibility among male sports fans." And Dana's statement might be more pessimistic still: "There are people who just don't want to hear sports from a woman under any circumstances, ever. They simply don't see it as credible." It should come as no big surprise, then, that this lack of legitimacy and credibility leads to a serious lack of confidence and a classic case of stereotype threat in many a sportista.

Lack of Confidence and the Presence of Stereotype Threat

Read what Samantha says: "Lack of confidence . . . easy to get intimidated. I believe that when a woman makes one mistake in this field it sticks with [her] much longer than if a male made a mistake." And this is how Jillian assesses this issue: "If I make a sports blunder . . . I am, on the one hand, easily forgiven because I am a girl, but on the other hand, I will now have to work twice as hard to regain the respect I had previously earned. And it is not guaranteed that I will ever regain it, actually."

In our interviews, we asked these young, accomplished, smart, and confident women if there were any other topics, such as politics, the arts, or general public affairs, let alone subjects studied in school, in which they felt in any way insecure when conversing with their male colleagues and classmates—whether, for example, when studying together for an examination, or watching a political debate on television, or a press conference, or really participating in any matter of their busy lives, these women experienced any anxiety about being "revealed" at some point, about not living up to expectations, about being frauds or imposters of sorts. The answer was a uniform no on all counts, with one exception: sports. Here, all of our sportistas harbored some sort of insecurity, a sense of being on guard, of being tested, of being watched and observed. Some experienced this more strongly than others did, and some appeared more self-conscious about this than others did, but all expressed some degree of unease bespeaking some sort of "foreignness" in a world that they had just crashed and in which their welcome, though finally granted, still seemed somehow conditional. They all felt that they had to prove themselves continually lest they be dismissed or chose to drop out themselves. These women knew that they always had the "exit" option, but between "voice" and "loyalty," they could only opt for the latter. Be happy to have gained entrance to the club, but remain unobtrusive in it, which—oddly enough—excludes passivity. Once again, here is Jillian:

> I think it is easier to be a passive sports fan if you are a man. You can watch the game when it's on, discuss it when you feel like it, and not be questioned if you want to attend a game. As a woman, it is harder to be a less intense fan. If you say you like sports, you are immediately questioned about why you do and how much you know and if you *really* like sports and are a *real* sports fan. So somehow, women always fall in the middle; we can't be *true* sports fans because we don't know enough, can't possibly understand it, don't care enough, or don't follow it 24/7. However, we also can't just simply like sports—our comments are called "cute" and our participation comical. This does not give us a lot of confidence in this male setting.

And Sarah has this to contribute:

> Men seem to have the ability to take more risk when discussing sports—in terms of speculation, commentary, etc.—than women, probably because it is taken for granted that when a man speaks about sports he has a baseline understanding of the material just because he is a man. Men are given an automatic pass for something that women may never quite attain in the same manner even if they know a lot . . . . Women can be totally fluent in a sports language but may never feel as if they speak it with the native ease that men do . . . What makes matters worse still is that even being known for having a working knowledge of sports does not guarantee a woman an entrance into the male-dominated conversation. Sports, and sports viewing in particular, have the

characteristics of an activity that is designed to be exclusive for men, as an escape from female accompaniment.

It is not surprising that this world of constant doubt, relentless suspicion, and reluctant welcome and acceptance provided a thriving milieu for a constant stereotype threat: Women are not supposed to be insiders of hegemonic sports culture, do not feel secure in it, and are constantly worried about reproducing all of the stereotypes that men have of them. So women actually do so, with some frequency, in their actual behavior.

Yet, despite women's obviously marginal and subordinate role in the male-dominated world of sports, men experience women's presence in it as strange, odd, even threatening. Let us look at a few comments from our interviewees emphasizing this aspect.

Challenging and Threatening to Men

In her detailed study of thirty-three top-level female sports journalists, Gillian Warmflash repeatedly encountered the phenomenon of sports-savvy women being threatening to men in her respondents' elaborations. She writes: "The interviewees are most personally reminded of sports' maleness, however, in their interactions with other sports fans . . . men unfamiliar with the interviewees' fandom and extensive sports knowledge generally react, both strongly and visibly—with surprise, with glee, with anger—to the presence of a rare woman well-informed about sports." A major sports writer at a leading East Coast daily who did not want her identity revealed had this to say to Warmflash: "I have always been viewed initially as a novelty by men. Their first impression when they hear I'm into sports is, 'Oh, how cute.' Even then, most [men] are uncomfortable arguing with me."[4]

Please note the terms "anger" and "arguing," which—either in these very forms or in those of various synonyms—appear constantly in our own subjects' responses as well. People, of course, argue about lots of topics, and arguments—like most things in our culture—are gendered. But men's reactions to women's presence in sports have a different quality than their reactions to women's presence in politics or culture or most other areas of interest, knowledge, and passion in that these reactions are comprehensive and one-sided and a priori *only* directed at women as the sole "other," nobody else. Indeed, it is notable how precisely the opposite pertains to such other major social markers as class, religion, or ethnicity. One of the immense emotive powers of hegemonic sports is that, like few, if any, other venues, they provide a true medium of understanding,

---

[4]Warmflash, "In a Different Language."

even brief moments of empathy and solidarity, between rich and poor, Jews and Gentiles, blacks and whites. Of course, divisions along these fault lines remain exclusive, massive, and even violent, as is—alas—still the case in European and Latin American soccer. Of course, there are "working-class" and "upper-class" teams, Catholic and Protestant clubs, and "leftist" and "rightist" sides. So suspicion and exclusion reign supreme in all sports. Indeed, that is the very nature of any partisanship, of team loyalty, of home field advantage. But when it comes to refraining from the partisanship of particular teams and joining the large body of sports as a whole, especially those constituting a country's hegemonic sports culture, men do not exclude other men at all. Indeed, regardless of their class, ethnicity, or religion, they *include* men with glee and delight, and without suspicion and anger and the need to test and compete. Maleness alone suffices as the requisite and uncontested entry requirement. Indeed, as we mentioned before, sports, more than virtually any other venue, offer men both bonding and bridging capital across major fault lines, such as class, ethnicity, and religion.

Here are some comments from our interviewees: "In college, you meet people . . . my friends introduce me as the sportswriter for *The* [Michigan] *Daily*, often saying, 'She knows more about sports than you do.' That's where the tension comes in immediately. They're waiting for some sort of new trivia to come up so they can catch you," said Nicole. She continued, "Now, when I talk to guys, and I know way more about sports than they do, they get really weird about it and try to out-do you." As Samantha informed us,

> Even my boyfriend, who I have dated for two years, enjoys watching sports with me, acknowledges that I know a lot about sports or more than any other girl he knows, but will never admit that I know more or that I am more of an insider than himself. I somehow feel that he could never do this. I feel like that [sports knowledge and being sports insiders] is something that men want to protect and they believe [it] is their expertise and theirs alone.

Courtney Mercier, the aforementioned varsity soccer player at Michigan who kept a diary for us of her experiences on the team that we mentioned earlier, added the following: "One male player joked around with me one time, saying that it was 'creepy' how much I knew about hockey. He was impressed by my knowledge but also threatened by it." Laura had this to say: "I was always conscious of being a female sports fan. I would never bring up sports around guys who didn't watch sports because I didn't want to insult their masculinity." Annie told us the following: "Out of romantic relationships, most of the guys I dated were athletes. However, I was recently told by a guy of interest—not a college athlete, I might add—that I intimidated him because I knew more about sports than he did. He said he felt that I wasn't making him seem as masculine and that's why he prefers girlie girls." Of additional interest to our argument in this book is the fact that it was a non-athlete who seemed intimidated by Annie's sports knowledge. Perhaps an athlete might have been less so. And here is Jillian on this topic: "My father would call me downstairs so that his friends could get a kick out of how much I understood about football. They would quiz me about certain things, ask me to call plays and try to make bets with me. They were very impressed and pleased but also somehow uneasy about my detailed knowledge of things. Maybe even a bit threatened." And Kate concurred: "As [for] my male friends and what they think of me being a knowledgeable sports fan: I think that it is a little of both; they most definitely feel threatened by it but also a bit amused." She continued, "Men make fun of me for knowing so much about the sport world. They will call me a 'tomboy' or they will argue with me and tell me that I don't know anything." The choice is clear: Either women are unfeminine or have to be defeminized—rendered into "tomboys"—to be taken seriously by men as equivalent interlocutors in sports, or they are coded as ignorant if they remain "real" (i.e., feminine) women.

Victorious women in all matters of hegemonic sports are particularly threatening to men. This pertains as much to events on the field as they do in the world of fantasy. Read what Fay told us: "Sometimes . . . in my online fantasy baseball league, when I won the first time, the men doubted me, thinking that one of their friends had invented my team. They didn't believe I was for real. A woman could not have beaten them in fantasy baseball. This was simply not possible. When I won a second time, they implemented new rules to take the power out of my team. This year, these changed rules are no longer in place, since one of them won last year."

Clearly, these tensions have costs to all involved: To the men who feel intruded on and threatened in one of the last remaining domains of unmitigated maleness in the world of advanced liberal democracies, but who, on another level, cannot relish treating women—often the closest humans in their lives in the form of their mothers, sisters, girlfriends, friends, colleagues—as inferior beings in an arena that is so important and central to them. There is tension all around. As Warmflash argues in her thesis,

> Overall, then, it is not only male fans who display uneasiness with the idea of women participating in a male-dominated world, but female fans who also express discomfort being female in this male arena, exhibiting a gender-driven self-consciousness in their interactions with the hegemonic, male-dominated sports culture. This persisting unease displayed by both men and women seems to make it unlikely that sports culture will become gender-neutral anytime soon.

And to render things much more complicated for sportistas than they already are, it turns out that they do not only constitute an imagined and experienced threat to men but also to women. Let us look at a few of the sentiments expressed in this direction by our sportista respondents.

Challenging and Threatening to Women

Here, all of the tangled issues concerning beauty, femininity, intelligence, knowledge, expertise, legitimacy, and credibility that we addressed in previous chapters emerged in full force. But so did women's rivalry for men. Sarah says, "My girlfriends get really jealous and threatened because whenever we're out or hanging with guys we inevitably start talking about sports. Many girls find that threatening because they can't interact with guys in the same manner, and feel out of the loop." Caitlin repeatedly felt that women who found out about her love and knowledge of, as well as interest in, sports "dismissed her as one of the guys." Jillian experienced that "sometimes women who do understand and know sports—or certainly could easily learn to—pretend that they are not interested at all and tout their ignorance to seem more feminine." There is, of course, what one could call the sportista's impatience, even arrogance, vis-à-vis the woman who embodies the typical female sports fan, whom we featured in Chapter 4. "As terrible as this sounds, I feel like I often treat females who claim to love sports as I myself am treated by males," said Samantha, meaning with impatience, contempt, and irritation, seeing them as ignorant imposters, who—and this is crucial—make the sportista's stand even more difficult than it already is, because, these regular female sports fans merely confirm all of the prejudices that men harbor against most women relating to sports, which, of course, includes the sportistas, whose distinction vis-à-vis the other women men will not need to acknowledge or respect. Laura had some fascinating things to say on this important topic:

> I tried not to talk about sports in front of girls when I was growing up. I still try not to do so to this day because I never want to put myself on a pedestal or be exclusive and appear somehow arrogant or a know-it-all.
>
> Sometimes girls think that because I like sports that makes me incredibly different from them so they don't feel like they can talk to me about other things. Indeed, they fear that because I like sports and know and care so much about them, I will not be available to do all kinds of girl stuff with them. They see sports as a direct competitor to such girl things . . . I've toned down my sports around girls because it hasn't always been taken well. I just remember in high school girls thinking I only liked sports because I wanted to talk to the boys. The

"girl sports fans" I knew wore pink jerseys and only had limited sports knowledge that was specific to one team. They set the standard for the norm which I didn't want to be associated with because these girls weren't genuine fans.

And here are Laura's concerns as to how beauty might ipso facto delegitimate expertise in her assessment of Erin Andrews's standing: "Erin Andrews makes me nervous because she knows what she's talking about but the emphasis is often on her looks and not the content of her reporting. I prefer Suzy Kolber, Michele Tafoya, Pam Ward or Andrea Kremer." It is, in fact, a matter of personal taste whether Erin Andrews is indeed more beautiful than these other very attractive female reporters. But there is no question that, by virtue of many factors way beyond the purview of our book, Erin Andrews has come to be perceived as a "babe," meaning that there is the widely held (though, of course, totally unfair) view that ESPN mainly employs her because of her looks rather than her sports knowledge, which, by all measures, is stellar and impressive and, as Laura rightly states, "she knows what she's talking about." Laura is merely articulating a widely held view of Erin Andrews and her role that makes Laura—and many of her fellow sportistas—uneasy: the sexualization of the female sports reporter and thus her concomitant delegitimation as a credible expert and consummate professional.

Of course, there exist sportistas who have absolutely no problem reconciling this important aspect of their lives with doing purely "girly" things with their girlfriends. Here is Samantha: "Although I am really into sports, it is not like my devotion to them has made me have less in common with my female friends, as we share other things in common still."

Sportistas clearly play a mediating, interpretive role between sports and their girlfriends. Alisa informs us:

Of course not all of my friends share the same passion for sports that I do . . . but I tend to gravitate towards girls that are interested in sports. In my mind, I equate "down-to-earth"-ness with sports. If I can strike up a conversation about Michigan football with someone, I somehow begin to think of her as less materialistic or dramatic . . . Because I feel the need to justify my involvement in a sorority and prove that I am not a stereotypical sorority girl, I use the fact that many of the girls gather in the TV room to watch college football on a Saturday night or watch the Tigers in the playoffs to show that we're not "girly girls." That being said, I don't make a point to watch sports with girls. My love for sports is not something that I share with my close female friends, but rather something that they lovingly tolerate.

Quite often, sportistas serve as resources for other women, who tap their expertise to get some information about sports that they want or need for a specific occasion or—often also—for a particular (usually male) person. As advanced speakers of the language of sports, sportistas serve as primers for other women by providing them with a basic speaking knowledge lest they get totally lost in this male-dominated cultural complex, as in an example given by one interviewee:

> "Nicole, we need you to give us a sports primer. Nicole, can you tell us what are the big things going on in sports? Can you also explain the basics of college football?" I had to teach them. I am getting texts from my girlfriends [saying], "What's THE game tonight?" or "Who won the Yankees game?" My girlfriends are always coming to me with all these sports questions. I am their resource. They want to know, but nothing in detail, nothing deep. They just want to be able to converse with the guys on a basic level, want to know vaguely what the guys are talking about all the time.

The aforementioned sports journalist from Warmflash's thesis who chose to remain anonymous had the following insightful comments about the distinction between "real" and "regular" female sports fans: "Real fans [our sportistas] follow sports, not just watch the events which everyone is 'supposed' to watch. I find that that [the latter] applies to most women, again, they view it as a social gathering vs. something they want to actually watch." And the journalist confides that she was never able to share her devotion to sports with her friends, male or female, while growing up. She saw herself as having been somewhat socially disadvantaged by virtue of her sports passion.

Sportistas like Jillian seek distinction by separating themselves from "regular" or "normal" female sports fans, whom she, as a sportista, does not regard as genuine, quite similar to how men view women, without bothering much to distinguish between sportistas and their sisters who are less conversant in sports languages. Jillian notes,

> Some of my girlfriends speak about sports to guys only by saying which athletes they think are cute. These examples, of course, are women who aren't really sports fans. The standards for a "real" female fan, I think, are lower. If a female is aware of the team's record and who they played last, men "applaud" her and think that this is this girl's real capability.

What Jillian, of course, implied with her comments was that men should indeed be impressed with *her* knowledge of, and commitment to, sports, which is indeed impressive. However, few men—beside Jillian's father, of course—might give her due credit for this achievement. Sportistas are engaged in a constant battle of not having their status and stature—their distinction—diminished by the lesser standards attained by regular female sports fans.

The tensions and complexities defining the relationship between sportistas and regular female sports fans, on the one hand, and sportistas and male fans, on the other, play out in the context of all hegemonic sports cultures and are in no way confined to the United States. The nature of the sports differs, but the substance of the struggle is well-nigh identical. Thus, for example, Katharine W. Jones's research on female fandom in men's professional football in England solidly confirms all of the patterns that we studied and described with our American examples.[5] First, just like in the world of the Big Four, women in English football stadiums "perform fandom with the knowledge that, to some male fans, their gender makes them inauthentic."[6] We are sure that this constant feeling of inauthenticity goes well beyond the purview of the stadiums and pertains to pubs, living rooms, attics, studies, pretty much anyplace in which men consume their beloved football (baseball, basketball, American football, and ice hockey, in their North American equivalents). Not having authenticity—which entails being without credibility and legitimacy—in any pursuit will shake anybody's confidence, even an otherwise confident person's. Thus, attaining such authenticity is of paramount importance, and anybody or anything impeding this acquisition has to be dismissed in no uncertain terms. Above all, the authenticity seeker will want to establish a clear distinction between herself, having undergone the trials and tribulations to attain such authenticity, and her former peers, who never did but whose very existence continues to threaten the newly anointed member's still precarious position. Here is Jones with findings from her English football examples:

> The interviewees in this category [Jones calls them "proper fans," which is tantamount to our sportistas] had strong ideas about which women should be considered real or authentic fans. Just like women in other male-dominated spaces, they distanced themselves from displays of emphasized femininity by rejecting women who, to their eyes, did not do fandom properly. Thus, they complained about women getting "dolled up" to go to football matches, wearing makeup and high heels or only going because their boyfriends had taken them. They also used language typical of male fans . . . to disparage some female fans—"they

---

[5]Katharine W. Jones, "Female Fandom: Identity, Sexism, and Men's Professional Football in England," *Sociology of Sport Journal* 25 (2008): 516–537.

[6]Ibid., 520.

just haven't got a clue what's going on [in] the game" . . . They told stories of women they knew who claimed to be fans but did not understand
the offside rule or who "let . . . us all down" by finding players attractive.
They were annoyed by "silly little girls" and "bimbos" who went to football to try to pick up a man because they gave "real fans" a bad name.
Thus, they disliked female fans who practiced emphasized femininity.[7]

Jones's research shows that English sportistas do not like emphasized femininity in fans because it, by definition, disqualifies them as "proper fans" and
codes them as "bimbos." That would be fine if such pejorative associations
were confined to these women and did not "bleed" further. But in the sportistas' view—and fear—it most certainly does affect all women and thus risks
tainting sportistas as unserious "bimbos" as well. Jones concludes, perhaps a
tad too harshly, but certainly not unreasonably, that "perhaps because of the
negative stereotypes of female fans, the gender negotiations of these interviewees [meaning sportistas] suggest that they sometimes did not want to be
reminded that they were women."[8]

Gauging from this presentation, it would appear that being a sportista is
mainly fraught with difficulties, tensions, and contradictions that make such
existence unpleasant and uncomfortable. Far from it: Being a sportista offers
much-valued social currency and provides distinction that is immensely positive and pleasing. The advantages of being a sportista are numerous.

Once a woman has established the elusive but all-powerful authenticity,
or "street cred," with the insiders of the sports world (i.e., men), she is fully
accepted as "one of the guys." Her views are fully respected, her voice is listened to; she will not be dismissed easily. She now has the freedom to commit errors without the risk of being excluded from the club. Entry established,
voice and loyalty are now guaranteed and the threat of exit banned.

"I know that being such a fan of sports has strengthened my relationships
with my male friends, because we always have something to talk about," said
Samantha. What she meant by "something to talk about" was, of course, something "meaningful," something "deep," to talk about—creating a hitherto in-
accessible bond with men, not one man, not dad, not uncle, not brother, not

---

[7]Ibid., 528. Very similar patterns exist in the world of German soccer. Only 30 percent of German
women express even the vaguest interest in the game, and many of those purportedly do so as a
medium to connect with men. Many do not know—and do not care about—the intricacies of the
game, its history, or its "language," and they are often more interested in commenting on the players' attractive or "cute" physical appearance than on their performance on the field. See Darya
Brjantzewa, "Replika: Hotjat li Zhenshiny Futbol," Deutsche-Welle-World, November 10, 2011,
available at http://www.dw.de/dw/article/0,,15517386.html (accessed November 12, 2011).

[8]Ibid., 529.

boyfriend, but *men*, plural. And as Liz mentioned in her comments, men really respect a woman and accept her in the fraternity of sports culture if she knows the "deep structure" of sports, meaning that she knows more than just superficial facts, the kind that Nicole's female friends always want to extract from her, just to be able to drop a few hints here and there, feigning interest in sports when talking to men. Liz states, "I have not found men to think that my sports knowledge is amusing, annoying or inferior. I think that is because I can talk strategy. So, knowing a few facts is one thing, but being able to talk strategy in a lot of sports is another, and I think men appreciate that aspect." Clearly, Liz qualifies as a sportista: She can talk strategy, she knows a lot of sports, she does not confine her sports identity to rooting for one or two teams—which she most definitely does, incidentally—but engages in a number of them, both on an emotional and, most importantly, on an intellectual basis.

After having featured the voices of some of our amateur sportistas whom we interviewed, we now would like to give a brief analysis of a fascinating and relevant new venue that will undoubtedly have a major bearing for both of our sportistas, professional and amateur: espnW. With ESPN having become a culture of its own and, without any doubt, *the* most important purveyor, communicator, and interpreter of sports in North America—the network's *SportsCenter* has become an indispensable part of contemporary American culture way beyond sports—it clearly has had a major impact on gender relations in the United States. Still a bastion of male discourse and culture, the network has also come to feature women as important cultural figures in the past two decades. Female reporters, like the aforementioned Erin Andrews, Michele Tafoya, Suzy Kolber, Pam Ward, Andrea Kremer, and—more important still—current and former anchors, like Cindy Brunson, Hannah Storm, Linda Cohn, Robin Roberts, Betsy Ross, Jane Chastain, Dana Jacobson, and Sage Steele, not only have been major pioneers for women in the world of sports journalism but also have actually become nationally known figures of decided public recognition and cultural importance of their own. So with this major and powerful network introducing a program named espnW—with the "W," of course, standing for "women"—it would be remiss on our part not to discuss this issue in a book focused on the interaction of women and sports in contemporary America.

The Sportista's Reflection on espnW

In October 2010, ESPN announced that it would soon be launching a new "brand" under its name. ESPN had, of course, been quite prolific in creating microcosmic versions of its sports coverage within the United States that focus on a specific category of sports consumer and a specific geographical region. Pertaining to the latter, a handful of major sports cities (New York, Chicago,

Boston, Dallas, and Los Angeles) have their own sections on ESPN's website (ESPN.com) and ESPN radio programs that feature all of the sports news concerning these metropolitan regions' teams. In addition, ESPN has also come to focus on particular levels of sport. Thus, for example, high school athletes have been specifically targeted by way of ESPN Rise, and college athletics are the sole focus of the cable channel ESPNU. The vast breadth of sports affords ESPN not only an unprecedented national stage to become culturally synonymous with sports but also plenty of opportunities to narrow its focus on only one city's sports (as in ESPN Boston, Chicago, New York, Los Angeles, and Dallas) or a particular demographic's (high school and college). The announcement in October 2010, though, was significant because it meant that ESPN would be aiming to capture a demographic that was not sought after and was not included—in fact, the very demographic that currently constitutes 24 percent of its television viewership: women.[9] The brand was to be called espnW, or ESPN "for women." Rather than becoming the medium of an already established and well-known clientele, with espnW's creation, the network entered uncharted waters in search of a hitherto neglected collective whose commitment to sports was—at best—unknown.

At the time of the announcement, espnW was described as "a brand marketed to women that will begin in the spring [of 2011] as a digital presence and could eventually expand to television."[10] Its homepage explains that "espnW is a destination for women who are passionate sports fans and athletes." In the examples of other ESPN variations just mentioned, the vectors of distinction that are employed in delineating each specialized subset within ESPN are clear, as is the purpose and message of the targeted focus. That is, what ESPNU "means" is clear: It will be a channel or section of ESPN's larger website that covers only college athletics. ESPN Boston is no mystery, either: It features the sports news related to Boston teams. ESPN Rise is a specific online brand whose content is meant for high school athletes. And there is, of course, ESPN Deportes, the Spanish language ESPN that specializes in sports particularly popular in the immensely diverse Latino community of the United States: soccer for folks hailing from South America, Mexico, and Central America and also baseball for those from the Spanish-speaking Caribbean countries and, of course, Mexico as well. ESPN also has an international presence, with variations in programming being reflective of cultural norms in each coun-

---

[9]Marcus Vanderberg, "ESPN Targeting Female Demographic with espnW," October 1, 2010, available at http://www.mediabistro.com/sportsnewser/espn-targeting-female-demographic-with-espnw_b1743 (accessed August 22, 2011).

[10]Katie Thomas, "ESPN Introducing espnW, a Digital Presence for Women," *New York Times*, October 15, 2011: B15.

try. There is ESPN America, ESPN's presence in Europe, broadcasting American sports on that continent with increasing success. ESPN.co.uk broadcasts American sports to British audiences and has grown to become a major presence in the local broadcasting of sports popular in the United Kingdom. And the network plays a huge role in the broadcasts of sports in Latin America and Asia. In each of these cases, the organization prides itself on following a well-designed strategy: Have an identical format everywhere, down to the globally iconic music accompanying the beginning of *SportsCenter*, the identical anchor desks, and other visuals, but vary the content from country to country, from culture to culture, featuring the local hegemonic sports cultures interpreted by local experts. If Argentinian soccer dominates ESPN's Argentinian variant, then soccer, rugby, and cricket are featured in its British version, and cricket in its Indian incarnation.

All of these obvious and very clear distinctions in each and every one of these cases remained blurred in espnW's. What exactly was to differentiate its content from ESPN's? ESPNU covers college sports, and ESPN Boston covers Boston sports; will espnW cover women's sports? Is it for women first, who may or may not have particular interest in all of its content (a targeted demographic, as in the case of ESPN Rise), or is it for all people, male or female, who are fans of women's sports? Or as Nicole, our interviewee, phrased it: "Who is this really for? If you're like, 'What's on your iPod?' I think that's fine, but I think it generalizes all women . . . Like people who would care about espnW might be some girl who listens to [pop singer] Ke$ha while working out."

The confusion that we faced on ESPN's announcement of this new "brand for women" was further extended by a possible third option: that espnW will be for female athletes or former athletes and will focus more on women's fitness and health.

We were confused. Is espnW a digital setting for increased coverage of women's college and professional sports? If so, will the site (or eventual television channel) cover any popular men's sports? Is it going to be a woman's "take" on popular (men's) sports, a sort of "safe haven" for female sports fans to escape the bullying and constant derision that they encounter on male-dominated sports sites? Is it even going to focus on popular sports at all, or instead will it cover participatory sports, offering advice about running, yoga, and Pilates? In Dan Levy's words, "Does espnW make [female fans] proud—a sign of sports fan solidarity—or the exact opposite?"[11] The sole thing that was clear at this time was that we were not alone in our confusion.

---

[11] Dan Levy, "ESPN Launches espnW. (Well, This Headline Sure Got Right to the Point.)," *Press Coverage*, December 6, 2010, available at http://presscoverage.us/media/espn-launches-espnw-well-this-headline-sure-got-right-to-the-point (accessed May 11, 2011).

In a blog post on December 16, 2011, Levy opined, "Let's say, for the sake of this example, the existing sports fan landscape is 80% men and 20% women. Is espnW hoping to get much of that existing 20% as its core audience, or will it be looking to grow from the birth of a new, female-only audience that has been yet untapped?"[12] "Do enough people care about women's sports to pay attention to espnW, or will the site be more 'a women's take' on all sports?" In a sportista's blog comically entitled "Same Size Balls," on December 6, 2010, in a post titled "What is the 'female sports fan'?" the author writes: "Is espnW espnW because it comes from a female perspective? Well, maybe, but there are many women sports writers. Is espnW espnW because it is written to a female audience? I would guess that that is the difference from ESPN.com . . . and other sports outlets. Perhaps the female-audience factor is at work in the site's content and that is the fundamental difference between espnW and other women's sports coverage." The author continues, "if it's not *just* about women's sports and if it's not *just* about women writers, then it must be about the way espnW figures the female sports fan tends to ingest sports."[13]

With an understanding of the demonstrably large difference between the *doing* and the *following* of sports, it is clear to us that the two parts of espnW's target demographic—female sports fans (sportistas) and female athletes—are most likely not going to have their needs met by the same things. Tina Johnson, editor-in-chief of espnW, explained in June 2011 that espnW's goal is "to inspire the female athlete and fan." The content is meant to cater to women, "as sports fans and athletes as well." It is Johnson's understanding that " the sports fan and the athlete are one in the same," at least when referring to espnW's core audience. "[The espnW woman] is a fan *because* she is or was an athlete; she probably watches sports because she played them," Johnson explains. Laura, one of our sportista interviewees, highlighted precisely why sportistas may take issue with this notion, when she explained: "[my fandom is] not inspired by my playing sports. Instead, being a fan inspires me to go play them."

In this work, we have amply highlighted the disconnect between the "doers," or athletes, and the "followers," or fans; many of the men (and women) who visit ESPN.com every day and watch *SportsCenter* every night are, in fact, far from being premier athletes themselves. To cater to the female athlete is not necessarily to cater to the female sports fan; "women sports fans" are, as we know, not necessarily "women's sports fans." If espnW is to be a place for more coverage and discussion of women's sports (which, as of 2009, only received

---

[12]Ibid.

[13]Same Size Balls blog, "What Is the 'Female Sports Fan'? espnW Attempts to Define," December 6, 2010, available at http://samesizeballs.wordpress.com/2010/12/06/what-is-the-female-sports-fan-espnw-attempts-to-define (accessed May 11, 2011). Emphasis in the original.

1.4 percent of *SportsCenter*'s total programming time), if it "can get people to care about women's college volleyball or softball or the WNBA," as Levy wrote, "that'd be great for those sports."[14] Finally, women's sports fans would have a place to get more in-depth analysis, commentary, and discussion on women's college and professional sports. That seems to be the only recourse of the aforementioned "options" or directions that espnW could pursue that would not bore, irritate, and embarrass a sportista, whether amateur or professional.

Each of the mentioned possibilities for espnW's content and angle present their own questions and potential problems. Let us briefly discuss them:

1. *espnW is about women's sports.* This new construct covers more closely women's college basketball, softball, WNBA, U.S. women's soccer, women's tennis, women's golf, and other major women's sports. Thus, it may very well represent a promising new medium, venue, and opportunity for such sports to gain more widespread attention. The truth is, though, that this channel or website would be a flop because people, men and women, simply do not watch women's sports in any significant numbers. The women's sports events (and teams) that generate sufficient public interest to amortize coverage expenses can already be found on "regular" ESPN because they involve stories that are popular and relevant to all sports fans. Take the immensely successful Women's World Cup in Germany in the summer of 2011, as an example. Coverage of this popular tournament, for which the women at the helm of espnW clearly had much enthusiasm, was divided between ESPN and espnW in peculiar, yet telling, ways. The coverage of the U.S. women's national team, the group on which espnW had been reporting for months leading up to the actual World Cup, was handled exclusively by the "big guns" at ESPN, once the tournament commenced for real. Coverage of all *other* teams competing in the World Cup, however, fell into the hands of the espnW writers and reporters. The point is clear: The more important an event's content becomes in terms of the breadth and depth of its popularity with the American public, the likelier it will be that ESPN will become this event's broadcaster. Things that remain exotic and less salient to the American public will remain the purview of espnW. Concretely, espnW was in charge of covering the women's national soccer team's preparations before the tournament itself. With very few people outside the still-small soccer community in the United States caring about the U.S. women's soccer team's regular games, apart from the World Cup competition, the product could be "relegated" to espnW. But once relevance emerged with the beginning of the competition in Germany, ESPN took over the event, with espnW

---

[14]Levy, "ESPN Launches espnW."

having to make do by reporting on England's national team and occasionally Australia's, Canada's, New Zealand's, and various others of little interest to any American sports fan, male or female. That is, if a woman's event is popular enough for the fan community at large to care, then ESPN "regular" will cover it. Perhaps, then, espnW will offer space for covering the less mainstream women's events. Though this option may seem like a positive opportunity to showcase women's sports—to give them a hitherto denied space—it might actually be detrimental to their fate concerning the broadening of their fan base and enhancing their popularity. There clearly is a danger of such sports' becoming marginalized and ghettoized.

Here is Michael A. Messner, an influential sports and gender sociologist, on precisely this issue concerning espnW: "Yes, it's going to give women's sports fans a place to go," he said, "but it might ultimately ghettoize women's sports and kind of take ESPN off the hook in terms of actually covering them on its main broadcast."[15] That is, the miniscule portion of ESPN's attention that women's sports have received might just get shifted to espnW, therefore further removing women's sports from the vision/view/milieu of the male-dominated hegemonic sports culture. It might mark women's sports as a clearly inferior "other," and consequently lessen them even more.

Many men hate when women's games intrude on *their* channel, in their sacred space, even if it is an NCAA championship game. Albertson lived for three years on the University of Michigan campus in a house full of sports-crazy males, and she amassed an extensive collection of anecdotes reflecting this particular male distaste for the unwelcome appearance of women's sports on ESPN. The Tuesday immediately after the NCAA men's basketball tournament's traditional Monday evening championship game—a time of year when the TV is always tuned to a postgame analysis of the men's final; interviews with members of the winning and losing teams; lengthy postmortems of the entire three-week "Big Dance," never mind the bevy of NBA and NHL games inching toward the playoffs in both leagues; various opening days in Major League Baseball; and previews of the impending NFL draft, which was barely two weeks away—one of the young men in the house switched the TV to ESPN (a move that was as much second nature to him and his peers as was brushing their teeth). A collective groan let out as the crowd in the room realized that on the screen was the women's championship game instead of any of the aforementioned possibilities, most, of course, featuring lots of talk instead of an actual game, however, involving men only. None of the young men present wanted to watch this game, which, after all, featured the two very

---

[15]Thomas, "Digital Presence."

best teams in women's Division I college basketball fighting for the national championship.

ESPN's decision to move the women's championship game to the Tuesday after the men's appeared as a triumph for the proliferation of the broadcasting of women's sports on American television. Indeed, viewership rose significantly in the years after the switch from the previous period, when the game was played on Sunday, sandwiched between semifinal Saturday and championship Monday, on the men's side. It bears mentioning in this context that there were plenty of empty seats in the arena in Indianapolis in which the women's championship was contested, something that was totally unthinkable in the male equivalent. What Albertson's anecdote reflects, though, is that it is doubtful whether the American, largely male, sports public—apart from the two areas from which the two contesting teams hailed—was clamoring to watch the women's game, but that it was effectively put right in their way, made unavoidable as they tried to continue with their normal sports programming. The women's game appears during prime time on ESPN, not a major non-sports network, like the men's (in this case, CBS), further strengthening the notion that the women's game's audience may indeed be partially accidental. Albertson's roommates were irritated, indeed aggravated, that the game was disrupting their normal routine, that they could not, for that night, see the normal ESPN programming that had become a part of their daily lives. While the move to Tuesday was clearly a prescient one in terms of drawing larger viewing audiences for the women's NCAA tournament, the increased audience may actually be a function of the fact that people are tuning in to watch ESPN anyway, and the game happens to be on.

Albertson's roommates did not change the channel immediately, but seized the opportunity (or ambush, as they characterized it) to point out all of the reasons why they do not watch women's basketball. In a pattern that is repeated during all kinds of women's sporting events—that is, the few that men bother to watch, even if only by accident—the game becomes an occasion for men to re-up all of the negative stereotypes that they harbor about the alleged inferiorities of women's sports. Men can finally point to all of the things that make women's sports worse, with the "proof" right there on the screen for all to see. This then serves for men to solidify their expertise and to gather more prima facie evidence, were such even needed, for the obvious inferiority of women's sports, which, therefore, are not worth watching. Watching one game per year renders these men experts in women's basketball, which they can now dismiss, although not as macho jerks but rather as informed analysts. What these young men once held as an unsubstantiated prejudice has now been legitimated by way of their stumbling upon the women's game. By creating a place for all women's sports, espnW might just be accidentally demoting them further, almost as if the network were doing the ESPN viewers a favor by getting rid of the girls, both on and off the court.

2. *espnW is going to cover popular sports (which means mostly men's), but cater more specifically to a female audience.* If this were indeed this new entity's raison d'être and mission, then one would assume it to emphasize the interpretive and writing prowess of female sports writers, created, perhaps, in a milieu separate from men. Still, the task remains murky. "If the site is meant to be more 'a women's take' on all sports, why shouldn't those writers be given equal billing to the other (i.e., male) writers on the main ESPN.com site?" Levy wonders.[16] "It shouldn't be about being a man or a woman; sports fans get their news from qualified sports writers of both sexes, and non-fans, well, they don't get sports news."[17] If espnW's intention is to employ female sports writers to write about sports for a female audience, similar problems that were identified in the first scenario may arise: a de facto ghettoization of female sportswriters or broadcasters who are looking for jobs in the industry, who would then be routed to the all-female espnW, a sort of natural home for women working in sports. ("You'd be GREAT for espnW!") If there is a specific place designated as being solely for women, then women might find it harder to compete with their male counterparts for equivalent or identical positions elsewhere.

Moreover, what does appealing to a "female audience" really mean? What does the female sports fan want that the male fan does not? How do female sports fans experience ESPN as deficient or lacking? To be sure, ample research reveals that women—in contrast to men—prefer sports coverage to take more of a human interest angle, to tell stories about the athletes as people rather than feature the games' final results and the various statistics attained by the players in the contest. While this has clearly been shown to be true of women in general, if employed by espnW, it would also typify the putatively preferred narrative of female fans. In terms of the sportista, the atypical woman in sports matters, her interest in the nature of sports coverage, as conventionally (and superbly) furnished by ESPN, does not differ from men's; the sportista, just like her male peers, does not much care about players' upbringing or their moms' cooking habits. Instead, she is merely concerned with the effectiveness of their outside game, their running the break, their jump shot, their assist ratio, and their deficiencies on defense. The presumption that the sportista's gender inevitably has her watching and enjoying sports differently than men do and that, therefore, the male-dominated conventional ESPN broadcasts leave her somehow wanting

---

[16]Levy, "ESPN Launches espnW."

[17]Ibid.

and dissatisfied, which in turn makes the creation of a female-centered sports medium essential, strongly implies a kind of essentialized view of all women's relationship to sports, which is, almost by definition, incompatible with men's. During a presentation at the 2011 convention of the AWSM in Charlotte, one participant, the radio play-by-play commentator for the Bemidji State women's varsity ice hockey team, asked Tina Johnson (editor-in-chief of espnW), "Why would I go to espnW for my NHL news if I was already getting it at ESPN.com?" Johnson answered immediately, nodding her head, "You wouldn't."

However, if espnW's coverage features the same games, stories, and players as ESPN's, then why does one even need this conceptually still murky, but decidedly female-centered, project? Creating something called espnW, an ESPN for women that covers the same big sports stories as its parent, ESPN "regular," renders the latter almost explicitly as being de facto *for men only* since women now have their own ESPN.

To wit: espnW featured a story about Kevin Durant, one of the most dominant players in the NBA and one of the league's unquestioned superstars. However, instead of addressing details of Durant's or his team's play throughout their impressive playoff run in the spring of 2011, which would surely be an absolutely central topic of a comparable player profile piece featured on ESPN. com, the espnW article's headline about Durant read: "Kevin Durant's Secret Weapon: Mom."[18] And the ensuing text's content corresponded to its headline.

This sounds like a stereotypically "female" style of sports coverage, and it is. But that constitutes precisely espnW's very raison d'être: to cater to the typical woman who, as research has amply shown, much prefers this type of "sports" coverage.[19]

If the espnW article on Kevin Durant's relationship with his mother is for women, then the more technical, on-court-related piece on Kevin Durant, the player, must be for men. It is simple: The designation espnW "others" women, thereby delineating their inferiority relative to "real" (i.e., male) sports fans. In other words, espnW informs women that, if they want to know what happened in game two of the Stanley Cup finals, there is a special place for them to do so, a place built for them by their kind of people who understand that they need something to be *different*—decidedly softer, less technical, much shorter—from the more widespread original coverage. Note to women: Get your sports in this place specially designed (and designated) for you, and please leave ESPN.com for the men.

---

[18]Andrew Gilman, "Kevin Durant's Secret Weapon: Mom," espnW, May 25, 2011, available at http://espn.go.com/espnw/news-opinion/6588029/mom (accessed June 4, 2011).

[19]Recall the earlier discussion on athletes being appreciated and followed as *celebrities*, focusing on areas of their lives that are less related to their "craft" and more to their personal story.

The difference between the typical female sports fan and her male counter-parts is the vastly different possession of sports knowledge and the subsequent capacity for interpretation that such knowledge affords. Given this pattern, it is easier to accept and understand espnW's choice to give abbreviated, simple "reports" of games, not bothering with any kind of deep analysis or interpretation that a person (woman) without knowledge is not yet capable of relating to or grasping. The kind of reporting seems to be for a person who wants to know what happened or what games are going to be of interest that night, but who did not herself watch the game and who most likely will not be watching any more tonight. These items are written for somebody who does not appear to be too interested in astute predictions, in-depth commentary on what teams or play-ers should do that night, or any form of analysis that goes beyond the surface level of simple factual reporting. The whole thing appears like those helpful CliffsNotes (formerly Cliffs Notes, originally Cliff's Notes; or Monarch Notes, preferred by some) that proved so handy in the passing of many students' exam-inations, but added little to their knowledge of literature, let alone the apprecia-tion of its beauty and lasting value. As Tina Johnson, editor-in-chief of espnW, explained, espnW "draw[s] from ESPN for the X's and O's, because they do that so well," but then "texturize[s] it by talking about the stories behind the story, about a player's family or personal history."[20] Johnson elaborates on espnW's goal: "ESPN.com does the game cap and the news break so well already . . . one of our biggest challenges is to come up with something *unique* to say about the game." One might wonder, why? Where is the audience for a "unique" report on a discrete sporting event? But, research clearly shows that there are people, mostly women (apparently *only* women, based on the moniker "espnW"), who have an interest in sports as a part of popular celebrity culture but not necessar-ily an interest in the games, competitions, and strategies themselves.

Additionally, feminizing sports reporting might represent a welcome change for some women and even attract them to sports, about which they cared little before the introduction of this new reporting. But it is doubtful that their numbers will be large enough to sustain such a novelty in the long run because we think it is a fair assumption that these converts to espnW sim-ply will not care about sports in a committed way that will make them regular consumers of this project. That is, the women who seek sports' human interest angle may appreciate the stories that they encounter, but this in no way means that they will also follow the essence of these sports, which, when all is said and done, still remains competition—battle, winners, losers, results, collective and individual achievements. If espnW amounts to "sports lite," it will defi-

---

[20]Tina Johnson, panel discussion at the 2011 Association for Women in Sports Media Conference, Charlotte, NC, June 25, 2011.

nitely fail to attract the extant sportista and will be unable to convert the current "regular" female sports consumer into one.

Lastly, it seems that there is, if ESPN wants to use it, space within the realm of "regular" ESPN for a different style of story. What if ESPN were just to incorporate this "softer" style of reporting in its coverage, creating a well-rounded product that could appeal to everyone, without alienating any particular tastes? Instead of designating this kind of human interest reporting as being explicitly for women and forcing any sports fan (male or female) who really *wants* to read about Curtis Granderson's favorite ice cream flavor to leave ESPN.com and find his or her way to espnW.com, why would ESPN not include this type of reporting on its larger site and let ESPN fans—both men and women—read or pass on such items at their own discretion? The results might very well be that women will constitute the overwhelming majority of readers of human interest pieces, but at least in this case, they would not have to feel as though they were demoted from the big boys' site and ghettoized in a second-rate version reserved solely for them.

The idea that sportistas might need sports programming specifically for them—that they do not get what they want and need from ESPN's "regular" content—might be a tad insulting, as it implies that somehow sportistas are not true sports fans in the same way that males are. "Is it fair to assume that any . . . sports fans who are women will visit espnW in addition to their regular stops elsewhere on the Internet just because there's a new site for 'them'?" Levy asks. "What does that even mean? Why would a site for 'them' look any different than the site for all of the rest of the world's (male) fans?" Sportistas do not seek to be singled out by their gender, especially not in a way that is meant to "account for" their gender as the most important determinant of how they consume sports. Contrary to what the vice president of espnW said, sportistas and other women interested in entering the world of sports consumption do not "see [ESPN] as their father's brand, or husband's brand, or boyfriend's brand," nor do they, in their daily visits to ESPN's multiple channels of programming, "recognize it's not theirs."[21]

To be sure, the majority of women do not much care about sports. They feel, correctly, that ESPN has little attraction for them. But it is unlikely that a feminized version will attract such women. Indeed, the danger is more realistic that such a project will alienate the sportistas who have already committed to making sports part of their quotidian culture. "Do we really need BCS, LeBron James and baseball winter meetings stories here?" asks Wendy Parker,

---

[21]Michael Hiestand, "ESPN Aims for Female Audience with espnW," 2010, available at www.usatoday.com/sports/columnist/Hiestand-tv/2010-09-30-espnW-baseball-tv-playoffs_N.htm (accessed June 15, 2011).

with some irritation, on her sportista-geared blog. "Women who are diehard sports fans know where to get this," and it is in a location no different from that where the men go to obtain their sports information.[22]

3. *espnW is going to be for women who play sports, with a focus on health, fitness, and participatory sports.* ESPN, at least to our knowledge and to our reading of its rich and sometimes turbulent history, never attempted to be a medium for the sports producer. From its origins in 1978 to this day, the network's raison d'être was to cater to the sports consumer.[23] The fact is that most of the people who have been ESPN's closest followers are *not* themselves athletes. (In fact, spending many hours on the computer and watching television, almost by definition, means that one does not accord fitness much importance.) If ESPN is looking to expand its coverage to include "participatory" sports (those that many sports fans are themselves doing, including working out at a gym, jogging, and yoga), then an appropriate name might be ESPN Body,[24] or perhaps ESPN Do. The problem with the inclusion and featuring of participatory sports on espnW is that these are then assumed to be only "for women," with the presumption that women "do" sports to take care of their bodies, while men "follow" sports and thereby add to the demise of theirs.

Plenty of people have interest in health and fitness, enough to buy and visit a myriad of magazines, websites, and programs devoted to exercise, nutrition, and beauty. Most of these products are specific to one gender, with different magazines for men's versus women's fitness, for example, but it is important to recognize that there are as many men's magazines in this category as women's and that concern with and interest in health and fitness are not exclusive to women. ESPN should, if it sees fit (as is does at least once a year in *ESPN The Magazine*'s annual "Body Issue"), extend its reach to include these topics in a number of possible venues, but putting health and fitness–related issues under the blanket of espnW does not seem to make sense, especially considering the other types of content within the brand. More women than men may very well have a greater interest in beauty, fitness, human relations angles on sports stories, women's sports, and other categories that are grouped together under

---

[22]Wendy Parker, "Now That espnW is up and Running, What Is It, Exactly?" blog post in *Extracurriculars*, December 6, 2010, available at http://www.wendyparker.org/2010/12/now-that-espnw-is-up-and-running-what-is-it-exactly (accessed April 20, 2011).

[23]James Andrew Miller and Tom Shales, *Those Guys Have All the Fun: Inside the World of ESPN* (New York: Little, Brown and Company, 2011).

[24]Once every year, *ESPN The Magazine* does pursue this topic, coming out with the "Body Issue." This issue usually features a scantily clad female athlete on the cover, with more photos of her and other women baring their bodies inside the publication, but it also contains articles about exercise and nutrition.

espnW's banner, but the labeling of those topics as ESPN's corner "for women" sends a message that the rest of its products and content are for men. If ESPN wants to expand the range and scope of its content, it might consider doing it in a nongendered way, for marking certain presumed writing styles and areas of interest as "female" effectively alienates the women who were already fulfilled by the "regular" content that ESPN provided in its original outlets.

The sportista is a woman who is likely to be concerned about the health of her body and equally likely to take active measures to maintain and augment her health. However, she also follows the Big Four sports avidly and probably belongs to various fantasy leagues. But these latter interests are not covered by espnW. The woman who is more interested in learning about stretching regimens or yoga techniques than in hearing about next week's draft predictions is not a typical ESPN consumer, and, before espnW, her interests were not specifically addressed by any of ESPN's content. If ESPN decides to target her and others like her, then the aim should be to reach other people—both men and women—with that set of interests. ESPN could appropriately name its different brands to reflect the specific interests or preferences that each encapsulates, instead of labeling a wide-ranging set of topics and variations based on the gender that is supposed to prefer it.

In October 2010, right after espnW's introduction to the world, Albertson called her mother to share her frustrations about the implications of this new entity. Mom returned Albertson's call a few days later, telling her that her anger and frustration about espnW were misguided and naïve. Albertson's mother proceeded to tell her daughter that she had consulted with her female friends and they all agreed that they would appreciate and welcome the existence of a more female-geared sports broadcast. Albertson was intrigued. Her mother explained that she and her friends have a hard time watching and enjoying sports games because so much of the commentary goes over their heads; they do not enter the broadcast with a workable knowledge of sports and therefore are quickly lost soon after the games commence. "If you don't know what an offensive line is, then you most likely won't find it interesting or useful to hear commentators discuss a 3–4 versus 4–3 offense or talk about protection in the pocket," Albertson's mother insisted. She and her friends want an option, a channel with its own unique commentators, which will allow them to watch sporting events (they do find enjoyment in watching major sports, especially, she reported, college football) without feeling as if the games are being broadcast in another language. They *want* to become better, more knowledgeable fans, but there is no way for them to transition into it at this point. And with the barrier to entry so stark and foreboding, the option to turn away and not bother becomes very real and attractive. After all, one does not best learn

French by reading Victor Hugo's *Les Misérables* in its original form before having embarked on the acquisition of some basics of French grammar, vocabulary, and elementary literature.

Albertson was genuinely intrigued, on a number of levels, by her mother's reaction. It was interesting that it was these kinds of problems that her mother and her friends contemplated and discussed when they first heard about espnW. That is, they never even assumed that espnW might be a network that covered women's sports, for, as Mrs. Albertson explained to her daughter, after being asked why she and her friends thought in this direction, "ESPN is about popular sports. And popular sports are men's sports." These "normal" (i.e., white, middle-class, educated, suburban) women assumed a priori that an ESPN channel "for women" would mean broadcasts with more basic explanations of the rules and strategies of the (men's) games, which somehow, almost by default, meant that they would be geared to women since most men were fully conversant with such rules and strategies.

In this work, we have already addressed the fact that such an expectation would not be completely erroneous, since most women, in fact, do not know sports that well and could be helped to appreciate them by becoming conversant with the basics. That being said, though, it is not in the interest of the woman who does, in fact, know the basics and then some, who actually is an advanced and nuanced sports speaker and a sophisticated consumer of sports, to have an elaborate new venue solely dedicated to explaining something that she already knows.

The best way to delegitimize sportistas and to make their already tenuous social position more brittle still is to call a watered-down version of sports broadcasting a "women's" version. The key in Mrs. Albertson's understanding of her daughter's frustration, though, was that this whole new venture should not be labeled "for women," for doing so implies that a *woman*, simply by virtue of her gender, cannot understand a "normal" sports broadcast. While this may be the case for most women, the sportista is alienated from the rest of the world's sports fans by the very idea of labeling the new entity espnW, an a priori gendering of an extant difference. Why not call it "ESPN Rookie"? It could be geared toward those lacking sufficient sports knowledge, toward novices of all kinds—children, recent immigrants, and, yes, women, too, as well as men, for that matter. By labeling the entity "ESPN Rookie," one denotes it by a level of knowledge, a degree of expertise, thus universalizing the handicap instead of particularizing it to a specific group, in this case, women. And it is only women whose category lends itself to such a particularization. Yes, there is ESPN Deportes, as we already mentioned, but here the particularization is by language—in this case, Spanish—rather than by such ascriptive categories as religion, ethnicity, or gender. Thus, for example, a JEWSPN would be unthinkable. Daniel Levy had this to say about such in his critical assessment of espnW's founding:

> There are some pretty good Jewish sites on the Internet and some of those sites cover sports. There's a niche out there, sure, but if ESPN started JEWSPN, am I logging on every day to see what Andy Katz or Doug Gottlieb has to say about the best Jews in college sports? (Note to ESPN, if you do eventually start JEWSPN and I'm not asked to be a part of that, heads will roll. Yarmulke'd heads will roll). Would JEW-SPN grow the audience of sports fans by suddenly adding more Jews who didn't previously follow sports, or would the site exist to engage us at the expense of the more traditional, and therefore "non-Jewish," sports sites, like ESPN.com?

One of the online directors at espnW admitted, "I almost wonder if we should have called it something besides espnW. That's where the heat has come from, not that people are upset about what we're producing, but that some women resent being typified, or kind of excluded, like that."[25]

It is obvious that the needs and desires of the advanced doctoral student in French literature writing a dissertation on Victor Hugo will be different from those of the freshman enrolling in an introductory French language course. Moreover, it is very likely that the former will quickly become bored, even irritated, by the material that the latter will find not only challenging but also absolutely necessary to become even minimally conversant in French. To follow this analogy for our topic, expert sports fans (predominantly male, but also comprising a growing segment of sportistas) want their advanced doctoral seminars in baseball, football, basketball, hockey, soccer, rugby, cricket—whatever the language of the respective hegemonic sports cultures might be. And they often display little patience when lesser advanced discourse is brought to bear on a game or other occasions. For example, Europeanized American soccer fans often disdain the elementary, even instructional, commentary used by some American soccer announcers, whom these fans see as ignorant of the game compared with their European or Latin American counterparts, whom these "soccer snobs" deem to have a more sophisticated understanding and appreciation of the game and whose commentary they thus prefer. Experts—even purported ones—will always use their expertise, often in the form of jargon or other exclusionary methods, to distinguish themselves from those whom they deem less knowledgeable or novices to their world. But all these

---

[25]Allison Creekmore, conversation with the authors, June 25, 2011.

expert communities, whatever their specific identity might be, ought to be much more welcoming to the growing constituencies solicitous of courses in beginning and intermediary sports language instruction, precisely because the existence of such courses bespeaks a willingness by the uninitiated to join the club of the cognoscenti.

So these are the "possibilities" and corresponding issues that were in place when we first heard about espnW. What, then, has come to fruition? What did the espnW team choose to pursue? It seems as if it had combined all of the above. In answer to the question "What is espnW?" its own website states that

> espnW is fully dedicated to serving female athletes and fans. We'll shine a brighter spotlight on women's sports, and give you added perspective on the sports stories of the day, while offering personal training tips and guidance from pro athletes, trainers and experts to help you connect with your inner athlete.[26]

This sounds like a perfectly fine idea in itself, but takes a different tone when one remembers that it is supposedly "for women," as consumers. A "brighter spotlight on women's sports" and more attention for exceptional female athletes are surely positive changes for women. "Added perspective" on popular sports stories and "personal training tips" comprise entirely appropriate topics for ESPN to branch out and begin covering. ESPN could enrich the content of the site and might even find that the new content reaches new audiences—female and, lo and behold, male, too. The issue that a sportista seems to have with the current espnW model is that these changes and additions are all justified as being specifically, if not exclusively, "for women." Maybe espnW's current content is for a (predominantly, but not necessarily, female) group that thirsts for more women's sports coverage; maybe it is for those who appreciate the "story behind the story" and would like a break from the same callous writing style that is typically used in sports journalism; maybe it is for gym rats and fitness buffs. The point is that all of these "types" could be women *and* men. The common factor in these different themes, topics, approaches, and target groups should not be assumed to be one's gender. It is in the lazy and facile gendering as a convenient solution to these complex problems that the sportista finds her frustration.

We would like to close this chapter with a very salient passage from the concluding section of Gillian Warmflash's fine thesis, which, we believe, captures superbly the gist of our current chapter as well as our book. With Warm-

---

[26]search.espn.go.com/espnw-women-+-sports-summit/ (accessed May 9, 2012).

flash having written her thesis under Markovits's guidance, we feel a kinship to her work that enhances ours:

I must return now, however, to the topic of sports language . . . since I believe that women's position in America's sports culture landscape could ultimately come down to this issue. Women are certainly capable of learning sports language, in the strictest, most technical sense of the word; that is, they are capable of learning sports jargon, rules, idioms, and statistics. My interviewees are proof of this point. Raised in sports fan families in sports-crazy cities, young girls can pick up sports language as easily as they can pick up Italian or Spanish. Yet fluency might be insufficient for their total inclusion in the fan landscape. Just as speaking German fluently does not make one a native-born citizen of Germany, so speaking sports fluently does not make one a native-born citizen of America's hegemonic sports culture.

This is the case because sports language is not merely a language of sports—it is a language of men, as the interviewees—and popular consciousness, really—make clear. [Thus, for example, Liz] Clarke [of the *Washington Post* in November 2003, when Warmflash interviewed her] and [Dana] Jacobson [of ESPN *SportsCenter* and ESPN News in November 2003, when Warmflash interviewed her] specifically make the point that sports language is a language of men. Clarke says that "sports are a currency among men, they're what you trade, they're what you talk about." Jacobson similarly argues that "most men have talked about sports most of their lives. They know that another guy will be interested, so it is a safe place to go." And [Margaret] Grossi [of *Real Sports with Bryant Gumbel* on HBO Sports in November 2003, when Warmflash interviewed her] stated that "sports are a common denominator for men." Due to the strong historical relationship between masculinity and sports . . . as well as men's domination of the sports fan landscape, male fans have the privilege of determining what type of sports language—both its vernacular and the manner in which it is used—serves as sports culture's "national language." As a result, sports language as jargon (and not players' personal stories) and sports language as a means of impersonal communication (and not expressive communication) rule. More importantly, however, beyond such textual connotations, sports language has meta-textual connotations. Due to the societal imperative for men to participate in and follow sports, sports language is integral to the way in which men relate to each other; indeed, it is like a secret handshake among fraternity members not to be shared with outsiders (i.e., women), a common denominator that unites the doctor, the cabbie, and the vendor. *Speaking sports is analogous to speaking "man,"* [our emphasis] and by virtue of men having to speak it, the language itself assumes a male quality. Put differently, there is a gendered component to sports language that one cannot acquire or understand except by being born male.

For these reasons, then, women might not even be able to experience native-born citizenship in American sports culture. Women's construction of sports language as vernacular, though it might include sports terminology, also includes players' backgrounds and stories, and women's use of sports language as a form of communication, though at times impersonal, is generally quite expressive. Their version of sports language thus overlaps with sports culture's national language, but does not perfectly coincide with it. More importantly, however, women lack the societal imperative to participate in sports and become fans. Sports language is not integral to their communication with each other. *Speaking sports is not analogous to speaking "woman."* [our emphasis]

Indeed, as our discussion of the sometimes tense relationship between sportistas, on the one hand, and regular female sports fans, indeed, women as a whole, on the other hand, clearly delineated, whereas the identities of "man" and "fan" are totally congruous and expected, the identities of "woman" and "fan" are anything but. Thus, speaking sports to men conforms to—and confirms—their expected gender identity. The exact opposite pertains to women's fluency in sports languages. The identities of "woman" and "sports fan" collide with each other, and, if they are not solidly incompatible, they most definitely are fraught with difficulties and contradictions in our hegemonic culture. Thus, to a certain extent, being a sportista at least tacitly implies muting, perhaps even downgrading, if not outright denying, one's femininity.

Back to Warmflash:

In many ways . . . in the modern sports landscape, achievement prevails. On the question of gender, however, ascription still appears to win out: One component of sports language remains elusive to women simply by virtue of their being female. Female fans, therefore, may remain "immigrants" or "naturalized citizens" in American sports culture, and as such speak with "accents" about sports. Since they were not "born on the home soil," however, native-born citizenship may evade them.[27]

---

[27]Gillian Lee Warmflash, "In a Different Language: Female Sports Fans in America" (unpublished honors thesis, submitted to the Committee on Degrees in Social Studies, Harvard University, Cambridge, MA, March 2004), 111–113. This reminded Markovits of a story that an Orthodox

All of this is much more pronounced in "speaking sports" than in "speaking physics" or math or engineering because the latter are elite pursuits, limited to a relatively small group of mainly male participants, whereas sports is arguably *the* most popular—thus most democratic—channel of intra-male communication, even more so than politics, religion, and other mass subjects, because all of these are fraught with tensions and conflicts that sports, as a whole, do not have. Above all, not all men purport to be experts in any of these fields the way that they do—and are expected to—in sports. Remember how male respondents to our sports survey at the University of Michigan, as well as at the German and Austrian universities, desperately pondered questions to which they did not know the answer, but felt compelled to try responding by virtue of some amorphous, yet keenly experienced, societal obligation that men, if true to their gender, are to know the details of sports history. None of the women on either side of the pond exhibited any such behavior. They blithely returned their questionnaires, not worried in the least that they might be ignorant of the players for the New York Yankees of the 1950s, the players of the Boston Celtics of the 1960s, or the members of the World Cup–winning German national teams of 1954, 1974, or 1990. Women did not feel even a modicum of shame for their lack of sports knowledge in the same way that at least some men on both sides of the Atlantic clearly did. To men, sports provides a widely accessible and commonly experienced "haze of male exclusivity," as *The Atlantic's* Ta-Nehisi Coates so properly called the possibly insurmountable hurdle that his wife's becoming a football fan encountered.[28] J. Danielle expands eloquently on this "haze of male exclusivity" as an essential marker of sports: "For some reason, men think they own sports. They think there is some innate thing that makes them inherently more knowledgeable and that women who watch sports are anomalies they should examine. Not only do men challenge a woman's knowledge of sports more than they challenge the knowledge of other men, they also find it their business to analyze a woman's intentions and behavior . . . If a man believes something is inherently male, then he doesn't feel compelled to take a woman seriously unless she jumps through

---

Jewish colleague shared with him about converts to his community. This person was immensely impressed by these converts' complete embrace of Judaism's detailed laws and strict rules, as well as their mastery of Hebrew and their knowledge of complicated texts. But what all these converts lacked was the meta-language of being Jewish, the occasional Yiddish expressions, the little nuances of the vernacular, the references to cultural tropes that were not religious at all but that "native" Jews, including non-religious or even anti-religious ones, simply knew and used as a matter of course in their daily language and culture.

[28] J. Danielle, "Female Sports Fans and the Men Who Judge Them," *Jezebel*, February 4, 2011, available at http://jezebel.com/5752163/female-sports-fans-and-the-men-who-judge-them (accessed April 20, 2011).

whatever hoops he puts up."[29] And as we have argued throughout this book, with the qualifications of sports expertise, the entrance into it, and the acceptance by its practitioners not being credentialed in any way, shape, or form, the hoops that men have put up for women in the world of sports consumption constantly vary in height, width, and shape. The bottom line is this: If love of certain teams, particularistic passion, and immediate partisanship are left unmentioned, no other venue of communication can serve male companionship and interaction better and more harmoniously than sports. Nothing emulates "speaking man" better than the languages of hegemonic sports culture. And maybe the world of hegemonic sports culture emulates a linguistic phenomenon that is found in Japanese, which, though formally a gender-neutral or gender-free language, like the Finno-Ugric cluster of Estonian, Finnish, and Hungarian, and like Persian, Chinese, Malay, Korean, Bengali, and Basque, distinguishes itself from these in that the language spoken by Japanese women is markedly different from that of men in its vocabulary use of idioms, grammatical structure, and pronunciation.

---

[29]Ibid.

Conclusion

So what if women speak sports differently than men do? After all, there are clearly many more gendered differences in our world in which the disadvantages still befalling women are a good deal weightier than their second-class status in the world of sports. Moreover, as we showed in many an instance in our book, there appears to be ample evidence that women *want* to speak sports differently than men do—or often not at all. We have no problem with either of these options as long as all women possess them completely and can take them at their own will. Our plea is for women to be genuine "free agents" in the world of sports fandom by always having the option to exit, voice, and loyalty, the triad of agency so brilliantly posited by Albert O. Hirschman[1]: that they be free not to participate in sports speak at all if they do not want to and not be stigmatized for that by anybody; that their voice be accorded respect, credibility, and legitimacy were they to opt for participating in this culture; and that they be seen as genuine and bona fide participants of the team on equivalent and equal footing with its male members.

Are there any current indications that this world of genuine gender equality in the world of the hegemonic sports culture might come to pass at some point in the future? Our book points to some encouraging signs. Thus, let us not forget the immensely impressive advances—presented in Chapter 3—that women have attained on the playing fields in the course of the past three to

---

[1] Albert O. Hirschman, *Exit, Voice, and Loyalty: Responses to Decline in Firms, Organizations, and States* (Cambridge, MA: Harvard University Press: 1970).

four decades. We have not done the requisite research, but we believe to be on safe ground in stating that nobody in the 1980s, let alone the 1970s and before, predicted that Women's World Cups in soccer would become global events, watched by many millions, barely two decades later; or that Division I women's basketball would draw thousands to large arenas and attract millions to their television sets. Quite possibly, we could experience similarly massive shifts in women's sports consumption in the course of the next three to four decades. As Christine Brennan so eloquently told us, men have a century-long head start in this world. Their proficiency in sports speak can be dated to the late eighteenth century, when cricket and golf became the first sports to deserve the sobriquet "modern." In the course of the latter half of the nineteenth century, sports really became integral to men's identities in the United States via baseball and (college) football; in Canada via ice hockey; in Britain—in so many aspects the home of modern sports—via both football (Association and Rugby—Union and League) and cricket; in Britain's formal imperial holdings via cricket and rugby; and in her economic sphere of influence, such as continental Europe and important parts of Latin America, via Association football, best known to Americans by that Oxbridge slang term of "soccer." These languages had different content, but their structure and their very essence were quite identical. And nothing rendered them more so than their complete dominance by men: All players, owners, coaches, managers (on the production side), followers in the form of fans, and reporters and interpreters in the form of journalists (on the consumption side) were men. This is a perfect case of what Paul Hoch has aptly called "sexual apartheid," though we would prefer the more inclusive term "gender apartheid."[2]

When queried as to how this might change, Christine Brennan became much more pensive. And who can blame her. Nobody knows the future. And all predictive guesses, no matter how educated, risk being proven not only wrong but also silly. Still, we would like to venture some tentative thoughts at this closing juncture of our book that might provoke a fruitful discussion among our readers.

First of all, there exists absolutely no compelling conceptual or structural reason for the very nature of sports to remain essentially unchanged, since their establishment between the late eighteenth and the late nineteenth centuries. After all, why should a world created by English students at elite public schools and at Oxbridge and in the industrial working-class areas of the Midlands, as well as their social counterparts in the United States, established more or less at the same time, last forever? Indeed, while these sports cultures

---

[2]Paul Hoch, *Rip Off the Big Game: The Exploitation of Sports by the Power Elite* (Garden City, NY: Anchor Books, 1972), 147–166.

remain immensely sticky, they have also proven to be quite malleable. Thus, there is absolutely no reason why China should not emerge as a major basketball power in the next three to four decades, why Italy and Holland could not become major baseball countries, or why the United States could not win a soccer World Cup in the men's game. One could even go further and argue that these very sports languages, which were, after all, creations of a specific time and space, and are thus random, need not persevere forever. Who knows? Maybe the real global game will be Quidditch in decades to come. After all, we have had Quidditch World Cup video games in which a team consisting of members hailing from the United States, England, France, Germany, and Scandinavia played a joint squad comprising players from Japan, Spain, Australia, and Bulgaria.[3] And sure enough, the two of us attended an inter-university Quidditch match between the University of Michigan and neighboring Eastern Michigan University in the fall of 2010 played in Ann Arbor's Arboretum, with proper teams, equipment, rules, referees—and about 100 spectators. Tellingly, the teams had an equal number of male and female players, which has become quite normal in intramural sports at many American universities, yet another change that would have been unimaginable a few decades ago.[4] And anybody attending some of these intramural games will have to acknowledge that the level of play is respectable, on occasion, even advanced, and that the contestants are far from pikers with little skill, less effort, and no competitive commitment to win.

Of course, it appears absurd to imagine that, in a century, 110,000 spectators will fill Michigan Stadium on Saturday afternoons in the fall to watch Quidditch contests instead of football games or that Quidditch will enter America's hegemonic sports culture in any meaningful way. But then again, who knows! In the fall of 2010, the Quidditch World Cup attracted forty-six college teams from sixteen states to New York City. And barely a year later, in November 2011, one hundred teams from around the world, featuring 2,000 athletes, contested the next Quidditch World Cup, again held in New York City, this time on Randall's Island, the well-known former location for world-class track and field meets, as well as eminent soccer games featuring some of Europe's and Latin America's finest clubs and most renowned players, including the legendary Pelé. In the few years of its existence, Quidditch has thus far advanced from obscure backyards to actual public fields, with real players and

---

[3]Indeed there exists a widely circulated *Intercollegiate Quidditch Rules and Guidebook*, available at http://sites.google.com/site/savannahquidditchleague/IQARulebook.

[4]We believe that the first truly national Quidditch tournament occurred in New York City's Central Park in the spring of 2010. (Karen Matthews, "Quidditch in Central Park: Harry Potter Game Comes to Life in New York," *Huffington Post*, May 30, 2010.)

spectators, to Central Park to Randall's Island. Could stadia be that far off? Our point here is merely that these sports and their cultures are social constructs that are constantly subject to change. Just think how horse racing and boxing, once absolute mainstays of American hegemonic sports culture, have slipped from their previous perch, the latter perhaps permanently replaced by Ultimate Fighting Championship (UFC, the biggest mixed martial arts league in the United States), as the seven-year network television contract reached in the summer of 2011 with Fox demonstrates.[5]

Second, one need not be an orthodox Marxist to accord changes in production pride of place and see such as precursors to equally big changes in culture. This certainly pertains to women's relationship to sports. After all, women—as we noted—played sports in a serious way well before they commenced to follow them in a commensurate manner. Thus, we dare submit the possibly blasphemous—and most certainly unconventional, though far from unheard of—notion of the normative desirability and empirical reality of having women compete together with men on mixed-gender teams at the highest levels of sports (i.e., the major leagues) and not just intramural college contests.

Why have sports remained our last legitimate bastion of "separate but equal?" And this starts at a very young age. When Michael Messner asked his American Youth Soccer Organization (AYSO) league in Southern California why the coed teams that had existed until 1995, in which his elder son had played when he was five years old, was abolished and replaced by gender-segregated teams, he was told that "during half-times and practices, the boys and girls tend to separate into separate groups. So the league thought it would be better for team unity if we split the boys and girls into separate leagues."[6] The fact that Messner's suggestion—that the separate clustering of Latino and white kids during halftime never led anyone at AYSO to create ethnically segregated leagues—was met with incredulity underlines gender's unique legitimacy as a segregating force in the world of sports, and sports alone. Our society and culture continue to tolerate a gender segregation in sports that has become unthinkable with any other collective, be it class, ethnicity, region, or religion.

Title IX has been nothing short of revolutionary in permitting women access to the production of sports. But there is still a strict gender separation. Title IX has accorded women the most basic level of equality: that of quantity, but nowhere close to the much more important metric of quality. It certainly

---

[5]"UFC Headed for Prime Time after Inking 7-Year Pact with Fox," available at http://sportsillustrated.cnn.com/2011/mma/boxing/08/18/ufc-fox.ap/index.html (accessed August 23, 2011).

[6]Michael A. Messner, "Barbie Girls Versus Sea Monsters: Children Constructing Gender" in *The Sport and Society Reader*, ed. David Karen and Robert E. Washington (New York: Routledge, 2010), 187.

has not provided them with any kind of cultural and social equality in terms of the sports that they produce. Why have few, if any, feminists—at least to our knowledge—never demanded that the quarterback position of the Green Bay Packers, the point guard position of the Los Angeles Lakers, and the short-stop position of the New York Yankees be occupied by a woman the way they have successfully lobbied that university presidents, doctors, lawyers, mathe-maticians, physicists, computer engineers, senators, and Supreme Court Jus-tices, be women? (And it certainly is not unrealistic to expect that a woman will become president of the United States before too long.) Or why have there not been any major movements afoot to create mixed-gender teams beyond those in tennis's mixed doubles (tellingly, far and away the least prestigious of the five tennis competitions, and only becoming an Olympic event in 2012) and two yachting categories, which—with the equestrian disciplines—furnish the only mixed-gender teams in this global showcase of thirty-five different sports and almost four hundred different events?[7] Why do we, as a society, per-mit such a clear gender separation—which, regardless of its sugar coating, in essence, amounts to a clear second-class role for women, no matter how equal their participatory numbers may be—at the highest echelons of sports (i.e., in the world of the physical) that we would never tolerate in the world of the mental or intellectual or political? The equivalent in education would be for us to foster gender-integrated elementary and secondary schools, but then to allow only men to enter and compete in the top four-year colleges and leading research universities, with women relegated to less prestigious institutions and community colleges, even though the value of their effort, in terms of degrees or championships attained, would be nominally equal; or, to offer an anal-ogy from the world of politics, women would only be allowed to run for local and state offices, but not national offices. We wholeheartedly agree with Eileen McDonagh and Laura Pappano's emphatic argument that separate is not equal in anything, including sports.[8]

Does the logic of *citius, altius, fortius*—"swifter, higher, stronger"—by def-inition, require our currently practiced gender apartheid that is perceived as totally legitimate at the very top level of sports, since the most accomplished men will always run faster, jump higher, and be stronger than the most

---

[7]There exists the Dutch game of "korfball," a kind of basketball with two freestanding baskets with no backboards that players can circle like goals in ice hockey. This game is played by four men and four women on each team. However, only men guard men and only women can play against women, thus, in essence, perpetuating the gender apartheid within the game itself. According to Wikipedia, the rules of korfball state that "a player is allowed to switch among opponents whom he/she is defending, *as long as they are of the same sex*" (our emphasis).

[8]Eileen McDonagh and Laura Pappano, *Playing with the Boys: Why Separate Is Not Equal in Sports* (New York: Oxford University Press, 2008).

accomplished women? If we continue to define "the best," which is such an integral part of any sport, by our current criteria, then this separate but equal world will quite possibly never change. But if we construct alternate logics to what constitutes "the best"—include metrics of cooperation and style, for example, in computing winners and losers, or create truly gender-integrated teams in which the women's output would be weighted more heavily (e.g., assign five points to baskets scored by female players as opposed to the two for baskets scored by males), thereby creating real incentives to have the women be welcomed as positive additions to these teams, as has been the case in the aforementioned intramural contests—then we might actually arrive at a truly integrated sports world, which would thus be congruent with virtually all important public institutions of our contemporary democratic world. And then we just might reach a situation in which women's excellence on the production side of "sports"—not "women's sports," which, like the use of the phrase "lady doctor," defines the normative and baseline case of sports as *not* female[9]—will, by necessity, create a commensurate change in women's consumption of sports, thus making the sportista the norm among women and men, and not the exception.

---

[9]We derive this analogy from Lori Kendall, "Nerd Nation: Images of Nerds in US Popular Culture," *International Journal of Cultural Studies* 2, no. 2 (1999): 262.

Appendix:
Lists of Interviewees

OUR THIRTY-THREE INTERVIEWEES
IN ALPHABETICAL ORDER

Emily Albertson
Nicole Auerbach
Christine Brennan
Sarah Brenner
Krista Clement
Allison Creekmore
Samantha Cook
Liz Elsner
Samantha Fink
Alisa Foti
Joanne Gerstner
Emily Green
Laura Hahn
Katrina Hancock
Leah Hsieh
Ann Killion
Shaelie Lambarth
Courtney Mercier
Vicki Michaelis
Sarah Ailie Moran
Michelle Pritchett
Paige Robnett
Kathryn Rosenberg
Jillian Rothman

Stephanie Schwartz
Margaret Segall
Fay Shutzer
Caitlin Tommasulo
Kate Toth
Dana Wakiji
Karen Wall
Annie Walton
Gillian Warmflash

GILLIAN WARMFLASH'S THIRTY-THREE INTERVIEWEES IN ALPHABETICAL ORDER

Dianne Aguilar
Leslie Andrews
Sandy Bailey
Lisa Bennett
Bonnie Bernstein
Nicole Boden
Liz Clarke
Erin Comella
Jessica Gelman
Margaret Grossi
Catherine Herman
Dana Jacobson
Kristin Johnson
Andrea Joyce
Athelia Knight
Suzy Kolber
Andrea Kremer
Ann Liguori
Jackie MacMullan
Naomi Marcus
Beth Mowins
Kathleen Nelson
Diana Nyad
Stacey Pressman
Liz Robbins
Robin Roberts
Diane Shah
Suzanne Smith
Molly Solomon
Shira Springer
Carol Stiff
Hannah Storm
Lesley Visser

Index

AAGPBL (All-American Girls Professional Baseball League), 76–78
ability: vs. appreciation, 25–29
achievement-choice model, 22–29; ability vs. appreciation in, 25–29; attributed value in, 24–25; self-perceptions in, 24
achievement motivation, 22; of scientists, 43
Ackerman, Val, 101
Acosta, R. Vivian, 81n
adolescent experiences, 13–17; collectivity vs. chaos in, 17–20; conformity vs. deviance in typology of girls in, 33–35; in development of sportista, 5–6; differentiation in self-perceptions of competencies in, 20–22; expectancy-value theory and achievement-choice model of, 22–29; and formula for fandom, 29–32; living proof of gender differences in, 13–15; playground dynamics in, 15–16; and social capital, 32–33; sports involvement and social standing as, 32–33
adult expectations: and gender behavior, 29–30
advancement: in science, 42–47
affective fan: knowledgeable vs., 127, 128
aficionado, 10; vs. fan, 119–120, 123n
age: of female sportscasters, 190
aggression: in boys vs. girls, 16; men's vs. women's enjoyment of, 163, 164, 165–166
AIAW (Association for Intercollegiate Athletics for Women): in governance of women's athletics, 79–80; and NCAA takeover, 82; on women's basketball, 75
Akers, Michelle, 97n
Albertson, Emily: on components of fandom, 126–27; on espnW, 231–232; as sportista, 134, 140–141; on sports talk among men, 132–133; on sports talk among women, 12, 201; on televised women's sports, 95, 224–225; on time deepening, 140–141
All-American Girls Professional Baseball League (AAGPBL), 76–78
Alomar, Robbie, 156
Ambady, Nalini, 60, 60n
American Federation of College Women, 78
American Youth Soccer Organization (AYSO), 242
Andrews, Erin, 215, 219
androgyny: of scientists, 43
Anthony, Carmelo, 112
appearance: and credibility, 191–195; of female athletes, 101–108; vs. intelligence, 169n, 196–198; of television sports journalists, 169–170, 184–187, 189–195
Appiah, Kwame Anthony, 2
appreciation: ability vs., 25–29
Arnot, Madeleine, 34, 34n
Aronson, Joshua, 61n
Associated Press Sports Editors (APSE): Racial and Gender Report Card of, 171–172

Association for Intercollegiate Athletics for Women (AIAW): in governance of women's athletics, 79–80; and NCAA takeover, 82; on women's basketball, 75

Association for Women in Sports Media (AWSM), 12, 174, 201–202, 227

athletes: as celebrities, 161–162; vs. fan, 8–9; female (*See* female athletes); gap between sports consumers and, 84–92; as sports journalists, 183

attendance: at live events, 136–137

attractiveness: and credibility, 191–192; of female athletes, 101–104; vs. intelligence, 169n, 196–198; of television sports journalists, 169–170, 184–187, 189–195

attributed value, 24–25; sports competence and, 24–25, 30

Auerbach, Nicole, 145, 145n

Austria: sexualization of women's soccer in, 100

AWSM (Association for Women in Sports Media), 12, 174, 201–202, 227

AYSO (American Youth Soccer Organization), 242

"babe" factor: ambivalence of, 189–195

Bagilhole, Barbara, 62–63, 62n

Bajramaj, Fatmire "Lira," 99

Baker, Michael J., 192, 192n

ban(s): on women's soccer, 72–73

"bandwagon" fan, 123

Barbie: soccer, 97, 99

baseball: women's, 76–78

basketball: "feminization" of, 72; invention of, 71–72; Lingerie League, 111; women in media for, 182; women's (*See* women's basketball)

Beanster's Group, 132–133

beauty: and credibility, 191–192; of female athletes, 101–104; vs. intelligence, 169n, 196–198; of television sports journalists, 169–170, 184–187, 189–195

Belle, Albert, 156

Ben-Zeev, Talia, 59, 59n

Bepperling, Maika, 31, 31n

Berenson, Senda, 68n, 72, 73, 74

Berman, Chris, 177, 183

Bhawe, Nachiket M., 59, 59n

"Big Four" sports, 94, 116; credibility of women journalists for, 181–182

Bilalic, Merim, 53n

Biltz, Laura Marie, 137, 137n

Bird, Larry, 126

blogging, 145–146

"blowout" games: men's vs. women's enjoyment of, 164

Blumenfeld, Phyllis, 13n, 29, 29n

Bodenhausen, Galen V., 57n

body image: development of, 30–31

"Body Issue," 230, 230n

Bolt, Usain, 2

bona fide occupational qualification, 40, 40n

bonding capital: sports as, 143–145

"bottlenecks": and perception of sports competence, 27, 27n, 28–29

Bourdieu, Pierre, 118–19, 118n, 122, 146

boy(s): aggressive behavior in, 16; favorability of maleness to, 34; gender roles of, 20; play of, 14, 15, 17; self-perceptions of competencies of, 20–22; soccer team names of, 20; sports knowledge of, 31; storytelling by, 17, 19

Boyer, Peter J., 188n

bracketology, 129–133

Brady, Tom, 85

Bray, Janna, 99–100, 100n

breeding grounds for discrimination: in natural sciences, 46–47

Brennan, Christine: on career as sportswriter, 173–174, 174n, 186–187, 206–207; father's influence on, 205; on future of women in sports, 240; on Title IX, 90–91, 90n; on Women's World Cup soccer, 92, 92n

Brjantzewa, Darya, 154n, 218n

Brooks-Moon, Renel, 182

Brown, Gary, 75n

Brunson, Cindy, 219

Bryant, Jennings, 163, 163n

Bryant, Kobe, 2

Burke, Doris, 182, 183

business: women in, 49–51

Cadinu, Mara, 57, 57n

Cahn, Susan K., 4, 4n, 105n

Carlson, Jennifer, 104, 104n

Carpenter, Linda Jean, 81n

Castillo, Jorge, 101n, 115, 115n

Caulkins, Ann, 174n

celebrities: athletes as, 161–162

Chabris, Christopher F., 52n

challenge: of sportista to men, 211–214; of sportista to women, 214–219

chaos: collectivity vs., 17–20

Chastain, Brandi, 95–97, 96n, 113, 182–183, 184

Chastain, Jane, 185, 219

chess: women in, 51–58

childcare responsibilities: of women scientists, 43

childhood experiences, 13–17; collectivity vs. chaos in, 17–20; conformity vs. deviance in typology of girls in, 33–35; in development of sportista, 5–6; differentiation in self-perceptions of competencies in, 20–22; expectancy-value theory and achievement-choice model of, 22–29; and formula for fandom, 29–32; living proof of gender differences in, 13–15; playground dynamics in, 15–16; and social capital, 32–33
Churchill, Gilbert A., 192, 192n
civilizing agents: women as, 68–69
Civil Rights Act: on bona fide occupational qualifications, 40, 40n
Clarke, Liz, 235
clothing: with sports logos, 147–148
Coates, Ta-Nehisi, 237
Cohn, Linda, 177, 191, 219
collectivity: vs. chaos, 17–20
Collins, Bud, 102
combative sports: men's vs. women's enjoyment of, 164–166
Comisky, Paul, 163, 163n
Commission on Intercollegiate Athletics for Women, 79
common denominator: sports as, 143–145
competencies: self-perceptions of, 20–22, 23–24
competition "bottlenecks," 27, 27n, 28–29
competitive aspect of game: focus on, 158–159
competitive games: of boys vs. girls, 17
confidence: of sportista, 209–211
conflict: in storytelling of boys, 19
conformity: by girls, 33–35
connoisseur, 10; vs. fan, 119–120
"converts," 157, 158
"cosmopolitan" aspects: of sports, 2
Costas, Bob, 183
"countercosmopolitan" aspects: of sports, 2
courses: and advancement in science, 45–46
Coussement, Sylvere H., 163–164, 164n
Crafford, Anne, 50–51, 50n
Crawford, Garry, 103–104, 104n
credentialing, 7–8, 38, 39–41; in science vs. sportscasting, 197–198
credibility: appearance and, 191–195; of sportista, 208–209; of women in sports media, 181–184
Creedon, Pamela J., 199, 199n
Creekmore, Allison, 233n
Cross, Simon, 62–63, 62n
cultural capital: obtaining of, 118–119, 118n, 121–122
cultural weight: of men's vs. women's college basketball, 132

culture: official (high-brow) vs. popular, 118–122
Cup Final, 144

dads: influence on sportista of, 202–206
Damenfussball, 73
Danielle, J., 237–238, 237n
Darke, Ian, 184
Darley, John, 59–60, 59n
Davis, Daniel Cochece, 192n
Davis, Patrick, 136n
Davis-Blake, Alison, 189, 189n
Deadheads, 118, 122, 123, 124
democratization: sports and, 2–3
Dennis, Mike, 116, 116n
D'Ettole, Claudio, 57, 57n
deviance: by girls, 33–35
DGWS (Division of Girls' and Women's Sports), 78–79
DiCicco, Tony, 184
Dietz-Uhler, Beth, 125n, 127–128, 136, 139, 148–149
"discourse of empathy," 69
discrimination: in sports media, 175–176
discussing sports: childhood exclusion from, 157–158; time spent, 138–139, 142–147; by women, 10
"diversity hires," 177, 179–181
Devine, Fiona, 43–45, 43n, 51
Division of Girls' and Women's Sports (DGWS), 78–79
"doing gender," 61–63, 62n; sports fandom as, 123–124
doing sports: vs. following sports, 84–92
Dorfman, Bob, 112
Dorrance, Anson, 82–83
Durant, Kevin, 162, 227

early childhood experiences, 13–17; collectivity vs. chaos in, 17–20; conformity vs. deviance in typology of girls in, 33–35; in development of sportista, 5–6; differentiation in self-perceptions of competencies in, 20–22; expectancy-value theory and achievement-choice model of, 22–29; and formula for fandom, 29–32; living proof of gender differences in, 13–15; playground dynamics in, 15–16; and social capital, 32–33
Eccles, Jacquelynne S.: on ability vs. appreciation, 25–27, 25n, 28; on childhood origins of gender differences, 13n, 21n; on expectancy-value theory and achievement-choice model, 22, 22n, 23; on formula for fandom, 29, 29n, 30

Edelman, Robert, 116, 116n
educational tools: and advancement in science, 45–46
elementary school: valuation of sports in, 27, 27n
Ellis, Rodney, 61
Elo, Arpad, 52n
Elo rating, 52–53, 52n
Elsner, Liz, 86–87
emotion: in popular culture, 120–121
emotional fan: knowledgeable vs., 127, 128
End, Christian, 125n, 127–128
engineering: women in, 6–7, 41–47
English football: female fandom in, 217–218
enthusiastic dilettante, 128, 128f
entrepreneurship: stereotype threat in, 59
entry (entrance) requirements: and exclusion, 39; for fandom, 122–123
equality: gap between parity and, 40–41
ESPN: audience of, 125
ESPN America, 221
ESPN.co.uk, 221
ESPN Deportes, 220, 232
ESPN Rise, 220
ESPNU, 220
espnW, 219–235; confusion about goals of, 219–223; is about women's sports, 222–226; is catering to female audience of popular sports, 226–230; is for women who play sports, 230–231
evaluation: of female scientists, 42–43
Evans, Cadel, 93
Evans, Simon, 110n
exclusion: credentialing and, 39–40; and entry requirements, 39
expectancies for success, 23
expectancy-value theory, 22–29; ability vs. appreciation in, 25–29; attributed value in, 24–25; self-perceptions in, 24
expectations: that adults place on children, 16
expert, 10; vs. fan, 119–120

factual knowledge. See knowledge
Fagot, Beverly I., 15–16, 16n, 23
fair-weather fan, 123
"family genre": of storytelling by girls, 17, 18
fan: vs. athlete, 8–9; female sports (See female sports fan)
fan culture, 121–122
fandom: components of, 126–129, 128f; formula for, 29–32; spectrum of, 127; in sports vs. other areas, 10–11
fantasy sports programs: participation in, 125, 213

fathers: influence on sportista of, 202–206
Favre, Brett, 85
female athletes, 66–117; appearance of, 101–108; in basketball, 73–76; beginning of organized sports for, 71–73; espnW is for, 230–231; future of, 112–115; and gender identity, 104–108; governance of, 78–80; identity and sexuality issues of, 9–10; "Kournikova effect" in, 102–104; in Lingerie Football League, 108–112; and NCAA takeover, 81–83; physical education and, 70–71; in professional baseball during World War II, 76–78; sexualization of, 97–102; in soccer, 83–84, 92–95; as sports consumers, 83–84; Title IX and, 80–81; in Victorian times, 67–70; women's advances as, 9–10
female domains: men in, 61–64
female sports fan, 118–166; and bracketology, 129–133; categories of, 157–158; and celebrity, 161–162; components of fandom of, 126–129, 128f; espnW is for, 226–230; finding, 133–135; knowledge of, 148–159; merchandise purchases by, 147–148; motivations of, 159–160; "normal," 10; as spectators at live events, 136–137; sportista's view of, 214–215; sportista vs., 216–218; sports talk by, 142–147; time deepening of, 139–142; TV watching by, 137–139; unique preferences of, 162–166
"feminization": of rules, 71
figure skating: men's vs. women's enjoyment of, 166; playing vs. following sports in, 87–88
Fiske, John, 119n, 121–122, 146
"Fit for You" line, 148
fitness: espnW is for, 230–231
following sports: playing sports vs., 84–92
football: Lingerie League, 108–112
Foudy, Julie, 97, 182–183, 184
Fox, Mary Frank, 46–47, 46n
Frach, Henrik, 98, 98n
Frauenfussball, 73
Freeney, Dwight, 112
full fan, 127, 128, 128f
Funk, Daniel C., 159n

GAA (Girls' Athletic Association), 91
games: played by boys vs. girls, 14, 15, 17, 163
Gantz, Walter, 139–140, 139n, 140n, 160
gatekeepers: of sports fandom, 118, 123
gender apartheid: in sports, 240
gender behavior: adult expectations and, 29–30
gender deviation: by girls, 33–35
gender equality: in the future of hegemonic sports culture, 239–244

gender identity: female athletes and, 104–108; of men in female domains, 61–63, 62n

gender mixing: on playground, 13–14

gender norms: of men in female domains, 61–63, 62n

gender roles: of boys vs. girls, 20

gender role stereotypes: and achievement motivation, 22–29; in sports ability vs. appreciation, 26

gender segregation: on playground, 13–14, 15

Genovese, Jason, 172, 172n, 180, 190

George, Phyllis, 185–186

Gerdes, Christer, 56–57, 56n, 57n

German soccer: ban on women in, 72–73; female fandom in, 218n; sexualization of women in, 97–100

Gerstner, Joanne: on appearance, 195; on career as sports journalist, 174–175, 176, 176n; on need for constant proof, 206–207, 206n; on sports talk among women, 201–202

Gessat, Kristina, 98

Gibbons, Sheila, 171n

Gilman, Andrew, 227n

girl(s): aggressive behavior of, 16; favorability of femaleness to, 34; gender roles of, 20; play of, 14, 15, 17; self-perceptions of competencies of, 20–22; soccer team names of, 20; sports knowledge of, 31; storytelling by, 17, 18; typologies of, 33–35

"girlies," 33, 34

Girls' Athletic Association (GAA), 91

Glickman, Mark E., 52n

global icons: teams and individuals as, 1–2

Gobet, Fernand, 53n

golf: stereotype threat in, 59–60

Gosling, Victoria K., 103–104, 104n

Gottlieb, Doug, 233

Graduate Record Examination: stereotype threat in, 58–59

Granderson, Curtis, 229

Grandmaster: in chess, 51–53, 52n

Gränsmark, Patrik, 56–57, 56n, 57n

Grix, Jonathan, 116, 116n

Grossi, Margaret, 145n, 235

"growth spurters," 21–22

Grugeon, Elizabeth, 15, 15n

Grundy, Pamela, 81n

Gupta, Vishal K., 59, 59n

Guttmann, Allen, 4, 4n

gymnastics: in Victorian era, 67–68

Hac, Keith, 110

Hagan, Richard, 16, 16n

Hahn, Laura, 89–90, 90n, 143n

hair: of female athletes, 106–108

Hamm, Mia: appearance of, 97, 97n; as crossover star, 9, 112; as sports commentator, 184; and World Professional Soccer, 113

Hamnik, Al, 110n

Hancock, Katrina, 90, 90n

Hanson, Sandra L., 42–43, 42n

Hardin, Marie: on age of female sportscasters, 190; on credentials of female sports journalists, 172, 172n; on discrimination and resentment, 175–176, 176n; on diversity hires, 180, 180n

Hargreaves, Jennifer, 3–4, 4n, 67n

Harold, Rena D.: on ability vs. appreciation, 25–27, 25n, 28; on formula for fandom, 29, 29n; on gender differences in children, 13n

Harrick, Elizabeth A., 125n, 127–128

Hartmann, Douglas, 203n

"Harvard Test of Inflected Acquisition," 21

"haze of male exclusivity," 237–238

health and fitness: espnW is for, 230–231

hegemonic sports: defined, 4; and doing vs. following sports, 8; gender equality in future of, 239–244; as leveler among men, 211–212; market forces in, 115; notions of femininity and beauty and, 9; women in, 103–104

"heroic-agonistic genre": of storytelling by boys, 17, 19

Hiestand, Michael, 125n, 229n

high-brow culture, 118–122

high culture, 118–122

high school: valuation of sports in, 27–28, 27n

Hingis, Martina, 102

Hirakawa, Sumiko, 159n

Hirschman, Albert O., 125, 239, 239n

Hoch, Paul, 240, 240n

Hollobaugh, Jeff, 193, 193n

homosexual players, 98

Hopkins, Jessica, 111

Houston, William, 190

Howard, Dennis, 159

Hrubesch, Horst, 154

Hsieh, Leah, 126n, 139n

Hugo, Victor, 232, 233

Hultstrand, B. J., 79n

human interest stories, 229

Hunt, Virginia, 75n

Ilyumzhinov, Kirsan, 52n

impersonal criteria: as selection measures, 39

inclusiveness: sports and, 2–3

"in crowd": in social capital of girls, 32–33

independence: of scientists, 43

Independent Women's Football League,
    110–111
Iniesta, Andrés, 96
insecurity: of sportista, 209–211
instrumentalization: of sports by female sports
    fan, 146
integration: sports and, 2–3
intelligence: beauty vs., 169n, 196–198
International Master: in chess, 52
"in the blood" fans, 157–158
intramural clubs, 78
investment banking firms: women in, 50–51
Inzlicht, Michael, 59, 59n
"it factor": in business, 51

Jacobs, Janis E.: on ability vs. appreciation, 25n,
    27–28, 27n; on expectancy-value theory and
    achievement-choice model, 23; on formula
    for fandom, 30; on gender differences in chil-
    dren, 21n
Jacobson, Dana, 219, 235
Jacobson, Lenore, 21, 21n
Jacquemotte, Lindy, 125n, 127–128
James, Jeffrey D., 158, 158n
James, LeBron, 229
James, William, 121
Jarque, Daniel, 96
Jenkins, Sally, 72n, 182n
Jensen, Joli, 119–121, 119n
Jeter, Derek, 2, 112
job discrimination: in sports media, 175–176
Johnson, Andre, 112
Johnson, Kristin, 142
Johnson, Tina, 222, 227, 228, 228n
Jones, Bill, 180
Jones, Katharine W., 217–218, 217n
Jordan, Michael, 9, 112, 207
Jordan Brand, 112
journalism jobs, 170
journalism students: women as, 170–171
journalists: sports (See sports media)
Joyce, James, 120, 123

Kaplan, Don, 148n
Karg, Adam, 136n
Katz, Andy, 233
Kendall, Lori, 155n, 244n
Kennedy, Jayne, 186
Kennedy, John F., 199
Kian, Edward (Ted) M., 176, 176n, 180, 180n
Killion, Ann: on covering non-hegemonic
    sports, 184; on doing vs. following sports,
    89n; on Women's Professional Soccer, 113n;

on Women's United Soccer Association,
    114, 114n
kinetic movements: development of, 30–31
Kirk, Mary, 155n
knowledge: assessing level of, 149–152; assump-
    tions about, 178; of boys vs. girls, 31; current,
    148, 150–151; as entrance requirement to
    true fandom, 123–124; and fandom, 10–11;
    of female fans, 148–159; historical, 148, 150,
    151–154, 155–156; self-evaluation of, 149–
    150; team-specific vs. generalized, 158
knowledgeable fan: emotional vs., 127, 128
Kolber, Suzy, 215, 219
korfball, 243n
Kournikova, Anna, 102–104, 115
"Kournikova effect," 102–104
Kraus, Rebecca S., 42–43, 42n
Krawczyk, Janielle, 192n
Kreisky, Eva, 4, 4n
Kremer, Andrea, 177, 215, 219
Kronsberg, Sandra, 16, 16n
Kulik, Carol T., 189, 189n

"Ladies Days," 68
ladies-only chess clubs, 54
Lady Geek, 155n
Lamarr, Hedy, 169n, 193
language arts competence: self-perceptions
    of, 24
language of sports: childhood exclusion from,
    157–158; fluency in, 156–157
Lannin, Joanne, 75n
Lanza, Stephanie, 21n, 23
Lawson, Kara, 182n
"learners," 157, 158
legitimacy: of sportista, 208–209; of women as
    sports journalists, 168–169
Lehmann, Jens, 153
Leinbach, Mary Driver, 16, 16n
lesbians: in women's soccer, 98, 107
Letterman, David, 96
Levey, Hilary, 27n
Levitov, Ilya, 52n, 56, 56n
Levy, Daniel: on espnW, 221–222, 221n, 223,
    226, 229, 233
Levy, Donald P., 125, 125n, 137–138
Ley, Bob, 183, 184
Lieberman, Nancy, 182
Lingerie Basketball League, 111
Lingerie Football League, 108–112
live event: spectatorship at, 136–137
locker rooms: access to, 175
Loick, Steffen, 31n
Long, J. Scott, 46–47, 46n

Longman, Jeré, 97n, 112–113, 113n, 114
Lustina, M. J., 61n
Lynch, Christian, 59–60, 59n

Maass, Anne, 57, 57n
Macrae, C. Neil, 57n
Madrigal, Robert, 159
Magnay, Jacquelin, 175
Mahoney, Sarah, 137n
Mahony, Daniel F., 159n
making an impression: in business, 51
male-dominated realms, 39–65; business as, 49–51; chess as, 51–58; credentialing in, 39–61; ROTC programs as, 47–48; science as, 41–47; sports as, 11; stereotype threat in, 58–61
"maleness": sports fandom and, 123–124
Manilow, Barry, 120, 123
March Madness, 163–164
market: for women's sports, 115–117
Markovitch-Elfassi, Dana, 199n
Markovits, Andrei S.: on bracketology, 129–135, 133n; on celebrity, 161; on components of fandom, 126–127; on "discourse of empathy," 69, 69n; on influence of sports on politics and culture, 2, 2n; on knowledge of sports, 150–154; on playing vs. following sports, 84, 84n; on talking about sports, 138
Martin, Courtney, 110
Martin, Karin, 105–106, 106n, 107
masculine gender affirmation: of men in female domains, 61–63, 62n
masculinity: sports fandom and, 123–124
math competence: self-perceptions of, 24
mathematics: women in, 6–7, 41
Matthews, Karen, 241n
max-out benchmarks: in ROTC, 47–48
MBAs: male vs. female, 49–50
McDonagh, Eileen, 3, 3n, 243, 243n
McDonald, Heath, 136n
McKay, Hollie, 111
McLeod, Peter, 53n
McManus, Jane, on number of women in sports media, 173
mechanized sports: men's vs. women's enjoyment of, 164–165
men: challenge and threat of sportista to, 211–214; in female domains, 61–64; instrumentalization of sports to gain access to, 146
mentor: in sports media, 175
merchandise, 147–148
Mercier, Courtney, 85–87, 85n, 212
Mesko, Zoltan, 161
Messi, Lionel, 2

Messner, Michael A.: on coed youth soccer, 242, 242n; on espnW, 224; on gender roles of boys vs. girls, 6, 6n, 20, 20n; on men in youth soccer organizations, 183n
Mewett, Peter, 157, 157n
Michaels, Al, 183
Middleton, Kate, 93
Miller, Cheryl, 182
Miller, James Andrew, 230n
Miller Lite Report on American Attitudes toward Sports, 160
Mink, Patsy, 80
"minority hires," 177, 179–181, 206
Mitrook, Michael A., 163–164, 164n
mixed-gender teams, 242–244
mixed martial arts, 242
Moore, Maya, 9, 76, 101n, 112, 114
Moran, Sarah, 148n
Morgan, Alex, 101
Morrison, L. Leotus, 79n
Mortaza, Mitch, 108, 110
mothers: influence on sportista of, 206
motivations: for attendance at live events, 136–137; for being fan, 128, 129; for engaging in sports consumption, 159–160
Mowins, Beth, 182
multitasking: during televised game, 139–142
Mumford, Lewis, 121
Murray, Harold J., 53n

"nailbiter" games: men's vs. women's enjoyment of, 164
Naismith, James, 71–72
Nakazawa, Makoto, 159n
narrative coherence: of boys vs. girls, 17
Nash, Steve, 86
National Amateur Athletic Federation: in history of women's basketball, 74–75
National Association for Girls and Women in Sport, 78
National Association for Physical Education for College Women, 78
National Collegiate Athletic Association (NCAA): and AIAW, 79–80, 82; popularity of men's vs. women's basketball in, 129–133; takeover by, 81–83; on women's basketball, 75, 225
national icons: teams and individuals as, 1–2
National Institutes on Sport, 79
nationalism, 92–93
National Joint Committee on Extramural Sports for College Women, 78
National Workshop on Intercollegiate Sports, 79

nature of attachment: in official vs. popular culture, 120–121

NCAA (National Collegiate Athletic Association): and AIAW, 79–80, 82; popularity of men's vs. women's basketball in, 129–133; takeover by, 81–83; on women's basketball, 75, 225

Nelson, Kathleen, 205, 205n

nerdettes, 155

nerd-type fans, 155, 155n

"nice girls," 33, 34

Nicolopoulou, Ageliki, 17, 17n, 162–163, 163n

Nixon, Richard, 199

novelty: sportista as, 211, 213

Nowitzki, Dirk, 93

NrrdGrrls!, 155

nudity: in Lingerie Football League, 109

nurses: men as, 63

object of desire: in official vs. popular culture, 119–120

observer-expectancy effect, 21

occupational qualifications: bona fide, 40, 40n

official culture, 118–122

"old boys' networks": in business, 49–50, 51

Olympics: chess at, 52n, 56; nationalism at, 93; women as sports journalists for, 175n, 182; women's basketball at, 75; women's sports at, 8–9

O'Reilly, Jean, 4, 4n, 105n

Orenstein, Peggy, 6, 6n

Osgood, D. Wayne, 21n, 23

Palin, Sarah, 143

Pappano, Laura, 3, 3n, 243, 243n

parity: gap between equality and, 40–41

Parker, Wendy, 229–230, 230n

Parmar, Belinda, 155n

particularistic criteria: as selection measures, 39

partisanship: sports and, 2

Patrick, Danica, 100, 102

Paul, Chris, 112

Peck, Carolyn, 182n

Pelé, 97n, 241

Penfield, Wilder, 157n

Perry, Elissa, 189, 189n

Pfister, Gertrud, 4

Phelps, Michael, 2

physical education, 70–71

physics lab: women in, 197

pink jerseys, 148, 215

Pittinsky, Todd, 60, 60n

play: of boys vs. girls, 14, 15, 17

Playboy: sexiest sportscasters in, 191, 191n, 195; women's soccer players in, 97–98

playground: gender mixing on, 13–14

playground dynamics, 15–16

playing sports: vs. following sports, 84–92

Podolski, Lukas, 153

Polamalu, Troy, 85

ponytail, 106–108

popular culture, 119–122

postgame shows: watching of, 138

Powers, Lindsay, 1n

Pratt, Mary, 76n

preferential hiring, 177, 179–181

pregame shows: watching of, 138

pressures: in sports media, 176–179

Prince William, 93

print media: female sports journalists in, 169, 171–172, 173, 176–179

Prinz, Birgit, 153, 154

privilege: in sports media, 199–200

promotion: of scientists and engineers, 42–47

protagonist: in storytelling of boys, 19; in storytelling of girls, 18

"proving oneself": in business, 50–51; as sportista, 206–208

"Pygmalion in the Classroom" experiment, 21–22

quantitative exam: stereotype threat in, 60

Quidditch, 241–242, 241n

quotas: for sports media, 181

Racial and Gender Report Card of the Associated Press Sports Editors, 171–172

radio: sports journalists on, 169

Rahn, Helmut, 153

Rapinoe, Megan, 113, 114

Rappold, Mariella, 100

reason: in high culture, 120–121

Reay, Diane, 33–35, 33n

Reitman, Frieda, 49–50, 49n

relationships: in storytelling of boys, 19; in storytelling of girls, 18

relevant credentials, 46

Rensmann, Lars, 2n

resentments: in sports media, 175–176

Rhem, James, 21–22, 22n

Rhodes, Richard, 169n

Ridinger, Lynn L., 158, 158n

Roberts, Lamar, 157n

Roberts, Robin, 219

Robinson, Denard, 88, 88n

Roethlisberger, Ben, 85

Rodgers, Aaron, 140

role-playing: by boys vs. girls, 17
Rooney, Wayne, 2
Rose, Judy, 174n
Rosenthal, Robert, 21, 21n
Ross, Betsy M., 80n, 219
Rossi, Paolo, 144
ROTC programs: women in, 47–48
Rothman, Jillian, 149
Rowe, Tracey, 50–51, 50n
Rudelic, Ivana, 98
rules: "feminization" of, 71, 72
Russell, Bill, 152

Sabathia, C. C., 112
salaries: in WNBA, 94, 94n
Salinas, M. F., 61n
Same Size Balls, 222, 222n
Sandler, Bernice, 80
Sargent, Stephanie Lee, 158n, 164–166, 165n
Schneer, Joy A., 49–50, 49n
Schultz, Brad, 173, 173n, 178–179, 192
Schwartz, Stephanie, 139n
Schweinsteiger, Bastian, 153
science: advancement in, 42–47; breed-
    ing grounds for discrimination in, 46–47;
    women in, 6–7, 41–47
second globalization, 2
Seidman, S. A., 188n
Seinfeld, Jerry, 93
selection mechanisms: fairness and inclusivity
    in, 39; nonquantifiable, inexplicit, and infor-
    mal, 41
self-confidence: of scientists, 43
self-perceptions: of competencies, 20–22,
    23–24, 30
"separate but equal," 3; sports as last bastion of,
    242–244
sex objects: women presented as, 188–189
sexual apartheid: in sports, 240
sexualization: in Lingerie Football League,
    108–112; sports bra incident in, 95–97; in
    Women's World Cup of 2011, 97–101
"sexually transmitted fans," 157, 158
Shackelford, Susan, 81n
Shahade, Jennifer, 56, 56n
Shain, Stacie, 175–176, 176n
Shales, Tom, 230n
shallow fan, 123
Shannon, John, 177
Sharapova, Maria, 103
Shattuck, Debra, 68n
Sheffer, Mary Lou, 173, 173n, 178–179, 192
Shepherd, Lindy T., 108
Shibutani, Alex Hideo, 87–88, 88n

Shih, Margaret, 60, 60n
"sideline hottie," 192
Silva, Jennifer, 47–48, 47n
Simic, Julia, 98
Simmons in Heels, 145–146
Sjomeling, Mike, 59–60, 59n
Smallbone, Kieran, 53n
Smith, David T.: and attendance at live events,
    136; on hegemonic sports culture, 135; on
    historic knowledge, 150; on playing vs. fol-
    lowing sports, 84, 84n, 134n; on television
    watching, 138
Smith, Shelley, 181
soccer: ESPN commentary on, 233–234;
    women in media for, 182–183, 183n, 184;
    women's (See women's soccer)
"soccer babes," 96
Soccer Barbie, 97, 99
soccer team names: of boys vs. girls, 20
social capital, 32–33
social currency: sports as, 143–145
social standing: sports involvement and, 32–33
softball: audiences and television ratings of,
    94–95; playing vs. following sports in, 86–87
"soft" credentials, 42–46
Solo, Hope, 101, 114
Sonnert, Gerhard, 41n, 46–47
"sorority sluts," 105
Spalding, A. G., 74
spectatorship: at live events, 136–137
"spice girls," 33, 34
Spitaler, Georg, 4, 4n
sponsorships: in science and engineering,
    44–46
sportistas, 201–238; as challenging and threat-
    ening to men, 211–214; as challenging and
    threatening to women, 214–219; defined, 5;
    and espnW, 219–235; influence of dads on,
    202–206; knowledge of, 5; lack of confidence
    and presence of stereotype threat in, 209–
    211; lack of legitimacy and credibility of,
    208–209; need for constant proof from, 206–
    208; vs. regular female sports fans, 216–218;
    as resource for other women, 216
sports ability: gender role stereotypes and, 26;
    vs. sports appreciation, 25–29
sports analyst: vs. sports newscaster, 187–189
sports anchors: women as, 171–172, 184–187,
    219
sports appreciation: sports ability vs., 25–29
sports blog, 145–146
sports bra incident: in World Cup soccer, 95–97
sports broadcasters: age of, 190; appearance of,
    189–195; women as, 169–170, 184–187

sportscasters: age of, 190; appearance of, 189–
     195; women as, 169–170, 184–187
SportsCenter, 219; female anchors at, 167, 219
sports commentator: vs. sports newscaster,
     187–189
sports competence: and attributed value,
     24–25, 30; decline in perception of, 27–28,
     28n; self-perceptions of, 24, 30
sports consumers. *See also* female sports fan;
     sportistas: gap between sports participants
     and, 84–92; motivation for, 159–160; women
     athletes as, 83–84
sports directors: women as, 171–172
sports editors: women as, 170–172
sports fan: female (*See* female sports fan); iden-
     tification as, 128; participatory activities of,
     160; reasons for being, 128, 129, 159–160
Sports Fan Motivation Scale, 159
sports involvement: and social standing, 32–33
sports journalists. *See* sports media
sports knowledge: assessing level of, 149–152;
     assumptions about, 178; of boys vs. girls, 31;
     current, 148, 150–151; as entrance require-
     ment to true fandom, 123–124; and fandom,
     10–11; of female fans, 148–159; historical,
     148, 150, 151–154, 155–156; self-evaluation
     of, 149–150; team-specific vs. general-
     ized, 158
sports language: fluency in, 156–157, 235–237
sports logos: merchandise with, 147–148
sports media, 11, 167–200; ambivalence of
     "babe" factor in, 189–195; avenues to cred-
     ibility in, 181–184; background as athlete
     in, 183; challenges with discrimination and
     resentment in, 175–176; coverage of non-
     hegemonic sports by, 184; credentials for,
     195; "diversity hires" in, 179–181; encour-
     aging figures on, 172–173; equality in, 167–
     168; hiding your brains in, 196–198; higher
     standards for women in, 177–179; history
     of beauty queens in, 184–187; legitimacy of,
     168–169; "living with your reality" in, 174;
     obstacles in, 168; pressures in, 176–179; print
     and radio vs. television, 169–170; privilege
     in, 199–200; reporting vs. commentary in,
     187–189; sports consumers' resentment of
     women in, 169; state of the art of, 170–172;
     wisdom from veterans of, 173–175
Sports Need for Achievement and Power Scale,
     159
sports newscast(s): viewers of, 125
sports newscaster: vs. sports commentator,
     187–189
sports omnivores, 84, 132–133

sports participants. *See* sports producers
sports producers, 66–117; appearance of,
     101–108; in basketball, 73–76; begin-
     ning of organized sports for, 71–73; espnW
     is for, 230–231; future of, 112–115; gen-
     der identity of, 104–108; governance of,
     78–80; identity and sexuality issues of,
     9–10; "Kournikova effect" in, 102–104; in
     Lingerie Football League, 108–112; and
     NCAA takeover, 81–83; physical education
     and, 70–71; in professional baseball dur-
     ing World War II, 76–78; sexualization of,
     97–102; in soccer, 83–84, 92–95; as sports
     consumers, 83–84; Title IX and, 80–81; in
     Victorian times, 67–70; women's advances
     as, 9–10
sports radio programs: callers to, 125
sports reporter: vs. sports commentator, 187–
     189; women as, 171–172, 173
sports section: readers of, 125
sports space, 94, 103
sports talk: childhood exclusion from, 157–
     158; time spent in, 138–139, 142–147; by
     women, 10
sports trivia, 155–156
sportswriters: women as, 169, 171–172, 173,
     176–179
"sporty girl" concept, 78
Stadtmiller, Mandy, 148n
Steele, Claude M., 53n, 58–59, 58n, 61, 61n
Steele, Sage, 219
STEM fields: women in, 6–7, 41–47
stereotyped expectations: that adults place on
     children, 16
stereotype threat, 58–61; in chess, 53, 53n;
     in computer science, 155n; of sportista,
     209–211
Stiff, Carol, 141
Stone, Jeff, 59–60, 59n
Storm, Hannah, 219
storytelling: by boys vs. girls, 17–20, 162–163
"street cred," 218–219
stylistic sports: men's vs. women's enjoyment
     of, 164–165
subjective credentials, 42–46
subjective task value, 23–24
subjective traits: in evaluation of scientists, 43
subject valuation, 23–24
Su-lin, Gan, 163–164, 164n
Super Bowl: watching on TV of, 137
superfan, 10–11, 127, 128, 128f
suspense: men's vs. women's enjoyment of,
     163–164
Swoopes, Sheryl, 76

Tafoya, Michele, 215, 219

talking about sports: childhood exclusion from, 157–158; time spent, 138–139, 142–147; by women, 10

Tebow, Tim, 88n

"Tebowing," 88, 88n

technology: women in, 6–7, 41

television: college softball on, 94–95; sports journalists on, 169–170, 171–172; sports on, 1; watching of, 137–142; women's basketball on, 76

tennis: beauty in, 102–104; in Victorian era, 69–70

Theberge, Nancy, 62n

Thirer, Joel, 32, 32n

Thomas, Katie, 220n

threat: of sportista to men, 211–214; of sportista to women, 214–219

time deepening, 139–142

Tirico, Mike, 183

Title IX, 3, 4, 80–81; effects of, 91–92; and gender separation, 242–243

Tobin, Larry, 111

Toffoletti, Kim, 157, 157n

tomboys, 33–35

Tomlinson, LaDainian, 145

Toro, Heather Michelle, 172n, 185, 192, 199

Tour de France: nationalism at, 93

Treadway, Dan, 112

trivia, 155–156

true fan: fair-weather vs., 123

Tsfati, Yariv, 199n

Tuggle, Charles A., 163–164, 164n

Turley, Taira, 110

Ultimate Fighting Championship (UFC), 242, 242n

United States Soccer Federation (USSF), 113

universalistic criteria: as selection measures, 39

University of Connecticut: women's basketball at, 9

Valentin, Iram, 80n

Van, Lindsey, 101, 101n, 102

Vanderberg, Marcus, 220n

Ventre, Michael, 102n

Verlander, Justin, 148

Victorian woman, 67–70

violence: men's vs. women's enjoyment of, 163, 164, 165–166

Vonn, Lindsey, 101

Wade, Dwyane, 112

Waismel-Manor, Israel, 199n

Wakiji, Dana, 89n, 183, 207–208

Waldman, Suzyn, 182

Walter, Fritz, 153

Walters, John, 195n

Wambach, Abby, 114

Wann, Daniel, 159

Ward, Pam, 182, 215, 219

Warmflash, Gillian Lee, 11; on challenge and threat to men, 211, 213; on fathers as influence, 205n; on mothers as influence, 92, 92n, 206; on "real" vs. "regular" female sports fans, 216; on sports language, 234–236, 236n–237n; on sports talk, 144; on time deepening, 141–142

WDNAAF (Women's Division of the National Amateur Athletic Federation): in history of women's basketball, 74–75

Weaver, James B., III, 158n, 164

Webb, Howard, 96

Weber, Max, 39

Weeks, Mark, 55n

Weich, Brigitte, 107

Wenner, Lawrence A., 139–140, 139n, 140n, 160

West, Candace, 62n

West, Mae, 196

Wick, Norma, 190

Wigfield, Allan: on childhood origins of gender differences, 13n, 21n; on expectancy-value theory and achievement-choice model, 22, 22n, 23; on formula for fandom, 29, 29n

Williams, Christine, 51, 51n, 62–64, 62n

Williams, Jean, 68n

Williams, Serena, 2, 101, 103

Williams, Venus, 101, 103

winning and losing: focus on, 158–159; in storytelling of boys, 19

Winter, Edward, 54n

WNBA (Women's National Basketball Association): future of, 112; salaries, 94, 94n

Woman Grandmaster: in chess, 52–53

women: challenge and threat of sportista to, 214–219

women athletes. See female athletes

women's baseball: in World War II, 76–78

women's basketball, 9; future of, 112–113; history of, 72, 73–76; at Olympics, 75; popularity of, 240; salaries in, 94, 94n; television coverage of, 76; in Victorian era, 68; in WNBA, 94, 94n

Women's Division of the National Amateur Athletic Federation (WDNAAF): in history of women's basketball, 74–75

Women's Football Alliance, 111

Women's National Basketball Association (WNBA): future of, 112; salaries, 94, 94n

Women's Professional Soccer (WPS), 88, 112–113

women's soccer: bans on, 72–73; future of, 113–115; lesbians in, 98, 107; playing vs. following sports in, 84–86, 88–89; sexualization of, 97–102; special nature of, 92–95; sports bra incident in, 95–97; in Victorian era, 68; Women's World Cup of, 92–94

women's softball: audiences and television ratings of, 94–95; playing vs. following sports in, 86–87

women's sports, 66–117; basketball as, 73–76; beginning of organized, 71–73; espnW is about, 223–226; future of, 112–115; gender identity in, 104–108; governance of, 78–80; "Kournikova effect" in, 102–104; Lingerie Football League in, 108–112; market for, 115–117; men's beliefs about inferiority of, 225; men's vs. women's knowledge of, 153–154; NCAA takeover of, 81–83; physical education and, 70–71; professional baseball during World War II as, 76–78; sexualization of, 97–102; soccer as, 83–84, 92–95; television coverage of, 224–225; Title IX and, 80–81; in Victorian times, 67–70

women's tennis: beauty in, 102–104; in Victorian era, 69–70

Women's Tennis Association (WTA), 102

Women's United Soccer Association (WUSA), 113

Women's World Chess Championship, 55

Women's World Cup soccer, 92–94; ESPN coverage of, 223–224; future of, 113–115; popularity of, 240; sexualization in 2011 of, 97–101; sports bra incident in, 95–97

Woods, Tiger, 2

World War II: women's baseball, 76–78

WPS (Women's Professional Soccer), 88, 112–113

Wright, Stephen D., 32, 32n

Wrigley, Philip K., 76–77

WTA (Women's Tennis Association), 102

WUSA (Women's United Soccer Association), 113

youth, 13–17; collectivity vs. chaos in, 17–20; conformity vs. deviance in typology of girls in, 33–35; in development of sportista, 5–6; differentiation in self-perceptions of competencies in, 20–22; expectancy-value theory and achievement-choice model of, 22–29; and formula for fandom, 29–32; living proof of gender differences in, 13–15; playground dynamics in, 15–16; and social capital, 32–33

Yu, Nan, 172, 172n, 180, 190

Zeeh, Julia, 100, 100n

Zelasko, Jeanne, 195

Zillmann, Dolf, 158n, 163–164, 164n

Zimmerman, Don H., 62n